the

OCEAN WISE

COOKBOOK

the

OCEAN WISE

seafood recipes that are good for the planet

COOKBOOK

edited by **JANE MUNDY**

whitecap

Ocean Wise.

A Vancouver Aquarium Conservation Program

The information in this book
is true and complete to the best
of the authors' knowledge.
All recommendations are made
without guarantee on the part
of the authors or Whitecap Books Ltd.
The authors and publisher disclaim
any liability in connection
with the use of this information.

Whitecap Books is known
for its expertise in the cookbook market,
and has produced some of the most
innovative and familiar titles found
in kitchens across North America.
Visit our website at www.whitecap.ca.

The publisher acknowledges the financial
support of the Government of Canada
through the Canada Book Fund (CBF)
and the Province of British Columbia
through the Book Publishing Tax Credit.

LIBRARY AND ARCHIVES CANADA CATALOGUING IN PUBLICATION
The Ocean Wise cookbook : seafood recipes
that are good for the planet / edited by Jane Mundy.

Includes index.
ISBN 978-1-77050-016-7

1. Cookery (Seafood). 2. Ocean Wise (Program).
I. Mundy, Jane

TX747.O34 2010   641.6'92   C2010-903170-9

ENVIRONMENTAL BENEFITS STATEMENT

Whitecap Books Ltd saved the following resources
by printing the pages of this book on chlorine free
paper made with 10% post-consumer waste.

TREES	WATER	SOLID WASTE	GREENHOUSE GASES
36	16,407	996	3,407
FULLY GROWN	GALLONS	POUNDS	POUNDS

Calculations based on research by Environmental Defense and the Paper Task Force.
Manufactured at Friesens Corporation

DESIGN: Mauve Pagé
PHOTOGRAPHY: Tracey Kusiewicz (except as
noted on the last page)
FOOD STYLING (TRACEY KUSIEWICZ PHOTOS):
Carol Jensson, Jane Mundy,
Tracey Kusiewicz, and individual chefs
ILLUSTRATIONS: Fish icons (pages 4–9) and
photo-illustrations (top of recipe pages)
by Mauve Pagé; "Preparing Fish and Seafood"
illustrations (pages 18–20) by Jennifer Sunday
EDITING: Naomi Pauls and Grace Yaginuma
PROOFREADING: Lesley Cameron, Viola Funk,
and Lana Okerlund

Printed in Canada at Friesens

10 11 12 13 14   5 4 3 2 1

Contents

FOREWORD

I've been fortunate enough to live my whole life on the coast in BC, with a father who is a self-described sailor. I developed a healthy respect and passion for the ocean and all its inhabitants, which led me to study marine biology at the University of Victoria. I continue to marvel at the ocean and its wonders. But even in my short life, I have witnessed changes in the marine environment.

As a child I was entranced by the abundant life in Boundary Bay—endless miles of sandbars filled with sand dollars, small fishes, eelgrass, and crabs—only to have a chemical spill render the same area lifeless when I returned the very next year. We are increasingly discovering that the world's oceans are in trouble. From climate change to ocean acidification, from plastic waste to ship pollution, we are putting huge pressure on the resiliency of our oceans. Above all else, fisheries have had, and continue to have, the greatest impact. Poor management and destructive fishing and farming practices have pushed marine and aquatic ecosystems to their limits, threatening the single largest habitat on the planet—our oceans.

Now more than ever, it is crucial to support fisheries that are conducted in a responsible and sustainable manner, and to avoid the others. I am reminded of Margaret Mead's famous inspirational quote: "Never doubt that a small group of thoughtful, committed citizens can change the world. Indeed, it is the only thing that ever has." We should never underestimate our power as consumers. What fisher would waste the time and energy to go out and catch something if we all refused to buy it? Knowing which fisheries to support is a problem, though. The science can be complicated or even contentious, and conflicting information can be downright confusing. Our understanding of fisheries can change quickly with new information; what was a good choice today can be a poor one tomorrow, and vice versa. Truly sustainable fisheries require a holistic, ecosystem-based management approach, because ecosystems are extremely complex, especially in the marine realm.

Understanding all the links and balances is not easy; many questions remain unanswered. And experts are still debating whether capture fisheries—the last true wild hunts on the planet—can be sustainable at all. So even scientists find it difficult to pinpoint what makes a sustainable fishery. Fortunately there are resources to help consumers.

In 2005 the Vancouver Aquarium started a unique program called Ocean Wise. Participation in the program is completely voluntary. The program helps businesses throughout Canada to identify and source sustainable seafood alternatives in order to create a market for sustainable seafood. When you visit a restaurant or market that participates in Ocean Wise, sustainable options are highlighted by a symbol on the menu that identifies the best choices you can make for healthy oceans. As demand for these products increases, it creates incentive for fishers and farmers to conduct their operations in a more sustainable manner, which then allows them to get more value for their products.

At the time of writing, Ocean Wise had over 2,700 partner business locations from Victoria to Halifax. Until participating businesses are in every neighbourhood, we hope this book will help consumers be more conscious about their choices. Jane Mundy has collected recipes from top Ocean Wise–supporting chefs across the country. All the recipes feature great sustainable seafood alternatives, and the book includes details on what seafood to buy, how to find it, and what to do when you get your hands on it. This book was designed to be the ultimate guide to sustainable seafood for the home cook—demystifying sustainable seafood and providing home chefs with all they need to prepare amazing seafood dishes at home. We certainly hope *The Ocean Wise Cookbook* leads you on a fabulous culinary journey into the world of seafood!

Mike McDermid
Ocean Wise Program Manager, VANCOUVER AQUARIUM

INTRODUCTION

I'll make no bones about it: I miss a lovely piece of Atlantic cod. I grew up in London, England, and for a treat my mum would send me round the corner to the local chippie, who wrapped up plump, battered cod and deliciously greasy chips in newspaper (that's dating me!). I could never wait until I got home to start gobbling up our meal. My mum tells me that I loved fish even as a baby—in fact, that's about all I would eat. She had to visit the fishmonger every day (we didn't have a fridge) to buy a fillet of plaice and poach it in milk.

I've also got some bad memories. Fish was a lot cheaper than meat in the 1950s and 1960s, especially herring, which was forced upon us kids in numerous ways: boiled "British" (for a very long time), smoked (as in bony kippers), and swamped in tomato sauce (canned pilchards heavily disguised). Wait, it gets worse—we even had to swallow a spoonful of stinky cod liver oil every day. It's a wonder that I still love seafood.

Recently I revisited herring at C, an upscale Vancouver restaurant, and, to my amazement, it was heavenly. Chefs Robert Clark and Quang Dang had 400 pounds of the little darlings delivered by their local fisherman that same day. Quang simply seared a few fillets in a little oil and butter for a few minutes, with a splash of lemon juice and salt.

Most of us have a favourite fish or seafood that is cooked in a certain way. Maybe for you, it's cod and chips, or an exquisite morsel of bluefin tuna sashimi, or beluga caviar on toast points. But these days many of us realize that because we have not responsibly managed the supply of these fish, they are in danger of disappearing. We must learn to take a more responsible approach to what we eat and consider how our individual choices affect the world.

Few days go by between lectures in the media on the importance of going green or buying local and organic. But we do need to consider the *s* word. It's not easy to play by the rules all the time, and when there's so much doom and gloom regarding the state of our oceans, it seems that an individual choice to eat sustainably is like a splash in the ocean. But if we all pull together to make a difference, I think there is hope.

In the past few years there's been a sea change in the demand for sustainable fish and seafood, mainly spearheaded by conscientious chefs—such as those who submitted recipes for this book. Suddenly we see underrated items appearing on the menus of great restaurants, both high-end and mid-range, and they influence our choices the next time we shop. Of course, increased demand for these items results in more supply, so these chefs greatly influence the livelihoods of their fishers and suppliers. In turn, fishers and suppliers can encourage chefs to try delicious but lesser known species that aren't endangered by overfishing. Now it's up to the home cook to rise to the same challenge, to explore new flavours and textures. And our pocketbooks may benefit as well as our palates. We lament the price of those fish high up the food chain—the cost of a big piece of halibut, for instance, can seem prohibitive. But, being in less demand, most sustainable products are relatively inexpensive, either because there's a lot of them in the sea or because they've been farmed responsibly.

HOW TO USE THIS BOOK

If you're using quality products it's hard to go wrong with the recipes in this book. You'll find some of them require more preparation than others, but if you have the time I think you'll agree that the effort is worthwhile. On the other hand, we've included plenty of recipes that can be assembled in the time it takes to drink a glass of wine— my preferred way to prepare dinner.

I encourage you to deviate from the "script"; the ingredients you have on hand, your personal taste, and, of course, the availability of fish and seafood are a good starting point for discovering new flavours. You'll find suggested substitutes for just about everything (well, an oyster is an oyster) so you can make your own choices. Bear in mind, though, that the seasons don't have to limit you—most Ocean Wise fish and seafood are available year round, thanks to sustainable fishing methods and modern-day freezers. I've also included serving suggestions (what goes with what) as well as tips on stocking a pantry, buying and storing fish and seafood, cooking your "catch," and other helpful suggestions.

Some people are intimidated by cooking fish and only tackle the familiar—shrimp, salmon, tuna, maybe halibut on occasion. This book is intended to expand your options and prompt you to look beyond old standbys. There are still plenty of fish in the sea—they're just not the fish we've been used to. Countless varieties of sustainable fish and seafood are taste delights, especially when you combine them with the right ingredients.

I hope the recipes in this book will help you to develop a passion for less familiar species. In addition to encouraging informed choices, this book is intended to make cooking fish and seafood at home a deliciously exciting experience—so dive right in, these fishes are fine!

CHEFS ROBERT CLARK
AND QUANG DANG INSPECT
A LOAD OF HERRING

Sustainable Fish and Seafood

The fish and seafood featured in the recipes in this cookbook have been sourced through sustainable fisheries or farms and are recommended as sustainable by Ocean Wise. They are also in either the "Best Choices" or "Good Alternatives" category of the Monterey Bay Aquarium's Seafood Watch program. Sustainable seafood refers to seafood (including fish) that is abundant, well managed, and caught or farmed in environmentally friendly ways.

Because fish and seafood stocks, our understanding of them, and their management are constantly shifting in terms of sustainability, some species could wind up on the "Avoid" list—even before this book is published—while others might become more sustainable. For this reason we recommend looking for the Ocean Wise symbol at partner restaurants and businesses wherever possible or checking the Seafood Watch website for the most current information before purchasing seafood. Those items to be avoided are caught or farmed in ways that harm other marine life or the environment.

Every business that participates in the Ocean Wise program—and every restaurant included in this book—has Ocean Wise icons on its menu, indicating which fish and seafood items are sustainable. Refer to the program's website, www.oceanwise.ca, for a Canada-wide list of member establishments. As well, the Seafood Watch program (www.seafoodwatch.org) offers wallet-sized printable cards for various US geographic regions to help you make a sustainable choice next time you buy fish or order seafood in any restaurant.

Some general notes:

» Eating small fish such as herring and mackerel has a big benefit: you eat low on the food chain because they survive on zooplankton. As well, they congregate in large schools so are caught with little bycatch of other species.

» Freshwater fish raised in land-based fisheries is a great option. Canada has freshwater fisheries for lake whitefish, northern pike, walleye (sometimes erroneously referred to as "pickerel"), rainbow smelt, yellow perch, arctic char, and more. For instance, Jim Giggie's Trout Farm purchases trout from land-based farms and supplies many restaurants in Toronto. The federal ministry of natural resources uses these trout farms as a standard of excellence when they test other fish farms, because unlike water in the Great Lakes, the ground source water in land-based trout farms does not harbour a particular virus to which the fish are susceptible.

» Cultured seafood like clams, mussels, oysters, and scallops are also great choices; there are many aquaculture sites, such as Island Scallops on Vancouver Island, that do not farm at high densities, which can cause disease outbreaks.

^ PHOTO TAKEN AT C RESTAURANT (VANCOUVER)

The following fishes and seafood are featured in this book; some sustainable items were not included, mainly because they come from very specific fisheries or farms and are seldom available nationwide. (Refer to location-specific pocket guides from Seafood Watch, and talk to your local fishmonger.)

Best = Seafood that is abundant, well managed, and caught or farmed in environmentally sustainable ways.

Good = Second-best choice. There may be some concerns with how the seafood is caught or farmed, or with the health of their habitat. Limit consumption to when seafood from the "Best" category is not available.

ABALONE Farmed abalone is nothing short of luxurious once it has been tenderized. You can either pound this univalve with a mallet for a few minutes, slice it very thinly, and drop it into a hot stock, or braise it in a low-temperature oven for a few hours with oil and aromatics. Overcooking will render abalone as tough as shoe leather.

‹ FARMED | BAMFIELD MARINE SCIENCES CENTRE AND HUU-AY-AHT FIRST NATION

ANCHOVY More than 20 different species share the name anchovy. The majority of the catch is canned, salted, turned into paste, or distilled to make Asian fish sauces. Fresh anchovies are very delicate and generally hard to find, but if you do come across a whole fish that is unbruised, it has a rich yet subtle taste and a soft texture.

‹ WILD

ARCTIC CHAR Arctic char is sometimes referred to as "salmon lite" because it is a member of the salmon and trout family, but it tastes more like trout, with a hint of vanilla and salt. The meat is moderately firm but has a finer flake than the meat of char's relatives. The Inuit have been freezing this fish and eating them like popsicles for hundreds of years. Now two-thirds of the world's char supply is farmed.

‹ FARMED

BARRAMUNDI A member of the sea bass family, barramundi is relatively new to the North American market, but Australia and parts of Southeast Asia have enjoyed its firm, moist texture and sweet, buttery flavour since Thailand started farming it in the 1970s. There are few bones in the larger fish and they are easily removed. US farm-raised barramundi are raised in recirculation aquaculture systems that are considered more environmentally friendly than other types of aquaculture.

‹ US | FARMED

CAPELIN This tiny fish is mainly caught for its roe, also known as *masago* when prepared as sushi. Similar to smelts, capelin can also be eaten whole.

‹ CANADA OR ICELAND | WILD

CATFISH Grain-fed channel catfish is one of the most sustainable seafoods available. Its meat is white and sometimes pinkish—don't buy it if it is reddish or slightly yellow. As a freshwater fish, it does not have an ocean odour;

‹ US | FARMED

uncooked, it almost smells like raw chicken. Catfish farmed in the US is preferable to basa or swai (river catfish farmed in Asia), because it is farmed in a more sustainable manner.

CLAMS There are three basic types of clams: soft-shell, razor, and hard-shell—the latter, such as manila clams and littlenecks, are usually preferred if you are going to serve them on the half-shell. Of course, most clams wind up in chowders, stews, and fritters. All good.

‹ FARMED
‹ WILD

COD, PACIFIC Pacific cod is smaller than Atlantic cod—the latter is a code red AVOID. Pacific cod is typically fished with traps in BC and by bottom longline in Alaska. Raw Pacific cod is opaque and creamy white, with a mild taste and higher moisture content than the overfished Atlantic cod.

‹ ALASKA | LONGLINE
‹ US | TRAWLED

CRAB Dungeness crabs are named after the small town of Dungeness in Washington state. From the ½ oz (10 g) shore crab to the spectacular Alaskan King, which can weigh up to 25 lb (10 kg), crabmeat is similar in taste worldwide, with a sweet, mineral-like flavour. Most every chef in British Columbia will argue, however, that west coast Dungeness is best. Food fight?

‹ DUNGENESS AND STONE CRAB
‹ BLUE, KING (US), OR SNOW
  IMITATION (SURIMI) CRAB

CRAYFISH The bulk of farmed crayfish comes from its native Louisiana, where they're also called crawfish, crawdads, or mudbugs. Make sure not to buy imported crayfish from China, where harvesting has caused considerable damage to the environment. Some people say that crayfish can be substituted for its ocean-going cousin, the lobster. It takes a lot of work and patience to get a small amount of meat out of a crayfish, but enthusiasts believe that makes the experience all the sweeter.

‹ US | FARMED

CROAKER, ATLANTIC The name comes from the croaking sound this lean and full-flavoured fish makes during mating season. It's about the same size and shading as a red snapper, only black and white, with firm flesh and edible skin. In most areas, it's quite inexpensive. Another type of croaker is the king croaker, also known as "white sea bass," which is on the "Best" list.

‹ NET-CAUGHT
‹ TRAWLED

GEODUCK The world's biggest clam, "GOO-ee-duk" is popular in Asia and, increasingly, mirugai (its Japanese name) is featured on North American sushi bar menus. Geoduck is similar in taste to abalone or conch but is much more sustainable.

‹ US OR CANADA | WILD (DIVER-
  CAUGHT) OR FARMED

HADDOCK The delicate flake and slightly sweet taste of haddock, also known as hake, is melt-in-your-mouth delicious—no wonder it's so popular throughout northern Europe for fish and chips. It's also sought-after in the cold-smoked product known as finnan haddie, which was invented in Scotland more than a century ago. Hook-caught haddock is a great substitute for Atlantic cod.

‹ US ATLANTIC | WILD

HALIBUT, PACIFIC Also known as "whales" or "barn doors" by fishers, Pacific halibut can weigh anywhere from 10 to more than 200 lb (4.5 to 90 kg). Because it retains moisture well, halibut freezes beautifully and keeps its texture when cooked. Its snow-white meat is mild, fine-grained, and dense, as long as you don't overcook it. Meat from a larger fish can be slightly coarser in texture.

< US OR CANADIAN PACIFIC

HERRING Most North Americans think of herring as pickled, smoked, or salted and usually consumed as kippers, rollmops, or canned sardines. Fresh herring, however, ranges from delicately flavoured small fish to larger fish with a fuller, oily flavour.

< ATLANTIC OR PACIFIC | WILD

JELLYFISH There are a lot of jellyfish. For centuries, Asians have known that jellyfish contains high levels of collagen, and they use it in vegetable dishes and salads. In Chinese cuisine, the umbrella (bell) part of a particular species is dried, then rehydrated, cut into strips, and served with chicken, cucumber, and soy. Jellyfish is bland on its own—it's more about the texture.

<

LINGCOD Not even a member of the cod family (it's a Pacific greenling), lingcod has had a bad rap: in the early 1900s it was called cultus cod (cultus means "of little worth" in Chinook). But a lingcod can grow to 90 lb (40 kg), although market size is about 10 lb (4.5 kg). The term "cod" was added to "ling" because the white flaky flesh and mild taste make this fish similar to cod.

< US OR CANADA | WILD (BOTTOM LONGLINE AND HOOK-AND-LINE)

LOBSTER In most parts of the world, lobster is an expensive luxury. There is much debate over which country has the best lobster, but if you can get one recently pulled from the sea and into your pot ASAP, its firm, sweet meat is nothing short of delectable.

< SPINY LOBSTER | US OR BAJA, MEXICO
< AMERICAN OR MAINE LOBSTER | NORTHEAST US OR CANADA

MACKEREL, KING AND SPANISH Mackerel is still underrated in North America, but Europeans love its rich, slightly metallic flavour, and small mackerel are excellent served as sashimi (saba or sawara) or preserved as gravlax. The raw fish looks grey and oily but becomes off-white and firm when cooked. Because of its high oil content, mackerel deteriorates quickly, so ask your fishmonger for a very fresh mackerel.

< US ATLANTIC OR US GULF OF MEXICO | WILD

MAHI MAHI Mahi mahi is the Hawaiian moniker—meaning "strong strong"—for dolphinfish. This beautiful fish has lean and firm meat, and it has a faint lemony, sweet flavour when cooked medium-rare. When buying mahi mahi look for hook-and-line- or troll-caught.

< US | WILD (HOOK-AND-LINE)

MUSSELS Some experts say they can taste the water where these bivalves grow, which may be true if they haven't been stored in a tank for long. The most common mussels—particularly those from Prince Edward Island—are

< WORLDWIDE | FARMED

farmed and seasonal. The best mussels are those you harvest yourself. Failing that, look for the big, plump, and juicy ones from British Columbia.

OCTOPUS In some parts of the world (Southeast Asia, Japan, China, and the Mediterranean) octopus is revered for its lobster-like taste and chewy texture. It is just catching on in North America, thanks to chefs who know how to tenderize and slow-cook this cephalopod. Smaller is better.

‹ BRITISH COLUMBIA OR ALASKA | WILD

OYSTERS There's nothing like the taste of oyster: it's the taste of the sea, to start, then sweet cream, finishing with a metallic taste. True oyster aficionados will say the only way to eat them is raw and naked, on the half-shell. But they are delicious with a few chosen condiments such as Tabasco and horseradish, smoked or grilled on a barbecue, or simply fried with a wedge of lemon. Or an oyster shooter with chilled vodka . . .

‹ WORLDWIDE | FARMED

PICKEREL The pickerel is a freshwater fish belonging to the same family as pike and muskellunge (muskie or musky). It looks like a diminutive pike, but don't let its homely appearance put you off—its taste is pure and sweet and irresistible. Ask any Manitoban.

‹ GREAT LAKES OR PRAIRIES | WILD

PIKE (NORTHERN PIKE) Sometimes called jackfish, the northern pike is a long, slender fish with sharp, backward-slanting teeth, duck-like jaws, and a long, flat head. Its back and sides are predominantly dark green to olive green, with yellow to white spots. In Alberta, northern pike have been known to weigh up to 50 lb (22 kg). The white flesh has a flaky texture, but is a bit boney.

‹ ALBERTA OR MANITOBA | WILD

POLLOCK Also known as "poor man's crab" because it is used in many fish "paste" products, such as imitation crab (*surimi*), pollock is a great way to get good fish flavour without breaking the bank. Perhaps that's because there is so much of it and because its dull grey colour is not that appetizing. But it's great gussied up and used in fish burgers (that's what you're eating at McDonald's), cakes, and sticks. Pollock is very similar to cod, minus the white flesh.

‹ ALASKA | WILD

SABLEFISH Known as black cod before a clever marketing tactic changed the name to sablefish, it is also called butterfish due to the melt-in-your-mouth, silky-rich meat. The high oil content gives sablefish a velvety soft texture. Look for trap-caught BC or bottom longline Alaskan for your best choice.

‹ ALASKA OR BRITISH COLUMBIA | WILD
‹ CALIFORNIA, OREGON, OR WASHINGTON | WILD

SALMON Five species of Pacific salmon are caught on the West Coast: chinook, coho, sockeye, pink, and chum. The jury is still out on which species are sustainable, particularly in the case of sockeye. As for pinks, Robert Clark of C Restaurant argues (see page 181) that pinks don't get the recognition they deserve. Just be sure to avoid farmed salmon from open-net pens.

‹ ALASKA OR BRITISH COLUMBIA | WILD

SARDINE   The sardine name is applied to several small fishes of the herring family, but it usually refers to the Pacific sardine. Sardines are often called pilchards in Europe (a pilchard is actually a sardine larger than 6 inches/15 cm) and *iwashi* when prepared for sushi.

‹ US PACIFIC | WILD ⟨fish⟩

SCALLOP   Raw scallop is a feature on most sushi menus, where it is known as *hotate*. Sea scallops are meaty, with a sweet, buttery flavour, while the smaller bay scallops are reminiscent of summer corn. Farmed scallops are another success story, like farmed catfish. They are available year round in or out of the shell and freeze well. The farmed Pacific scallop is a relative newcomer but equally as delicious as its wild counterparts—plump and silky. Avoid calico scallops—they're nasty. They are treated with chemicals and taste like iodine, and stocks are over-harvested.

‹ BAY, SEA, AND PACIFIC SCALLOP | FARMED ⟨fish⟩
‹ PINK SWIMMING SCALLOP | BRITISH COLUMBIA | WILD ⟨fish⟩

SHRIMP   Pot-caught shrimp have little impact on the environment and bycatch is minimal, as opposed to the impact of larger-scale trawl methods. Shrimp are small with a unique flavour profile, very sweet and tender. Simply steamed, fried, or roasted, they are delicious no matter how they are prepared.

‹ PINK SHRIMP | OREGON | WILD ⟨fish⟩
‹ NORTHERN SHRIMP | US OR CANADA | WILD ⟨fish⟩

SMELT, RAINBOW   This ubiquitous smelt species (there are several) is relished for its fresh odour, reminiscent of freshly mowed grass and cucumber, hence the nickname "cucumberfish." Small smelts can be eaten bones, skin, and all.

‹ LAKE ERIE | WILD ⟨fish⟩

SPOT PRAWN   Spot prawns are the largest—and arguably the most delicious—prawns on the West Coast. They are best bought fresh and live, but also freeze well. Order them as *amaebi* in sushi bars. No matter how you cook them—poached, grilled, boiled, steamed—they have a wonderful, sweet, delicate flavour and firm texture.

‹ BRITISH COLUMBIA | WILD (TRAP-CAUGHT) ⟨fish⟩

SQUID (CALAMARI)   What a bargain. Most of this abundant cephalopod is edible, and fresh or frozen doesn't affect the quality. Properly cooked (i.e., quickly, or stuffed and braised in a low-temperature oven), squid is both tender and toothsome.

‹ LONGFIN SQUID | US ATLANTIC | WILD ⟨fish⟩
‹ CALIFORNIA OR ARGENTINA | WILD ⟨fish⟩

STRIPED BASS   Farmed striped bass, called *suzuki* when prepared for sushi, is a hybrid of wild and white bass, yet milder and more delicate than wild striped bass. The translucent raw meat turns opaque white when cooked and its oil content keeps the fish moist, as long as it isn't overcooked.

‹ FARMED OR WILD ⟨fish⟩

STURGEON   The prehistoric sturgeon was sought after worldwide for its roe, which was processed as caviar. Most sturgeon now is farm-raised and the quality is consistently good. Its flesh is similar in texture to chicken breast, not at all fishy.

‹ NORTH AMERICA | FARMED ⟨fish⟩

SWORDFISH Swordfish steaks have a firm, meaty texture with a mild, subtle aroma. The rule of thumb is the fattier the fish, the more flavourful and moist, so it won't dry out when broiled or grilled. (Any albacore tuna recipe will work well for swordfish.) Make sure to avoid pelagic longline-caught swordfish, a highly unselective fishery.

‹ US OR CANADA | WILD (HARPOON OR HANDLINE)

TILAPIA Mild-tasting and delicate tilapia has been farm-raised for decades and is the second-most cultured group of fish worldwide, after carp. Tilapia is similar in taste to catfish: the cooked meat is white and lean, with tender flakes.

‹ US | FARMED

TROUT, RAINBOW All rainbow trout on the market is farmed. Trout farming is the oldest aquaculture industry in North America, dating back to the 1880s. The pinkish flesh of rainbow trout has a nutty flavour and a delicate flake when cooked. It's best sautéed quickly or smoked.

‹ FARMED

TUNA, ALBACORE Tuna: chicken of the sea, steak of the ocean. And albacore is known as the highest-grade "white meat" canned tuna. (Note that *bluefin* tuna is on the AVOID list!) Although its meat is not as firm as that of yellowfin tuna, which makes it less desirable for sashimi, albacore's mild yet rich taste and meaty texture appeal to meat lovers, and it is outstanding barbecued.

‹ US OR CANADA | WILD (TROLL- OR POLE-CAUGHT)

URCHIN, SEA Red and green sea urchins are fished primarily for their delicate, salty yet sweet roe. The roe is sold as *uni* when prepared for sushi. Urchin is served in various ways, including raw, with rice, preserved in brine and alcohol and salt, and in casseroles.

‹ CANADA | WILD (DIVER-CAUGHT)

WALLEYE It's also known as yellow pike, yellow pickerel, dory, and more, but walleye is *not* related to the pikes or other pickerels—rather confusing. Whatever name it goes by, walleye is considered to be the best tasting of any freshwater fish and is, of course, very popular with anglers.

‹ LAKE ERIE | WILD

WHITEFISH, LAKE This silvery, small-mouthed freshwater fish is related to salmon and trout (although the cooked flesh is white) and is traditionally the species used for gefilte fish. Its roe is considered exceptional, and its high fat content makes for an excellent smoked product.

‹ LAKE SUPERIOR, LAKE HURON, OR LAKE MICHIGAN | WILD (TRAP-NET)
‹ WILD (SET GILLNET)

YELLOW PERCH Considered the "ultimate pan fish" by many, yellow perch is a favourite freshwater fish—perhaps only rivalled by walleye—at northeastern restaurants. Loved for its versatility and lack of fishy odour, yellow perch can be cooked by literally any method, just as long as it isn't overcooked. Most recipes suggest preparing this with the skin on.

‹ LAKE ERIE | WILD

SPECIES TO AVOID

The following popular fish are to be avoided; use the sustainable alternatives instead.

AVOID	SUBSTITUTE
Atlantic cod	cobia (farmed), Pacific cod, pollock
bluefin tuna	albacore tuna
Chilean sea bass	halibut, sablefish, cobia (farmed)
clams, mussels, or oysters (wild)	clams, mussels, or oysters (farmed)
grouper	mahi mahi, striped bass, tilapia
marlin	mahi mahi, swordfish
monkfish	mahi mahi, sablefish
orange roughy	halibut, tilapia
red snapper	tilapia, sablefish, Pacific cod
salmon (open net–farmed)	salmon (wild), arctic char
skate	bay scallops (farmed)
sole or flounder	tilapia, catfish
tiger prawns	cold-water shrimp or prawns (sidestripe, spot)

Farmed versus Wild

Mike McDermid, Vancouver Aquarium

Many chefs who submitted recipes for this book use farmed fish and seafood. Don't ring the alarm—most of us have a misconception about farmed fish. One reason is that in recent years, especially on Canada's west coast, non-governmental organizations have been so good at educating the public about the perils of farmed salmon that "farmed" has become the new *f* word.

Some people no longer discern between types of farming—they just see that the fish or seafood is farmed and they won't buy it. Some of the time, however, farmed options are far more sustainable than their wild counterparts. This is especially true of shellfish such as farmed mussels, oysters, and scallops, and even of some fin fish. And as consumer demand increases, these farmed varieties are fast becoming available to the consumer from coast to coast. There have also been many improvements made to aquaculture methods and technology.

Fin fish are frequently raised in closed-containment land-based farms, which makes them excellent options. Take sturgeon, for example. Many species of wild sturgeon are endangered worldwide because of the demand for caviar, and it is now illegal to bring wild sturgeon products into Canada. Fortunately, this ancestral fish has been farmed successfully and sustainably across North America for the past decade. Businesses have developed systems in which freshwater sturgeon is

^ LAND-BASED TROUT FARM

farmed on land in closed containment tanks. There is no pollution of the environment and the process takes the pressure off wild stocks, thereby allowing the population to recover. Great success stories for farmed fish also include tilapia, rainbow trout, catfish, and barramundi.

When we talk about "bad" options or "poor" choices, we need to know how the fish is farmed so we can understand whether it is a bad option and, if so, why. Case in point: farmed salmon. It isn't farming salmon per se that is bad, but the way it is done. Farmed salmon is usually raised in open-net pens (as opposed to land-based, as is the case with sturgeon) that are part of the surrounding marine environment, creating serious concerns with regard to effluent (waste) and disease or parasite transfer to wild stock. A large buildup of effluent on the sea floor creates a situation where it can look like a bomb has exploded under the pens. With nothing able to live there, the area becomes a wasteland.

If we want to maintain our passion for eating salmon, we need to figure out how to farm it sustainably. Otherwise, we will wipe out the wild populations, which would be more devastating than we can comprehend. We know salmon is intrinsically linked to the health of our marine ecosystems because other fish and mammals rely on salmon for food. In addition, we are beginning to understand the role salmon plays in our coastal rainforest ecosystem. In some areas, over 40 percent of the nitrogen that fertilizes the rainforest is derived from the marine environment through bears and eagles and wolves dragging salmon carcasses into the forest, where they decompose. In other words, the salmon are fertilizing the forest, so if we lose them, will we also lose our rainforest?

We can all help by supporting producers who are fishing or farming in a sustainable manner. By doing so, as I mentioned in this book's foreword, we will create a demand for such fish and seafood—both wild and farmed—that will trickle down to the fishers and farmers, allowing more of them to conduct their operations in a sustainable manner.

A number of land-based fish farms nationwide currently supply restaurants, farmers' markets, and fishmongers with exceptional farmed products. Next time you dine at an Ocean Wise restaurant, try a farmed option. For instance, Raincity Grill in Vancouver showcases Swift Aquaculture's smoked coho, which is phenomenal. Bruce Swift's Agassiz, BC, farm is land-based, so it does not affect wild salmon stocks. Because of the farm's limited size, Swift sells its salmon to only a select group of restaurants. But that might change in the near future if consumers begin to request land-farmed salmon.

So the next time you see or hear of a farmed product, please don't rush to judgment. Some of these items should definitely be avoided, but many of them make an excellent choice. When in doubt, ask your fishmonger if the farmed food you see is Ocean Wise—increasingly, retailers are getting on board. As is the case in restaurants, it will get easier and easier to spot the Ocean Wise symbol when you shop. Take a good look at the display case and quiz the vendor, and you may go home with a great—and surprising—new sustainable seafood option.

⌃ SALMON

Fresh versus Frozen

Most of us assume that fresh seafood is always preferable to frozen. But depending on where we shop, frozen fish and seafood may be a better option. Fortunately, many fishers and reputable fishmongers across Canada have raised the bar on seafood quality in the past few years. Bob Fraumeni, for example, started fishing halibut in the 1970s on the West Coast. Back then he got it from ocean to high-end restaurant tables in Vancouver and Victoria within a few days.

In 1977 Fraumeni started out with a fleet of fishing boats, selling most of his seafood products to the Asian market. He opened the first Finest at Sea—a boutique-sized fish shop in Victoria, BC—in 2003, selling Ocean Wise seasonal fish and shellfish to the public.

In 2006 he opened two more locations in Vancouver. Products for sale include fresh sea gem oysters, clams, crab, Quadra Island mussels, and spot prawns, along with frozen fish, including albacore tuna, lingcod, and sablefish. Most are frozen at sea, within hours of being caught, so they don't have a chance to spoil during the long journey back to port. Many sustainable fish stocks, such as Alaskan pollock and sablefish, are caught and frozen at sea in this way.

Fraumeni had his eyes opened on the fresh versus frozen debate by a friend from Norway. "Years ago I started making gravlax from fresh spring salmon in the winter and it became a Christmas tradition in my family," he recalls. "When I asked my 86-year-old Norwegian friend to try my gravlax, I thought he would love it; instead he looked at me with great disdain and said, 'Absolutely not, this is fish of the grave.'

" 'What the heck do you mean?' I replied. He explained to me that in Norway, whenever the fish was going bad, they made it into gravlax, which literally means 'fish of the grave.' Fish stores turned their rotten fish into gravlax; it was disguised with a lot of salt and spices. People didn't have freezers then. By turning the fish into gravlax,

it would keep for another three weeks or so and eventually sell."

That's what we get when we buy frozen fish most of the time—old fish, Fraumeni says. If it isn't frozen at sea (FAS), it's usually way past its shelf life. Often the fish packer or processing company will freeze it rather than chuck it, just as they masked the fish that turned up as gravlax in the olden days. No wonder people who buy frozen fish are not that crazy about it.

On the other hand, much "fresh" fish is not fresh at all, Fraumeni explains, and that may be why it is not more popular. "Let's speak realistically," he says. "When my boats go out fishing, they run to the Charlottes and fish for three to seven days, take a 24-hour run back to Port Hardy, a day to unload the boat, a day to truck it [their catch] to Vancouver, a day to distribute it in Vancouver . . . You do the math—how fresh is the fish? That's why I promote frozen-at-sea products, and all my customers are believers, including high-end chefs."

Fraumeni also sells some fresh fish in his shops, but not much. One of his boats, the *Ocean Pearl*, only keeps fresh sablefish for the last day of a 30-day trip; everything else is frozen on board. That way the fish is only two or three days old when it gets to the Finest at Sea stores.

"Halibut fares better. It can be kept whole and heavily iced for a few weeks," says Fraumeni. "But there is no other fish on the planet that I know of that has a decent shelf life."

Despite the continuing image of frozen fish as second-rate compared to fresh, it can actually be superior, if it has been caught and frozen in peak condition. "My customers not only have an understanding of FAS, they even demand the product," says Fraumeni. "Last year I heard a lady ask if we had any FAS lingcod, even though we had fresh at the time. That was music to my ears—finally the public is getting it!"

Switch It Up (But Stay Wise)

With advances in freezing techniques such as "individually quick frozen" (IQF), "blast freezing," and "frozen at sea" (FAS), and advances in aquaculture, it is now possible to get quality "fresh" seafood year round. However, depending upon where you live and the time of year, you may find yourself shopping for fish that is not available or find that your local restaurant no longer has your favourite fish on the menu. Seasonality in seafood commonly refers to times when particular items can be caught "fresh" in a given area. Season openings are dictated by the migration patterns of the species (i.e., when the fish return to spawn or feed, as for salmon, herring, or sardines). Season openings may also be dictated by openings and closings of the fishery, which is managed to avoid times when populations are susceptible to overfishing, such as breeding season for BC spot prawns.

Fortunately most seafood in a given recipe can be substituted for another item with great results—with a few exceptions. Nothing can replace an oyster on the half-shell or a lobster just hauled from the sea and put into the pot. And jellyfish is jellyfish. But in a pinch you could try edible seaweed or sea asparagus to replace jellyfish, and crab is similar to lobster; just don't *pretend* it's lobster!

Until a few years ago some fish and seafood were relatively unknown or considered inedible by North American standards (such as halibut cheeks!). Fortunately these choices are now surfacing to replace favourite seafood staples that have either risen too high in price—often due to rising foreign consumption—or have become unsustainable for a variety of reasons. Increasingly chefs are opting for common fish varieties that have been used less often, and they are creating wonderful dishes from otherwise neglected species.

It's for this reason that a greater variety of seafood is showing up on restaurant menus, such as the Blue Water Café's "Unsung Heroes" (see page 41). Don't be afraid to try out new seafood and experiment. Substitutes listed on the following page are suggestions only and may not work with your particular recipe, but they are chosen based on flavour and texture.

‹ FINEST AT SEA FISHER "BAGGS" LANDS AN ALBACORE TUNA

OCEAN WISE FISH OR SEAFOOD	YOU COULD ALSO USE . . .
abalone	squid
anchovy	small herring smelts
arctic char	salmon rainbow trout
barramundi	striped bass catfish
capelin	smelts
catfish	sea bass tilapia
clams	mussels
cod, Pacific	haddock pollock
crab (Dungeness and stone)	pollock other sustainable crab species
crayfish	shrimp lobster
croaker, Atlantic	mullet
geoduck	abalone clam
haddock	Pacific cod hake (South Africa) pollock
halibut, Pacific	large Pacific cod sea scallops tilapia
herring	mackerel
jellyfish	edible seaweed sea asparagus
lingcod	Pacific cod halibut
lobster, spiny	crawfish crab
mackerel, king and Spanish	large herring sardines (fresh)
mahi mahi	albacore tuna striped bass
mussels	clams
octopus	squid (calamari)
oysters	none
pickerel	walleye yellow perch

OCEAN WISE FISH OR SEAFOOD	YOU COULD ALSO USE . . .
pike, northern	walleye lake whitefish rainbow trout—in a pinch
pollock	Pacific cod haddock (but why bother substituting pollock?)
sablefish	swordfish sturgeon
salmon	another salmon species such as pink or chum arctic char mahi mahi swordfish rainbow trout
sardine	mackerel herring
scallop (bay, sea, Pacific, or pink swimming)	none
shrimp, northern	crayfish tails another shrimp species crabmeat if recipe calls for cooked shrimp meat
smelt, rainbow	herring lake whitefish
spot prawn	shrimp
squid (calamari)	bay scallops halibut cheeks
striped bass	arctic char smaller salmon
sturgeon	albacore tuna swordfish
swordfish	halibut yellowfin tuna
tilapia	catfish
trout, rainbow	arctic char salmon
tuna, albacore	yellowfin tuna swordfish
urchin, sea	none
walleye	yellow perch pickerel
whitefish, lake	rainbow trout salmon
yellow perch	Pacific cod walleye

Purchasing and Storing Fish

Warren Geraghty, West Restaurant, Vancouver, BC

When it comes to buying fresh fish, one of the most frequently asked questions is how to tell if a fish is actually fresh. The best advice I can give is to shop at a reputable market or fishmonger.

Restaurants develop trusted relationships with their suppliers, and so can you. Ask your fishmonger which fish is the freshest and ask which is actually fresh or thawed. For the freshest fish, always buy whole—or from whole—whenever possible. Asking for an appropriate portion of a whole fish to be filleted is normally acceptable at a quality fish shop.

Here are a few tips for determining whether or not fish is truly fresh:

» The fish should have a fresh ocean scent, not an overly fishy smell.
» The eyes should be clear and slightly bulging.
» If the fishmonger allows, press the meat with your finger—the flesh should feel firm and bounce back when touched.
» The gills should be wet and a bright red or pink colour (not like a faded brick).
» If the head has been removed, look inside the fish's cavity; there should be bright red fresh blood along the bone and around the opening.
» If you are buying pre-portioned fish, firmness of the fillet is very important.
» The flesh should have a translucent appearance.
» Avoid fish with any discolouration—brown or yellow edges or drying around the edges.

Obviously sourcing fish and seafood that are local and seasonal is your best way to ensure freshness. Be aware of which species are advised as sustainable and ethically fished. At West we refer to the Vancouver Aquarium's Ocean Wise program.

QUESTION: *Once I bring a fish home from the market, I don't always have time to prepare the fish right away. How long can I keep it before cooking?*

Of course it's best to use fresh fish right away to guarantee that wonderful fresh taste and great texture. However, as long as the fish was purchased fresh, you can store it in the refrigerator at 42°F (6°C) for two or three days. Store the fish on top of a perforated tray with a layer of ice overtop, making sure that the water will not touch the fish as it drains away.

QUESTION: *Is there a rule of thumb when purchasing fish with bones? Any special way to remove them?*

A general rule is that saltwater fish have larger bones, and freshwater fish have finer bones. I typically bone a saltwater fish before cooking, and I would prepare a freshwater fish—such as a trout—on the bone, and then remove the skeleton in one easy motion after the fish is cooked. Normally your fishmonger is happy to fillet the fish for you. If the small pin bones are still in the fillet (you can also request these bones be removed), use a small pair of needle-nose pliers or tweezers to pull them out. Always pull them toward the head to remove them cleanly and easily. Give it a whirl!

For more information, go to *www.oceanwise.ca/seafood shopping.*

Preparing Fish and Seafood

For how-to videos depicting many of the following techniques, please visit the Ocean Wise website at www.oceanwise.ca/video.

KITCHEN EQUIPMENT

You can certainly muddle through life equipped with only a few pots and pans, a decent knife, and a wooden spoon, but if you want to get creative and passionate about cooking—and have a whole lot of fun in your kitchen—it's worth investing in the right kitchen equipment. A few good-quality items will save you time and effort. Kitchen gear, especially the non-essentials, can get pricey. To augment your collection, consider second-hand stores, Craigslist, etc., particularly after Christmas.

Good knives make a big difference in how well you can perform in the kitchen. You can get by with a chef's knife or an Asian-style vegetable knife, such as Japan's all-purpose *santoku-bocho*; a straight 3-inch (8 cm) paring knife; and a serrated knife. You'll also need a sharpening steel.

These are some must-haves for the seafood chef:

» Good pair of scissors for cutting off fins
» Lobster cracker for lobster and crab
» Lobster pick
» Oyster shucker (also called oyster knife)
» Ring molds, 2-inch (5 cm) and 4-inch (10 cm)
» Tweezers or needle-nose pliers to remove pin bones

⌄ OYSTER AND SMELT

HOW TO SKIN A FISH

To skin a fillet:

» Place it skin side down on the cutting board.
» Sprinkle some coarse salt on your fingers; it will help you to get a better grip on the fillet.
» With the knife held at a slight angle, begin approximately one quarter of an inch from the tail end and cut the flesh from the skin.
» Hold the tail flap with your free hand to steady the fish, and turn the knife so the blade is flat. The knife should now be between the skin and the flesh.
» Hold the skin tightly and carefully slide the knife all the way down the fillet, using a gentle back-and-forth sawing motion. This should separate all of the flesh from the skin.

To skin a cooked fillet:

» Grab the skin at the tail end with tongs as soon as the fish is done; the skin of most fish will easily peel away.

To skin a whole fish:

» Make a shallow incision at the base of the tail, without cutting through any meat.
» Scrape the skin with the blade of the knife and free the skin enough to allow you to grasp the fish firmly with your fingers.
» With your free hand, hold the body of the fish down. Use the other hand to pull the skin toward the head, and finally over it.

HOW TO FILLET A FLATFISH

» To fillet a flatfish such as halibut, place the fish dark side up on your cutting board. Make an incision with a sharp, flexible knife down the middle, and cut along the spine from gill to tail. Then score through the skin along the fins on each side, cutting from tail to head.

» Now cut the bone in an arc shape just behind the head and visceral cavity. This will give you a shorter fillet from this side of the fish.

» Slide your knife into the cut, beginning at the head, and use long strokes to separate the flesh from the bones. Peel back the meat as you work toward the centre cut, until all the fillet is released from the bones.

» Do the same for the second fillet, working from the centre cut out toward the fin edge. Remove all the viscera and turn the fish over. Repeat these four steps to get two more fillets on the other side.

HOW TO FILLET A ROUNDFISH

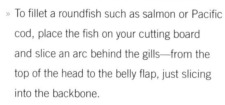

» To fillet a roundfish such as salmon or Pacific cod, place the fish on your cutting board and slice an arc behind the gills—from the top of the head to the belly flap, just slicing into the backbone.

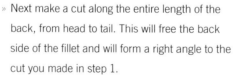

» Next make a cut along the entire length of the back, from head to tail. This will free the back side of the fillet and will form a right angle to the cut you made in step 1.

» Aiming the blade toward the tail, cut into the fish until you feel the central bone with your knife blade. Using the ribs as a guide, slice along the length of the fish.

» As you slice along the length, peel back the flesh—this will free the meat from the rack. Now remove the head and tail and turn the fish over to repeat steps 1 through 4.

www.oceanwise.ca/salmon

^ SALMON FILLET

If you prefer steaks, use a sharp, heavy knife to remove the head from a whole roundfish. Make a diagonal cut right behind the gills, severing the backbone. Starting a few inches (5–8 cm) from the head end, cut steaks crosswise, about 1 inch (2.5 cm) or so in thickness.

HOW TO FILLET MACKEREL

» If you prefer your fish to be boneless, remove the line of pin bones that runs down the centre of each mackerel fillet. To do this, run your finger down the line toward the tail, to make the bones stand up a little. Then, with the tip of a sharp knife, cut along one side of the bones at a 45-degree angle, going down to, but not through, the skin.

» Repeat this technique on the other side of the bones.

» You should then be able to lift out a V-shaped bit of flesh, with all the bones in it, leaving a neat channel in the fillet. The fish can be filleted several hours in advance; refrigerate until ready to cook.

www.oceanwise.ca/mackerel

HOW TO PREPARE TILAPIA

Meeru Dhalwala, Vij's, Vancouver, BC

» You can usually buy tilapia trimmed and boned. If not, trim the fillets by cutting off the skimpy, whitish edges that are mostly skin, about ¼ inch (6 mm) on each side.

» Using a large knife, scrape any fish scales off the skin—there shouldn't be too many on tilapia.

» Cut each fillet lengthwise down the middle and check for bones. You can normally cut the bones out quite easily.

» Rinse the tilapia fillets and set aside on a tray or in a colander to dry for a few minutes. Cut them into smaller pieces, about 6 inches (15 cm) long and 1½ to 2 inches (4 to 5 cm) wide. You should have a total of 12 small fillets, with 2 fillets per serving.

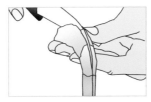

HOW TO SHELL, DEVEIN, AND BUTTERFLY SHRIMP AND PRAWNS

» Twist off the heads. Using a small, sharp knife, make a slit between the swimmerets (legs).

» Peel off the shell and legs, leaving the shell on the tail. If desired, squeeze the tail to remove it from the body.

» Once the shell is off, you may find a black line running down the back. This is the intestinal tract, which is black when full. It is not harmful but can be gritty, and the prawn looks better without it.

To devein a prawn (remove the intestinal tract), use a small, sharp knife to make a slit along the middle of the back to expose the dark vein. Pull out the vein. If you don't want to cut the back, use your fingers to gently pull the vein through the opening at the head end to remove.

» If you want to go one step further, butterfly your prawns by cutting along the back, just enough to spread the halves open.

› SPOT PRAWNS

HOW TO PREPARE A LIVE OR COOKED CRAB

» If you're cooking a live crab, place it back side up on your cutting board. Position a large, heavy knife in the centre of the crab and hit the back of the knife with a mallet; the crab will be killed immediately.

» Now start to clean it—either raw or cooked. With your knife point, break off the belly flap on the crab's underside.

» Flip the crab over and firmly grasp the top shell. Lift off the shell by pulling firmly from the rear. Discard the shell if you aren't going to use it. (Some recipes, such as Stuffed Dungeness Crab and Sautéed Crab Legs, page 70, use the shell for presentation, and there are uses for the crab tomalley and liver; don't be in a hurry to throw them away.) Once the shell is removed, you will see the spongy gills, which must be removed and discarded. If your crab is raw, rinse the rest of the body under cold water.

» Cut the crab body in half and twist off the legs and claws.

» Now quarter the crab body. If it's raw, rinse again. Remove the pockets of meat from a cooked crab with a metal pick or small fork. To remove meat from the cooked claws, crack along the edge of the shell with a heavy knife.

www.oceanwise.ca/crab

HOW TO CLEAN A SQUID

» Remove the head and tentacles from the squid body (also known as the hood). The entrails will be attached and will come away in one gentle tug.

» At the top of the body cavity, feel for a hard and transparent quill. Remove it and any remaining innards.

» Place the head and tentacles on a cutting board and cut the tentacles from the head, just below the eyes, leaving just a part of the head so that the tentacles are still joined. Keep the tentacles.

» Peel back the transparent, speckled membrane from the body and discard. Turn the body inside out and rinse under cold running water.

» Now you can slit the bodies and score the inside surfaces with diagonal cuts (preferred method for grilling and if the squid is small), cut into rings, or leave the squid whole for stuffing.

www.oceanwise.ca/squid

HOW TO KILL AND CLEAN A LOBSTER

» Don't remove the rubber bands yet! Wearing rubber gloves, centre your lobster on a cutting board. Grab the body with one hand and the tail with the other and flatten it out.

» Now take a heavy knife (ideally a 10-inch/25 cm chef's knife) and aim the tip of the knife about an inch (2.5 cm) from between the eyes and the tail, with the tail toward you.

» You are going to cut the lobster in half, down the centre. (This is the most humane and painless way to kill a crustacean.)

» Press the point of the knife into the head until it goes all the way through the head to the cutting board and bring the blade down between the eyes. Now you can remove the rubber bands.

» Twist the lobster in half to remove the tail from the body. Break a tip off one of the antennae and insert it into the vent at the base of the tail. Make a half-turn twist and pull it out. The vein and all its contents should now come out with the antenna. Discard the contents and antenna. Rinse the lobster until all the green blood is removed. Refrigerate the tails until ready to use.

www.oceanwise.ca/lobster

HOW TO CLEAN A FRESH LIVE SCALLOP

Julian Bond, Pacific Institute of Culinary Arts, Vancouver, BC

» Hold the scallop firmly in your hand, with your thumb near the hinge. Carefully slide a butter knife into the space between the two shells and pry open gently. Use your thumb to hold the shell open wide enough that you can slip the knife in. Working slowly, scrape the bottom of the shell with the butter knife to separate the scallop from the shell.

» There will be a point where you know that the scallop is no longer alive. Open the shell completely and continue to scrape the base of the shell to separate the meat from the shell.

» Holding the meat of the scallop, pull the stringy bits from the body. You will be left with the "nugget" (the silky meat) and the coral, which is the roe, a crescent-shaped part of the inside flesh. Refrigerate cleaned scallops wrapped in a damp tea towel or damp paper towel for up to 24 hours. Discard any whose shells are tightly closed, or that don't close tightly when tapped. Alternatively, you can freeze cleaned scallops for up to three months in a sealed container.

www.oceanwise.ca/scallop

HOW TO PREPARE AN OCTOPUS

Your fishmonger usually sells octopus cleaned, cut, and cooked, but some frozen octopus is sold whole and requires preparation. Chef Scott Pohorelic at the River Café, in Calgary, wrestles with 50-pound-plus cephalopods, but you'll likely purchase one weighing only a few pounds.

» Give the octopus a good rinse and turn the body inside out to remove the entrails and bone-like strips.

» Find the stomach sac—about the size of a golf ball—and cut it out and discard. Now turn the octopus right-side out.

» Locate its beak in the middle of the tentacles and, with your finger, push it out. Cut the soft flesh that surrounds the beak, removing the beak, and rinse the whole octopus under cold running water.

www.oceanwise.ca/octopus

HOW TO CLEAN ABALONE

William Tse, Goldfish Pacific Kitchen, Vancouver, BC

» Pry the whole abalone from its shell with a blunt tool such as an oyster knife. The abalone attaches to its shell with a solid round muscle at the bottom, and everything else is just clinging to the shell. Pry open a section between the abalone and the shell, and then work a thin spatula around and along the shell until the abalone detaches. Push against the shell with the tool rather than against the abalone to keep it whole and easier to release.

» Slide the abalone from its shell and set aside. Scrub the shell (to use for serving if you like).

» Hold the main body of the abalone and let the viscera (guts) hang down. Cut off the viscera with a sharp knife and discard it.

» Next, scrub off the black film along the sides of the abalone. (You can also cut this off, but it scrubs off easily, and this method preserves more abalone meat.) Cut off and discard the curled edges (a.k.a. the lips) and the tough, pointed end. You're left with a whole abalone, ready to prepare. If you like, scrub the shell and air-dry it and serve abalone in the shell.

HOW TO SHUCK AN OYSTER

Daniel Notkin, Oysterologist, Old Port Fishing Company, Montreal, QC

So you wanna open an oyster! It's a great idea. But there are some things you should know. Unlike those workers in industrial shucking facilities, I'm not going to make it easy and suggest you use a hammer. No, you're going to use skill and a proper oyster knife, and you're gonna be smart about it.

First let's look at the big picture—the goal, if you will—of opening an oyster. The ideal shucked oyster (and "shucking" is the proper term for opening an oyster) is presented intact on its lower, or cupped, shell, severed from all ties to said shell and looking as perfect and untouched as when it was happily closed and sitting in the ocean, with no cut marks, no bruising, and no scrambling. How, you ask, is this possibly accomplished?! It's simple (after you've done 20,000 oysters. Before that, you need practice . . .).

Important notes for both methods:

» If you are new to oyster shucking I encourage you to place a cloth over the top of the oyster, large enough for the material to be draped over the part of your hand facing the knife. This will protect your hand from the knife breaking through the shell or skipping over it for any reason.

» Go slow. You are likely not in a competition yet. The oyster is not going anywhere. And you cannot impress anyone from the waiting area of an emergency room.

» Use a proper oyster knife. These are readily available at fish markets. Even the simplest of knives are fine to start with. A knife also does not have to be sharp. You will be doing more scraping than slicing. Sharpened screwdrivers are highly advised against. (See note 2!)

Anatomy

You must understand the anatomy of the oyster to understand what you need to do to open it. There are two shells to an oyster, the bottom shell (or cupped side) and the top shell (the slightly more flat side). There are also two distinct sides. One side is the "lip" of the oyster (the wider, more rounded side) and the other the hinge (the more tapered, slightly pointed side, a.k.a. the back). The belly of the oyster is located toward the hinge, tucked right in by it; the "mantle" that filters all the nutrients is out in front, lining the inside of the lip. The most important part is the adductor muscle that the oyster uses to keep its shell closed. (With the "belly" down, draw an imaginary line down the centre of the oyster. The adductor is located slightly beyond the midpoint of the line and to its right.) Releasing, scraping, or cutting this muscle is your goal. Once this muscle is cut, the oyster will fall away from the shell.

www.oceanwise.ca/oyster

‹ DANIEL NOTKIN

› DAILY CATCH AT THE LOBSTER MAN, GRANVILLE ISLAND

Method 1

There are two main ways to open an oyster. The first is popular on the East Coast from New York northward and also on the West Coast. This is the hinge technique; it involves first prying the oyster open at the back (the slightly pointed part). This is done by inserting your oyster knife at 45 degrees into the slight gap between the top shell and bottom shell. Apply forward pressure similar to the amount you would use when sharpening a pencil. Your goal here is to wedge the knife in. Twisting the knife too much is a common mistake. If you do this, the shell will crack and fragment and your oyster will be full of crunchy bits. A good steady, forward motion and just a bit of torsion to wiggle the blade into the hinge is all you need.

Once your knife has found the sweet spot (a good test is that when released from your hand it will stand on its own), you can then apply a little bit of wrist action and torsion to crack the shell open. Twisting the knife will "pop" the shell open. Wedge the shell open with the knife only about ½ inch (1 cm), and then hold it open with the fingers of the hand holding the oyster. Imagine holding a dog's mouth open while trying to brush its teeth. Only open the hinge a little—much more and you risk tearing the meat and muscle inside.

Now take your knife and insert it into the oyster. Recalling where the adductor muscle is, insert the knife as far in as possible to the right of the muscle. Then, with the knife at a 30-degree angle toward the top of the shell, scrape the top of the shell in one swift motion toward you. Insert your knife toward the right and scrape left. The goal is to cut the muscle; in doing so, the rest of the meat will fall away from the top shell.

A couple of additional cautious scrapes are completely acceptable. As a result, the top shell should simply come off, leaving the oyster inside. Now you need to release the "foot" or bottom part of the adductor muscle on the cupped side. Do this by turning the oyster so that the hinge is now facing your other hand, and in one fell swoop, angle the knife under the oyster and scrape the muscle from the bottom half of the shell. Check for bits of shell in the oyster.

Look for consistent colouring (grey spots are not great). Getting to know your oysters, you will get to know colouring, opacity, and characteristics, but anything that looks like discolouration might be a sign of unhealthiness. Keep in mind, however, that the stomach is located near the hinge of the oyster and its colouring is a deep brown. Additionally, if the oyster appears grey in some parts, look at the shell. If the shell is coloured grey in the same manner, then this is a colouring the oyster grew up with. However, if the oyster is grey and the shell is white, discard.

Smell the oyster, and if it reminds you of the ocean, tip her back and chew her up and enjoy. If it reminds you of low tide in summer, discard. If you're unsure, you can always just sip the liquor (the water in the oyster). You will know immediately whether the oyster is okay to eat.

Method 2

The other technique for shucking an oyster is used often on the East Coast from Wellfleet, Massachusetts, southward as well as in Europe. The goal is always the same, only these shuckers use a thinner knife and slide it into the side of the oyster closest to the adductor, slice forward, and finish as in the first method. This is not a method suggested for first-time or even novice shuckers, as the seam for the oyster is hard to find, and the knife can easily slip upward and over and go through your hand. If you do feel like trying this method, wearing a thick leather glove is a must.

Well, that's Oyster Shucking 101!

Enjoy and be careful . . .

Cooking Methods for Fish and Seafood

The recipes in this book generally call for fish and seafood to be braised, fried, grilled, poached, roasted, sautéed, or steamed, although some recipes suggest more than one method.

Whatever technique you decide upon, keep this mantra top of mind: don't overcook. I prefer—and I'm sure most chefs would concur—to undercook fish, because it doesn't stop cooking when you remove it from the heat. Many of us grew up with our parents overcooking seafood because they were afraid of undercooking it. Don't worry about that. You aren't going to get worms from undercooking fish—we aren't talking about land mammals here.

Whether you grill, sear, or bake seafood, most recipes recommend that you start the dish off on high heat to sear in the juices and then reduce the heat. These recipes offer timing guides, but give or take a minute because a lot depends on your oven. To determine whether fish is cooked, look at its flesh, which will change from translucent to opaque. Fried food will turn a golden brown around the edges. Give the fish a poke with your finger—if it feels firm and resilient, it's done. If you're still not sure, don't be afraid to take a knife and slice into that luscious and expensive halibut fillet. It should glisten in the centre; you don't want it completely cooked all the way through. Keep in mind that you can always put that lovely piece of salmon back on the heat if medium-rare is not to your liking, but if you overcook it, there is no going back.

If you find yourself confused about what cut you want when shopping for fish, tell your fishmonger how you are going to cook it. He can cut large fish into steaks for grilling, fillet a fish for poaching in oil, or clean and tenderize octopus. If you're pressed for time, leery of sharp knives, or squeamish, he can even shuck your oysters and boil your lobster.

Here is an overview of the main methods used to cook fish and seafood.

BRAISING

This is a no-muss, no-fuss method because fish, liquid, and vegetables are cooked together and the liquid becomes the sauce. Typically, fillets are braised in a large, shallow pan on the stovetop and larger, whole fish go in a roasting pan in the oven. The idea is to cook the fish slowly, until it's tender.

‹ BEST TO USE: ANY FISH CAN BE BRAISED, BUT WHOLE FISH AND STEAKS ARE IDEAL.

FRYING

Food doesn't get much tastier than a white-fleshed fish, whole or filleted, pan-fried in a little butter or oil or a combination of both. Finished with a splash of lemon juice, this dish is heaven. You must control the temperature, however—too low and your fish will get soggy, too high and you'll wind up with burnt bits.

‹ BEST TO USE: ANY LEAN FISH, ESPECIALLY FRESHWATER FISH LIKE WALLEYE, OR CLAMS, SCALLOPS, SHRIMP, OR SQUID.

There are a few rules when it comes to deep-frying: Use a good-quality vegetable oil and make sure the depth of the oil in the pan is at least 2 inches (5 cm). Keep the temperature at about 375°F (190°C) unless otherwise indicated and use a heavy pot. If you can't live without homemade fish and chips on a regular basis, consider buying a deep-fryer.

GRILLING

When it's summertime, the eatin's good, especially when you fire up the barbecue. Cooking over coals and/or wood chips imparts a deep, warm, and satisfying flavour to just about any seafood, whether it's marinated first or simply brushed with oil and seasoned with a pinch of salt and pepper. Indoors, a smoking-hot cast iron griddle will do the trick any time of year (make sure your fan is working). It sears in all the juices and gives the fish a crispy skin.

‹ BEST TO USE: OILY FISH SUCH AS MACKEREL, SALMON, AND TUNA, IDEALLY WITH THE SKIN ON, AS WELL AS SCALLOPS, SHRIMP, AND SQUID.

POACHING

Poaching is a very healthy method of cooking; it doesn't involve butter or oil but keeps the fish deliciously moist. The seafood is gently cooked in liquid, either on the stovetop or in a pan in the oven; the seasoned broth, wine, or coconut milk concoction remains at a simmer.

‹ BEST TO USE: LEAN FISH FILLETS, STEAKS OR WHOLE. AVOID OILY, DARK-FLESHED FISH, BUT POACHED SALMON IS TERRIFIC.

ROASTING

There is a difference in degrees between baking (about 350°F/180°C) and roasting (400°F to 450°F/200°C to 230°C). Pan-roasting is another option. The term means you sear the fish first in a smoking-hot cast iron grill on the stove top and then finish it in the oven.

Fish can be roasted with aromatics such as sprigs of rosemary and thyme, with oil as the only liquid. Or try roasting a whole fish in salt—just make a paste with kosher salt and water, cover the fish, and slide it into the oven for about an hour. None of the juices can escape, making a moist, delectable dish that's also a conversation piece.

‹ BEST TO USE: DENSE FISH FILLETS SUCH AS SALMON OR PACIFIC COD AND SMALLER WHOLE FISH.

SAUTÉING

This method is basically frying, but with less fat. You lightly cover the bottom of a pan with a little oil or butter (or both), and then sear the fish over medium-high heat, lowering the heat to finish. You may sauté raw fish or seafood naked. Alternatively, dredge it in seasoned flour, panko, or breadcrumbs, and then shake off the excess before placing it in the pan.

‹ BEST TO USE: SMALL WHOLE FISH (UNDER 1 LB/500 G) SUCH AS TROUT, SKINLESS FILLETS, OR SEAFOOD.

STEAMING

Steaming, either in a steamer basket perched over a wok or in any tightly covered container, will result in delicate, pure-flavoured seafood. Many Asian recipes use this method. Clams and mussels are usually steamed in a little liquid—like a splash of white wine and aromatics—until they open.

‹ BEST TO USE: ALL LEAN FISH, INCLUDING SMALL WHOLE FISH SUCH AS SEA BASS, AND SHELLFISH. AVOID MEATY, OILY FISH.

APPETIZERS

RESTAURANT
2 Chefs and a Table

CHEFS
*Allan Bosomworth
and Karl Gregg*

TYPE
tuna

LOCATION
Vancouver, BC

Ancho-Spiced Tuna Tartare with Tomatillo Purée

This mix of smoky spice with the tomatillo sweetness pairs well with local albacore tuna—such a great product. *Serves 8*

NOTE: If fresh tomatillos are not available you can substitute canned, found in the Mexican food section of your local supermarket. Drain and rinse before using.

SPECIAL EQUIPMENT: Eight 4-inch (10 cm) ring molds

TOMATILLO PURÉE

Preheat the oven to 350°F (180°C). Toss the tomatillos and canola oil together in a medium bowl. Place the tomatillos in an ovenproof dish and roast them in the oven for 10 minutes, or until they are soft. (If you are using canned tomatillos, skip the first two steps.) Place the tomatillos, sugar, half the cilantro, and the salt and pepper in a food processor and purée until smooth. Press the purée through a fine-mesh sieve into a small bowl using a spatula. Let the purée cool in the refrigerator, covered, before using it.

» 8 to 10 tomatillos, husks removed
» 2 Tbsp (30 mL) canola oil
» 2 Tbsp (30 mL) sugar
» 2 Tbsp (30 mL) chopped cilantro
» ¼ tsp (1 mL) salt
» ¼ tsp (1 mL) freshly ground
  black pepper

TUNA TARTARE

Mix the avocado, half of the lime juice, the olive oil, and salt and pepper in a small bowl and set aside. Mix all the remaining ingredients together, including the rest of the lime juice, in a separate bowl.

» 2 large avocados, peeled, pitted,
  and diced
» ¼ cup (60 mL) fresh lime juice
» 3 Tbsp (45 mL) olive oil
» ½ tsp (2 mL) EACH salt and freshly
  ground black pepper
» ¼ cup (60 mL) finely diced jicama
  (a crispy, sweet root also known
  as Mexican yam)
» ¼ cup (60 mL) finely diced
  red pepper
» ¼ cup (60 mL) finely diced
  English cucumber
» 1 tsp (5 mL) ancho chili powder
  (or regular chili powder)
» 1½ lb (750 g) sashimi grade
  albacore tuna, finely diced

Set out eight small plates. Place a 4-inch (10 cm) ring mold in the centre of each plate. Spoon one-eighth of the avocado mixture into the mold and flatten it with the back of the spoon. Repeat the same process with the tuna mixture. Remove the ring mold. Spoon some of the tomatillo purée around the tartare and garnish the plate with the remaining chopped cilantro.

PAIRING SUGGESTION: See Ya Later Ranch Gewürztraminer (BC). The sweetness paired with the dish's acidity will hold well together. *Tom Firth:* Tawse Pinot Noir or Kacaba Vineyards Reserve Syrah (both Ont).

RESTAURANT		TYPE
Cactus Club Cafe		tuna
CHEF	LOCATION	
Rob Feenie	Vancouver, BC	

Tuna Tataki with Green Papaya Slaw

This recipe showcases a beautiful piece of albacore with sweet and sour flavours. I consider sweet and sour the yin and yang of cooking. This dish features an extremely acidic sauce you keep wanting to go back for. *Serves 4*

NOTE: Yuzu is a Japanese citrus that tastes like a mix of lemon and lime. If you cannot find yuzu juice, lime juice is a good substitute. Green papaya is available at Asian supermarkets.

TUNA

Heat the oil over medium-high heat in a large frying pan. Pat the tuna loin dry with paper towel and season it with salt and pepper. Lightly sear all sides of the tuna for 10 seconds each. Wrap it tightly with plastic wrap and refrigerate. When it is fully chilled, slice the tuna loin into ¼-inch (6 mm) slices.

» 2 Tbsp (30 mL) vegetable oil
» 1 lb (500 g) tuna loin
» Salt and pepper

GREEN PAPAYA SLAW

Whisk the soy sauce, rice wine vinegar, yuzu juice, vegetable oil, lemon juice, and garlic together in a small bowl. Season to taste with pepper. Put the julienned daikon, carrot, and green papaya, Thai basil, and mint in a large bowl. Pour the yuzu vinaigrette over the slaw (reserve about 2 Tbsp/30 mL for finishing) and toss until the slaw is well mixed and evenly coated.

» 1 Tbsp (15 mL) soy sauce
» 1 Tbsp (15 mL) rice wine vinegar
» 2 tsp (10 mL) yuzu juice
» 1 Tbsp (15 mL) vegetable oil
» 1 tsp (5 mL) fresh lemon juice
» 1 tsp (5 mL) minced garlic
» 2 Tbsp (30 mL) julienned daikon (white radish)
» 2 Tbsp (30 mL) julienned carrot
» 2 Tbsp (30 mL) peeled, seeded, and julienned green papaya
» 1 tsp (5 mL) chopped Thai basil
» 1 tsp (5 mL) chopped mint

Set out four plates. Mound the dressed green papaya slaw on each plate. Garnish it with the orange segments, diced avocado, diced ripe papaya, and pine nuts. Fan the tuna slices over the slaw and drizzle it with the remaining yuzu vinaigrette. Top with whole leaves of cilantro.

PAIRING SUGGESTION: *Tom Firth:* Thirty Bench Small Lot Riesling "Triangle Post Vineyard" (Ont) or Mission Hill Reserve Sauvignon Blanc (Okanagan Valley, BC).

» 1 medium orange, peeled and segmented, membrane discarded
» 1 avocado, peeled, pitted, and diced
» ½ cup (125 mL) ripe papaya, peeled, seeded, and diced
» 1 Tbsp (15 mL) pine nuts
» Cilantro leaves

SOURCE
*Vancouver Aquarium Catering
and Events*

TYPE
tuna

CHEF
Myke Shaw

LOCATION
Vancouver, BC

Herb-Crusted Tuna Loin with Celeriac Remoulade, Swiss Chard, and Potato Latkes

The dense quality of tuna makes it almost meat-like. Be sure not to overcook the loin, which marries well with nutty celeriac, slightly acidic Swiss chard, and rich potato latkes. *Serves 8*

NOTE: The celeriac remoulade can be made a day ahead and stored in an airtight container in the refrigerator. The tuna can also be prepared one day ahead: wrap the loin tightly with plastic wrap and place it in an airtight container in the refrigerator.

CELERIAC REMOULADE

Combine the mayonnaise, celeriac, capers, Dijon mustard, parsley, and tarragon in a bowl and mix them together thoroughly. Season the remoulade to taste with salt and pepper and refrigerate it, covered.

» 1 cup (250 mL) mayonnaise
» ½ cup (125 mL) grated celeriac (celery root)
» 2 Tbsp (30 mL) finely chopped capers
» 1 tsp (5 mL) Dijon mustard
» 1 Tbsp (15 mL) finely chopped Italian flat-leaf parsley
» 1 tsp (5 mL) finely chopped tarragon
» Salt and pepper to taste

SWISS CHARD

Heat the oil in a medium non-stick frying pan over medium-high heat. Add the Swiss chard and stir it in the pan until it is completely wilted. Season it to taste with salt and pepper and set it aside to cool. Squeeze out any liquid.

For the garnish, finely julienne the Swiss chard stalks and place them in an ice bath until the stalks form curls. Drain off the water, pat the curls dry, and refrigerate.

» 2 Tbsp (30 mL) vegetable oil
» 1 bunch Swiss chard, roughly chopped, stalks removed (reserve stalks for garnish)

TUNA LOIN

Mix together the vegetable oil, the dill and parsley, and a pinch each of salt and pepper in a small bowl. Coat the tuna loin with the herb mixture and refrigerate until you're ready to cook it.

Sear the tuna in a non-stick frying pan over high heat for 1 or 2 minutes per side, or until the fish is firm and slightly springy. Set it aside to rest for 2 minutes. Using a very sharp knife, cut the loin into eight even slices. Cover the tuna slices and set them aside.

» 2 Tbsp (30 mL) vegetable oil
» 2 Tbsp (30 mL) finely chopped dill
» 2 Tbsp (30 mL) finely chopped Italian flat-leaf parsley
» Pinch salt and pepper
» 1 lb (500 g) sashimi grade albacore tuna loin

POTATO LATKES

Mix together the potatoes, onion, flour, egg, salt, and pepper in a medium bowl. Heat the oil in a non-stick frying pan over medium-high heat until it is hot. Working in batches, drop a heaping teaspoon (>5 mL) of the potato mixture into the oil and, using the back of the spoon, flatten each mound into a thin pancake. Cook the latkes, turning them once, until they are crisp and golden brown on both sides, about 5 minutes. Transfer them to a plate lined with a paper towel to absorb any oil. Cool them slightly before assembling the appetizer.

» 1½ lb (750 g) russet potatoes, peeled, grated, and squeezed dry
» 1 large yellow or white onion, finely chopped
» 2 Tbsp (30 mL) all-purpose flour
» 1 large egg, beaten
» ¼ cup (60 mL) vegetable oil
» 1 tsp (5 mL) salt

TO SERVE

Place the potato latkes on eight individual plates. Layer each one with the Swiss chard and a slice of seared tuna, and top with a dollop of celeriac remoulade. If you wish, garnish each plate with a curly Swiss chard stalk and a dash of salt and pepper.

PAIRING SUGGESTION: Nk'Mip Cellars Riesling (Okanagan Valley, BC) or R&B Brewing Sun God Wheat Ale.

RESTAURANT
West Restaurant

CHEF
Warren Geraghty

TYPE
arctic char, clams

LOCATION
Vancouver, BC

Pan-Seared Arctic Char with Grilled Fennel Coleslaw and Hollandaise

This dish is a great example of how to incorporate different textures in larger fish. Here you have the firm and sweet gravlax, the tender and juicy raw part, and the crisp and intense-flavoured skin—each part complemented by the elements of the dressing and accompaniments. *Serves 4*

TO CURE THE CHAR

Place the fillet skin side down on a plastic or stainless steel tray. Evenly sprinkle the kosher salt, maple sugar, lemon zest, and dill over the flesh. Cover the fish with plastic wrap and refrigerate for 1¼ hours. Gently rinse off the curing mixture and pat the fillet dry with paper towel. Cut it into four even portions and set them aside. (Refrigerate them if not planning to serve as soon as you have prepared the hollandaise.)

» 20 oz (600 g) arctic char fillet, skin on
» 3 Tbsp (45 mL) kosher salt
» 3 Tbsp (45 mL) maple sugar (or brown sugar)
» Zest of 1 lemon
» 2 sprigs dill, finely chopped

HOLLANDAISE SAUCE

Combine the wine, vinegar, and four-fifths of the sliced shallots in a small saucepan over medium heat. Bring the mixture to a simmer and reduce it by two-thirds. Cool and strain.

Whisk this shallot reduction, the egg yolks, cream, and a pinch each of salt and pepper together in a medium metal bowl. Place the bowl over a pot of boiling water and continue whisking the hollandaise until it begins to form ribbons. Slowly add the extra virgin olive oil in a steady stream, and then add the dill oil (if using). Season the sauce to taste with more salt and pepper if necessary. Chill the hollandaise in the refrigerator before serving.

Check to make sure that the hollandaise is set before use. Pour the hollandaise into a whipping canister that is set with a CO_2 charger and place the canister in an ice bath. (Alternatively, you may serve the hollandaise just chilled by spooning it onto the plate. We prefer the CO_2 method because more air lightens the hollandaise—it's not as heavy.)

» 1 cup (250 mL) white wine
» 1 cup (250 mL) white wine vinegar
» 5 shallots, sliced
» 3 large egg yolks
» ⅓ cup (80 mL) whipping cream
» Salt and pepper to taste
» ⅓ cup (80 mL) extra virgin olive oil
» 3 drops dill oil (optional)

continued . . .

GRILLED FENNEL

Finely slice half the fennel and cut the other half into small dice. Reserve the trimmings and diced fennel. Preheat a grill to high heat. Toss the sliced fennel in the olive oil and season with salt and pepper. Grill the slices, turning them once until grill marks appear on them, a few minutes. Place the grilled fennel in a small bowl, toss it with 1 tsp (5 mL) of the lemon juice, and add more seasoning if necessary. Reserve in the refrigerator.

» 1 large fennel bulb (reserve a few fronds for garnish)
» 1 Tbsp (15 mL) olive oil
» Juice of 1 lemon

TO SEAR THE FISH

Heat the olive oil in a large, non-stick pan over medium-high heat. Place the char fillets in the pan, skin side down, and sear them until the skin is golden brown and crisp, about 4 minutes. (You want the cooking to progress one-third of the way into the fillet, giving you three textures of char: cooked, raw, and cured.)

Remove the fillets from the pan and place them skin side up on a kitchen or paper towel.

» 2 Tbsp (30 mL) olive oil

BACON-CLAM DRESSING

Heat 1 Tbsp (15 mL) of the olive oil in a medium saucepan. Add the remaining sliced shallot and fennel trimmings. Sauté until the shallots are translucent. Add the clams, give them a toss, then add the white wine and vermouth. Place the lid on the pan and cook the clams, shaking them occasionally, for 2 to 3 minutes, or until they open. Pour the clams into a fine-mesh sieve, reserve the liquid, then strain the clam broth through a cheesecloth. Discard any unopened clams.

Heat the remaining 1 Tbsp (15 mL) of olive oil in a small frying pan over medium heat. Add the bacon and diced fennel and cook until the fennel is soft. Add the reserved clam liquid, and reduce it by half. Add the clams and simmer them gently until they are warmed through. Add the tomatoes, chives, and remaining lemon juice, and season the sauce to taste with salt and pepper.

» 2 Tbsp (30 mL) olive oil
» 1 lb (500 g) clams, scrubbed (about 12 small littleneck clams)
» ¼ cup (60 mL) white wine
» 2 Tbsp (30 mL) dry vermouth
» 1¾ oz (50 g) bacon, cut into small dice
» 2 medium tomatoes, peeled, seeded, and diced
» 3 Tbsp (45 mL) chopped chives

TO SERVE

Set out four plates. Place a small amount of grilled fennel just off the centre of each plate. Spoon an equal amount of chilled hollandaise in the centre of the plate and set a piece of seared char on top. Spoon the bacon-clam dressing over the fish, and garnish with a few drops of dill oil and fennel fronds.

PAIRING SUGGESTION: *Tom Firth*: Granville Island Brewery Cypress Honey Lager, Vineland Estates Elevation Chardonnay (Ont), or La Chablisienne Petit Chablis (France).

RESTAURANT
Coast Restaurant

TYPE
halibut

CHEF
Josh Wolfe

LOCATION
Vancouver, BC

Halibut Fish and Chip Roll with Japanese Tartar Sauce

This recipe is a Japanese expression of an English classic, fish and chips, with all the main components of the dish prepared with Japanese ingredients—a perfect marriage of the two cultures. The hand rolls are great as canapés or finger food on any occasion. *Makes 10 hand rolls*

NOTE: Shichimi togarashi (see page 295) is a commonly used Japanese seven-spice blend that typically includes red chili pepper, roasted orange peel, yellow and black sesame seeds, Japanese pepper, seaweed, and ginger. The mixture is used to flavour soups or noodles and yakitori, and Coast's fish and chip roll. Tempura flour is available at Asian supermarkets, as is tobiko (flying fish roe; also sold at Asian fishmongers).

JAPANESE TARTAR SAUCE

Combine the mayonnaise, pickled daikon, chopped capers, shichimi togarashi, and citrus pepper in a small bowl and mix well. The tartar sauce will keep for up to one week in the refrigerator.

» 1 cup (125 mL) mayonnaise
» 2 Tbsp (30 mL) chopped pickled daikon (white radish)
» 1 Tbsp (15 mL) capers, drained and chopped
» 1 tsp (5 mL) shichimi togarashi (Japanese seven-spice, page 295)
» Pinch citrus pepper

RICE

Place the rice in a rice cooker with a one to one ratio of water and cook for one cycle. Alternatively, in a medium pot, bring water and rice to a simmer and reduce to low heat. Cook, covered, for 30 minutes.

Once the rice is cooked, transfer it to a large bowl. Add the seasoned rice wine vinegar, sugar, and salt. Fold the rice gently, being careful not to squish or damage the grains, until it is well mixed. Allow the rice to cool for 15 to 20 minutes at room temperature.

» 1 cup (250 mL) sushi rice
» 3 Tbsp (45 mL) seasoned rice wine vinegar
» 2 Tbsp (30 mL) sugar
» 1 tsp (5 mL) kosher salt

continued . . .

POTATO STICKS

Heat the vegetable oil to 350°F (180°C) in a deep fryer (or large pot). Working in batches, carefully add the julienned potato to the hot oil and fry for 45 seconds, or until the sticks are golden brown. Remove the potato sticks from the oil using a strainer or slotted spoon and drain them on a kitchen or paper towel.

» 8 cups (2 L) vegetable oil
» 1 russet potato, peeled and julienned

HALIBUT TEMPURA

Increase the heat of the same oil used for the potato sticks in the deep fryer to 375°F (190°C). Place two-thirds of the tempura flour in a medium bowl and gradually whisk in the water until the batter becomes almost uniform in consistency. (You should still see a few small lumps in the batter.) Season the halibut strips with salt. Dredge each one in the remaining flour then dip it in the tempura batter. Carefully place each piece in the hot oil and fry for 1 minute, or until the batter is a light golden brown colour.

» ¾ cup (185 mL) tempura flour
» ½ cup (125 mL) water
» 10 oz (300 g) skinless halibut fillet, cut into ½-inch × 2-inch (1 cm × 6 cm) strips
» Salt to taste

TO SERVE

Cut the roots off the radish sprouts. Place a sheet of soy paper in the palm of your hand. Take 2 Tbsp (30 mL) of the sushi rice and place it in the centre of the soy paper. Top the rice with six potato sticks and drizzle them with 1 tsp (5 mL) of the Japanese tartar sauce. Add a piece of halibut tempura and six radish sprouts and then roll the sheet of soy paper diagonally into the shape of a cone. Garnish with about 1 tsp (5 mL) of tobiko and serve.

PAIRING SUGGESTION: Mission Hill s.l.c. Sauvignon Blanc/Semillon (Okanagan Valley, bc). *Tom Firth:* Creemore Springs Premium Lager or Road 13 Viognier Roussanne Marsanne (Okanagan Valley, bc).

» 1 package radish sprouts
» 10 sheets soy paper (or nori sheets)
» 3 Tbsp (45 mL) tobiko

Unsung Heroes of the Deep

Frank Pabst, Blue Water Café and Raw Bar, Vancouver, BC

Many of the fish I grew up with in Northern Europe—and took for granted at the time—were later fished out or became severely depleted: John Dory, monkfish, turbot, Atlantic cod, and Dover sole, to name a few.

That saddens me. But other fish I remember have remained sustainable and are still delicious resources. The fish of my childhood in Germany and Belgium—sardines, mackerel, and especially herring—along with some new items such as sea cucumber, octopus, jellyfish, geoduck, and sea urchin—live in abundance along the BC coast. They are often overlooked in favour of better-known varieties, although they can be highly tasty and nutritious.

In 2004 I introduced these "Unsung Heroes" to our Vancouver restaurant, Blue Water Café. The concept was simple: avoid species that are overfished, or fished in ways that damage the sea floor or cause unnecessary bycatch, by introducing diners to new flavours and experiences.

Yet this simple concept turned out to be a hard sell. Many of our North American guests were apprehensive about committing to the full tasting menu we were offering. And it was a challenge to source the "Heroes." Suppliers didn't know where to procure them, especially when they were still fresh. Most fishers would catch and immediately freeze them. Even nowadays some Heroes wind up as feed in aquariums throughout North America, while others are processed for pet food or, in the case of Humboldt (jumbo) squid or giant Pacific octopus, used as bait.

Soon perceptions—and misconceptions—about the Heroes began to change. We introduced a "small plates" menu, which was a little less intimidating and allowed for guests to share a variety of items, while leaving them enough room for items from our regular menu. I enjoy the challenge of creating dishes that combine the familiar and the unfamiliar to entice our guests: smoked herring with pickled Honeycrisp apples; sea cucumber stir-fry with fresh vegetables; and red sea urchin taglierini pasta with sea urchin sauce and broccoli flowers.

Our service staff is well trained in introducing these dishes, and if at first there was some resistance, familiarity has bred enthusiastic acceptance. Due to popular demand, some of the dishes have now been incorporated into our menu year round. And with the increasing prevalence of octopus or sardines on many mainstream menus, one could argue that these heroes are no longer "unsung."

The success of Unsung Heroes shows that chefs have the power to change the way people think, alter how suppliers behave, and even influence what fishers catch and how they catch it. Although there is a long way to go, Ocean Wise chefs aren't taking baby steps anymore. By popularizing what once were forgotten species, we can also take the pressure off more popular ones, and in turn allow them the chance to become more sustainable.

In my experience, if you ask your fishmonger for a certain sustainable-caught, Ocean Wise product and they don't have it, they will try to have it available next time you shop. And once you know a reliable fishmonger, they might suggest a fish you hadn't considered cooking—perhaps an unsung hero.

RESTAURANT
Wilfrid's Restaurant,
Fairmont Château Laurier

TYPE
mahi mahi

CHEF
Geoffrey Morden

LOCATION
Ottawa, ON

Grilled Mahi Mahi Kabobs with Mango-Lime Mayo and Chili-Radish Salad

These skewers are a perfect backyard appetizer for summer entertaining. Mahi mahi is a firm and tasty fish that lends itself well to grilling. The dip and salad offer a refreshing contrast to the rich flavours of the fish. We serve a variation of this in Zoé's Lounge in the Fairmont Château Laurier. *Serves 4*

NOTE: Fresh mango is easily puréed in a blender or food processor.

MANGO-LIME MAYO

Mix the mayonnaise, mango purée, 1 tsp (5 mL) of the ginger, 1 tsp (5 mL) of the garlic, lime zest and juice, and cilantro in a small bowl. Add salt and pepper to taste. Set aside.

» ½ cup (125 mL) mayonnaise
» ½ cup (125 mL) fresh mango purée (or use canned)
» 1 Tbsp (15 mL) grated fresh ginger (peeled)
» 2 tsp (10 mL) minced garlic
» 1½ tsp (7 mL) lime zest
» 1 Tbsp (15 mL) fresh lime juice
» ½ cup (125 mL) chopped cilantro
» Salt and pepper to taste

CHILI-RADISH SALAD

Combine all the salad ingredients and the remaining ginger and garlic in a medium bowl. Add salt and pepper to taste. Set aside.

» ¼ cup (60 mL) julienned daikon (white radish)
» ¼ cup (60 mL) julienned common radish
» ¼ cup (60 mL) julienned English cucumber
» ¼ cup (60 mL) julienned red pepper
» 3 Tbsp (45 mL) chopped fresh red chili pepper
» ¼ cup (60 mL) mirin
» 2 Tbsp (30 mL) canola oil
» 1 tsp (5 mL) sesame oil
» 1 tsp (5 mL) sesame seeds

continued . . .

BARBECUE SAUCE AND MAHI MAHI

Soak 16 bamboo skewers in water for at least 10 minutes (longer is better) before you prepare the recipe. Warm the marmalade and tangerine juice in a small saucepan over medium heat. Bring the mixture to a simmer, stirring occasionally, then remove from the heat and set aside.

Coat the mahi mahi with the canola oil and then season it with black pepper. Place two or three pieces of mahi mahi on each skewer. Cover the fish with plastic wrap and refrigerate until ready to barbecue.

Preheat the barbecue to 400°F (200°C). Brush the skewers with the barbecue sauce and sprinkle with a pinch of salt. Grill the mahi mahi for 1 minute per side.

» ¼ cup (60 mL) orange marmalade
» ¼ cup (60 mL) freshly squeezed tangerine (or orange) juice
» 1 lb (500 g) skinless mahi mahi fillet, cut into 1-inch (2.5 cm) cubes
» 2 Tbsp (30 mL) canola oil
» Freshly ground black pepper to taste
» Pinch salt

TO SERVE

Hot off the grill, serve the mahi mahi with the chili-radish salad and the mango-lime mayo on the side for dipping.

PAIRING SUGGESTION: A lighter-style North American Pinot Noir. *Tom Firth:* Mission Hill Five Vineyards Pinot Noir (Okanagan Valley, BC) or Le Clos Jordanne Vineyard Pinot Noir (Ont).

‹ AS SERVED AT WILFRID'S RESTAURANT

RESTAURANT
Squamish Lil'wat Cultural Centre (café)

TYPE
salmon

CHEFS
Albert Kirby, Eva Maria Joe, and Ken Wright

LOCATION
Whistler, BC

Blueberry-Candied Wild Salmon

Candied salmon is a product of curing and smoking fresh salmon to preserve it for months after the fishing season has ended. This recipe uses only natural products and is a healthy alternative to store-bought "salmon nuggets," which can contain nitrates, MSG, liquid smoke, and preservatives. The blueberry glaze simply adds a sweet flavour to the salmon after it is smoked. Without the glaze, the candy's appearance is less inviting, and the salt from the brine tends to create a white dust on the salmon once it is dried. *Makes 2 candied fillets*

CANDIED SALMON

Being careful not to cut through the skin, cut several 1-inch (2.5 cm) vertical slits into each salmon fillet, then grasp each end of the fillet and stretch the skin so that all of the slit opens up.

Place the salmon fillets on a large baking sheet that will fit in your refrigerator. Stir 1¼ cups (310 mL) of the brown sugar and the kosher salt and pepper together in a medium mixing bowl until they are well mixed. Evenly pack the mixture onto each fillet by hand, making sure to get between the open slits.

Place the fillets in the refrigerator overnight to cure. The dry cure will begin turning to liquid as the salt draws moisture from the fish. Once the salmon is cured, rinse all the remaining curing mixture off the fillets and allow them to air-dry for 1 hour.

Turn one burner of a gas barbecue on to low heat, about 100°F (38°C). Place an aluminum pan of alder, hickory, or cedar wood chips on the lit burner to create smoke. Place the fillets up high on a second-level rack if available (or on any rack), on the other side of the barbecue, above the unlit burner, and prop the barbecue lid open a little to allow air flow. Smoke the fillets for 1 hour. The objective is to smoke the fillets and not cook them. Try to keep the temperature under 120°F (50°C) for the entire hour.

» 2½ lb (1 kg) wild salmon fillets, skin on, pin bones removed
» 1½ cups (375 mL) brown sugar
» 1 cup (250 mL) kosher salt
» 1 Tbsp (15 mL) freshly ground black pepper

continued . . .

BLUEBERRY GLAZE

Combine the remaining ¼ cup (60 mL) of brown sugar, the honey, blueberries, and pepper in a small bowl. Mash the blueberries with a potato masher and add the boiling water to help melt the sugar. Stir the glaze to form a sticky sauce and brush it over the fillets once they are smoked. Leave the fish in the barbecue for 2 more hours with the burner off and the lid closed to allow the glaze to dry.

» 2 Tbsp (30 mL) unpasteurized honey
» ½ cup (125 mL) fresh blueberries
» 1 tsp (5 mL) freshly ground black pepper
» 3 Tbsp (45 mL) boiling water

TO SERVE

Slice the smoked salmon into bite-sized pieces or long strips and arrange on a platter lined with salad greens if you like, and scatter a handful of blueberries on top.

PAIRING SUGGESTION: *Tom Firth:* Okanagan Springs Pale Ale or most Pinot Noirs, such as one from See Ya Later Ranch or Church & State Hollenbach Family Vineyard Pinot Noir (Okanagan Valley, BC).

» 2 cups (500 mL) salad greens
» ¼ cup (60 mL) fresh blueberries

Salmon Tartare with Candied Salmon Tartine

This simple starter or light lunch is quick and easy. Tartine is a French term for something spread on bread—in this case, a salmon tartare, or raw minced salmon, flavoured with tartar sauce. I love this dish for a quick snack, especially when camping, with the bread toasted over the fire. *Serves 6*

CROSTINI

Preheat the oven to 350°F (180°C). Brush the baguette slices with oil on both sides and toast in the oven for a few minutes on each side.

» 1 baguette (preferably sourdough), thickly sliced
» 2 Tbsp (30 mL) olive oil

SALMON TARTARE

Mix together the dill, parsley, mustard, horseradish, Worcestershire sauce, and hot pepper sauce in a small bowl. Add the minced salmon to the herb and mustard mixture. Cover the salmon tartare and refrigerate until ready to serve.

» 2 Tbsp (30 mL) chopped dill
» 2 Tbsp (30 mL) chopped parsley
» 1 Tbsp (15 mL) Dijon mustard
» 2 tsp (10 mL) freshly grated horseradish (or 1 tsp [5 mL] prepared hot horseradish)
» 2 tsp (10 mL) Worcestershire sauce
» 4 dashes hot pepper sauce
» ½ lb (250 g) wild chum or spring salmon, skinned and pin bones removed (you can ask your fishmonger to do this) and minced

continued . . .

CANDIED SALMON TARTINE

Blend the candied salmon, mayonnaise, and pepper in a food processor until the mixture is smooth. If you do not have a food processor, mash the salmon with a fork, then stir in the mayonnaise. Add pepper to taste.

» ½ cup (125 mL) candied salmon
» ¾ cup (185 mL) mayonnaise
» Freshly ground black pepper to taste

TO SERVE

Spread the tartine on the crostini, then top with a dollop of the salmon tartare. Garnish the dish with the sliced onion and serve immediately.

PAIRING SUGGESTION: *Tom Firth:* Thornhaven Estates Gewürztraminer (Okanagan Valley, BC) or Rosehall Run Pinot Noir Rosehall Vineyard (Ont).

» Red onion, sliced thinly into rings, for garnish

RESTAURANT
2 Chefs and a Table

CHEFS
*Allan Bosomworth
and Karl Gregg*

LOCATION
Vancouver, BC

TYPE
sardines

Pacific Sardine Escabeche

We served this dish at one of our wine drinker dinners (more low-key and fun than your typical wine-pairing event). Sardines are great on top of your favourite salad or with tomato bruschetta, but you must use fresh or frozen sardines and not canned ones. Escabeche is a typical Mediterranean dish that usually involves putting the fish into an acidic marinade, then either poaching or frying it and finishing it with a drizzle of the marinade. *Serves 8*

MARINADE

Combine all the marinade ingredients in a large stockpot over medium heat. Reduce the liquid by half (this should take 15 to 20 minutes). Remove the pot from the heat and let the stock cool.

» 3 cups (750 mL) chicken stock
» 2 cups (500 mL) apple cider vinegar
» 1 cup (250 mL) dry white wine
» 2 cloves garlic, chopped
» 1 small white onion, chopped
» Zest of 1 lemon
» 1 tsp (5 mL) fresh thyme leaves
» 1 tsp (5 mL) chopped parsley
» ½ tsp (2 mL) cumin seeds
» ½ tsp (2 mL) fennel seeds
» ½ tsp (2 mL) red chili pepper flakes
» 4 whole black peppercorns
» 2 bay leaves

SARDINES

Heat the canola oil in a large frying pan over medium-high heat. Meanwhile, combine the flour, salt, and pepper in a shallow dish. Dredge the fillets in the flour mixture and shake off any excess. Fry two fillets at a time on both sides until golden, 1 or 2 minutes per side. Remove from the frying pan, pat dry with a kitchen or paper towel, and place in an airtight container in a single layer. Pour the marinade over the sardines and marinate them in the refrigerator for a minimum of 12 hours. They will keep for a week in the marinade.

» ¼ cup (60 mL) canola oil
» ¼ cup (60 mL) all-purpose flour
» 1 Tbsp (15 mL) salt
» 1 Tbsp (15 mL) pepper
» 8 large whole sardines, cleaned, heads removed, and filleted (ask your fishmonger to do this for you)

TO SERVE

Place the sardines over a mixture of your favourite salad greens or as a pairing with tomato bruschetta and top with a drizzle of the marinade.

PAIRING SUGGESTION: Château Gaudrelle Vouvray (Loire Valley, France). *Tom Firth:* Pentâge Chenin Blanc (Okanagan Valley, BC), or a Mediterranean beer such as Mythos or Moretti.

RESTAURANT
*The Cannery Seafood Restaurant
(1971–2010)*

CHEFS
*Frédéric Couton
and Wayne Sych*

TYPE
tuna, salmon, scallops

LOCATION
Vancouver, BC

West Coast Trio of Tartare with Soy Wasabi Dip

This tartare can be made with any fish, but The Cannery's popular appetizer deliciously integrates the flavours of salmon, tuna, and scallops. Make sure to mix together the seafood and seasoning at the last minute. Otherwise, the salt and lime will make the seafood look as if it has been cooked. *Serves 4 (12 appetizer quenelles)*

NOTE: If using fresh seafood, freeze it for 24 hours beforehand.

NORI CHIPS

Preheat the oil to 350°F (180°C) in a deep pan. Cut the nori sheets into six strips and hold them under gently running water for 2 seconds. Pan-fry the nori, one piece at a time, for 30 seconds per side or until it is crisp. Drain each chip on a kitchen or paper towel and reserve for garnish.

» ¼ cup (125 mL) canola, peanut, or sunflower oil
» 2 nori sheets (dried seaweed)

SOY WASABI DIP

Combine the wasabi powder and one-quarter of the soy sauce together in a small bowl to form a paste. Stir in the honey and the remaining soy sauce.

» 3 Tbsp (45 mL) wasabi powder
» 1 cup (250 mL) soy sauce
» 1 Tbsp (15 mL) honey

continued . . .

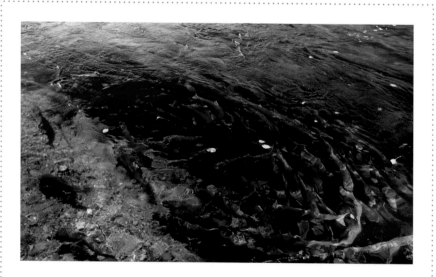

‹ SOCKEYE IN THE ADAMS RIVER
(NEAR CHASE, BC)

TARTARE

Combine the tuna, salmon, scallops, shallot, and chives in a medium bowl. Season the mixture with salt and pepper. Add the olive oil and lime juice, then toss everything gently. Let the tartare mixture sit for a few minutes.

» 5 oz (150 g) skinless albacore tuna loin, cut into ¼-inch (6 mm) dice

» 5 oz (150 g) skinless wild sockeye salmon fillet, cut into ¼-inch (6 mm) dice

» 5 oz (150 g) scallops, trimmed, cleaned, and cut into ¼-inch (6 mm) dice

» 1 Tbsp (15 mL) finely chopped shallot

» 1 Tbsp (15 mL) chopped chives (reserve a few unchopped chives for garnish)

» Salt and pepper

» 2 tsp (10 mL) extra virgin olive oil

» 1 tsp (5 mL) fresh lime juice

TO SERVE

Divide the tartare mixture onto four individual plates. Serve the dip in a small ramekin on the side of the plate. Garnish the tartare with the nori chips.

Alternatively, form the mixture into 12 oval quenelles using two soup spoons to mold them, and arrange them evenly on a chilled platter or in individual hors d'oeuvres spoons. Sprinkle the reserved nori chips on top. Lay a chive stick on each quenelle, and serve the dip in a ramekin on the side or drizzle it over each portion.

PAIRING SUGGESTION: JoieFarm Riesling (Okanagan Valley, BC). *Tom Firth:* See Ya Later Ranch Non Vintage SYL Brut Sparkling Wine (Okanagan Valley, BC).

RESTAURANT
Goldfish Pacific Kitchen

TYPE
anchovies

CHEF
William Tse

LOCATION
Vancouver, BC

Tempura Chili Anchovies with Spicy Soy Dipping Sauce and Five-Spice Sea Salt

Anchovies have a mild, slightly oily flavour. The skin is completely edible, and they are high in omega-3 fatty acids. Deep-fried and combined with a little bit of spice, anchovies are a great addition to any meal. At Goldfish we enjoy the crispness of the tempura combined with the spiciness of the chilies and garlic. *Serves 4*

NOTE: For the batter, use ice-cold water. Colder water inhibits the gluten in the flour, thereby creating a lighter batter.

SPICY SOY DIPPING SAUCE

Place all the ingredients in a bowl and mix well. Store covered in the refrigerator. Serve cold.

» 1 cup (250 mL) soy sauce
» 2 Tbsp (30 mL) sambal oelek (Asian chili sauce)
» 1 Tbsp (15 mL) fresh lime juice

FIVE-SPICE SEA SALT

Place the sea salt, five-spice powder, star anise, and dried chili in a frying pan over medium heat. Heat the salt mix until it is warm to the touch, about 10 minutes. Do not overheat or it will burn. The heating process allows the natural oils of the spices to flavour the salt. Remove the salt and spice mixture from the heat and let it cool.

» 1 cup (250 mL) sea salt
» 1 Tbsp (15 mL) five-spice powder (see Note page 55)
» 1 whole star anise
» 1 whole dried chili (preferably a Thai bird chili)

continued . . .

TEMPURA CHILI ANCHOVIES

To make the tempura batter, place the egg in a large mixing bowl and beat it until it starts to froth. Whisk in the water. Add all the flour, roasted rice powder, salt, white pepper, baking powder, and soy sauce. Whisk the mixture until all the ingredients are incorporated. Do not overmix or the batter will be tough. Cover the batter and place it in the coldest part of the refrigerator until ready to use.

Heat the oil (reserving 2 Tbsp/30 mL for later use) to 375°F (190°C) in a large pot over medium heat. Make sure the oil is only halfway up the pot so it will not overflow when you fry the anchovies. While the oil is heating, place the flour in a medium bowl. Coat each anchovy with flour, making sure to shake off the excess, and then dip in the tempura batter. Working in batches, cook the fish for 5 to 6 minutes. Remove them from the oil with tongs and place them on paper towel to drain. Do not crowd the pot, for this will lower the temperature of the oil and the batter will not be crispy.

- » 1 large egg
- » 1 cup (250 mL) ice-cold water
- » 3 cups (750 mL) all-purpose flour
- » 2 Tbsp (60 mL) roasted rice powder (available at Asian supermarkets)
- » 1 Tbsp (15 mL) salt
- » 1 tsp (5 mL) pepper (freshly ground white pepper works best)
- » Pinch baking powder
- » 2 dashes soy sauce
- » 10 cups (2.5 L) vegetable oil for deep-frying (reserve 2 Tbsp/30 mL for pan-frying)
- » 2 cups (500 mL) all-purpose flour
- » 4 lb (1.8 kg) fresh whole anchovies (about 10 per pound/500 g)

TO SERVE

Heat a medium frying pan over high heat. Add the reserved oil and the shallots, garlic, and Thai bird chili and jalapeños to the pan. Sauté them for 1 minute, and then add the tempura-battered anchovies to the pan. Sprinkle the fish with the green onions, garlic chips, and five-spice sea salt. Serve immediately with the spicy soy dipping sauce and a grinding of pepper on a platter.

PAIRING SUGGESTION: Gewürztraminer is a great wine with this dish. Full-bodied and high in sugar, with hints of lychee, this wine is a perfect match for spicy dishes and those with Asian flavours. Riesling is also an excellent choice for this dish. High in acidity, with hints of apple and pear, it pairs well with the spicy and savoury character of this appetizer. *Tom Firth:* Hillside Estate Gamay Noir or JoieFarm Rosé (both Okanagan Valley, BC), or The Organized Crime Riesling Reserve (Ont).

- » ¼ cup (60 mL) sliced shallots
- » 1 Tbsp (15 mL) chopped garlic
- » 1 fresh Thai bird chili, sliced
- » 1 Tbsp (15 mL) sliced jalapeños
- » ¼ cup (60 mL) sliced green onions
- » 2 Tbsp (30 mL) garlic chips (available at most Asian supermarkets, or see recipe next page)

RESTAURANT
Goldfish Pacific Kitchen

TYPE
capelin

CHEF
William Tse

LOCATION
Vancouver, BC

Crispy Fried Capelin Tossed with Five-Spice Sea Salt, Crispy Capers, and Garlic Chips

Capelin are like little fish french fries and very similar to smelt. Growing up I ate a lot of crispy fried smelt tossed in sea salt— simple, yet very tasty. Capelin are quite small but they are rich, so eight per person is ample. *Serves 4*

NOTE: When you buy capelin, ask the fishmonger to remove the blood and internal organs. Mirin, garlic chips, and five-spice powder (a combination of star anise, cloves, cinnamon, Szechuan pepper, and ground fennel seeds, commonly used in Asian cuisine) are available at most Asian supermarkets. You can also make your own garlic chips following the instructions in this recipe.

TO MARINATE THE CAPELIN

Rinse each fish thoroughly. Drain them well in a colander and pat dry with a paper towel. Place the capelin in a large bowl. Add the soy sauce and mirin and toss the capelin until they are evenly coated. Set them aside to marinate for 20 minutes.

» 32 capelin
» 2 Tbsp (30 mL) light soy sauce
» 2 Tbsp (30 mL) mirin (sweet rice wine)

TO PREPARE THE GARLIC CHIPS

Slice the garlic cloves on a mandoline (⅛ inch/3 mm or thinner). Place the slices in a small saucepan, cover with the coconut milk, and let marinate for 1 hour. Bring the garlic-coconut milk to a boil and remove from the heat. Drain the garlic slices in a fine-mesh sieve, discarding the milk. Pat the garlic slices dry on a kitchen or paper towel.

Heat the oil in a saucepan to 300°F (150°C). Fry the garlic slices for 5 minutes, or until the chips are a light golden brown. (Keep in mind they will continue to cook once out of the pan—don't allow them to get too brown.) Drain the garlic chips on a kitchen or paper towel. Garlic chips can be made ahead and stored in an airtight container at room temperature for one to two days.

» 15 cloves garlic, peeled
» ½ cup (125 mL) coconut milk
» 2 cups (500 mL) canola oil for deep-frying

continued . . .

TO PREPARE THE CAPERS

Heat the canola oil to 375°F (190°C) in a large pot over high heat. Put the capers in the oil, taking care to stand back a little as their moisture will cause the oil to splatter. Fry the capers until they pop and change colour, 1 to 2 minutes. Remove them from the oil with a metal strainer and drain them on a plate lined with a kitchen or paper towel.

» 8 cups (2 L) canola oil for deep-frying capers and fish
» ¼ cup (60 mL) small capers, drained and patted dry

TO FRY THE CAPELIN

Mix together the cornstarch and freshly ground white pepper in a medium bowl. Lightly coat the capelin one at a time, making sure to shake off the excess cornstarch. Working in batches, carefully drop each capelin into the hot oil. Do not crowd the pot, for this will lower the temperature of the oil and the batter will not be crispy. Deep-fry the fish for 5 to 6 minutes, then drain them on a plate lined with kitchen or paper towel. Sprinkle them with the five-spice powder and sea salt immediately. (The salt will only stick to the fish right after it comes out of the oil.)

» 1½ cups (375 mL) cornstarch
» 1 tsp (5 mL) freshly ground white pepper
» 2 Tbsp (30 mL) five-spice powder
» 1 Tbsp (15 mL) sea salt

TO SERVE

Place all the cooked fish in a large serving bowl and toss them with the capers and a handful of the garlic chips. Serve immediately.

PAIRING SUGGESTION: Sauvignon Blanc is the best wine to accompany this dish. It is high in acidity and is always tangy, tart, nervy, racy, or even zesty, pairing well with the saltiness of the dish. *Tom Firth:* White Bear Sauvignon Blanc (Okanagan Valley, BC) or Cloudy Bay Sauvignon Blanc (New Zealand).

RESTAURANT
The Observatory/Grouse Mountain Visitor Food Services

TYPE
mackerel

CHEF
Dino Gazzola

LOCATION
North Vancouver, BC

Marinated Mackerel with Mackerel Tartare, Pickled Onions, and Carrot–Blood Orange Reduction

The rich, oily taste of mackerel in this dish lends itself beautifully to tartare in this out-of-the-ordinary appetizer. The mackerel is marinated in two ways: in a champagne vinaigrette and in a spiced crème fraîche. And the pickled onions and caraway seeds add a distinctive Scandinavian edge. The carrot–blood orange reduction offers a somewhat sweet undertone to complement the rich flavours. *Serves 4*

TO PREPARE THE MACKEREL

Cut the mackerel fillets in half lengthwise. Dice the end pieces and reserve them for the tartare, leaving the thicker body for marinating. Keep the fillets covered in the refrigerator in a non-reactive (glass or ceramic) bowl until you are ready to make the tartare.

» Four 4 oz (175 g) skinless mackerel fillets

MACKEREL MARINADE

Process the butter lettuce, parsley leaves, and cucumber to a fine purée (ideally in a juicer or food processor). Pour the juice into a small, non-reactive bowl and whisk in the champagne vinegar, olive oil, and lemon juice. Reserve 1 tsp (5 mL) of the marinade for the tartare. Pour the marinade over the mackerel fillets and refrigerate them, covered, in a glass dish or Ziploc bag, for 1 hour.

» ¼ head butter lettuce
» ¼ cup (60 mL) Italian flat-leaf parsley leaves
» ½ English cucumber
» 3 Tbsp (45 mL) champagne vinegar
» 2 Tbsp (30 mL) extra virgin olive oil
» 1 Tbsp (15 mL) fresh lemon juice

continued . . .

PICKLED ONION

Combine the white wine vinegar, water, sugar, salt, and 2½ tsp (12 mL) of the toasted caraway seeds in a small saucepan over medium heat. Bring the mixture to a boil, then remove it from the heat. Place the sliced onion in a small bowl. Pour the pickling liquid over the onion and let it cool completely.

» ¼ cup plus 8 tsp (100 mL) white wine vinegar
» 3 Tbsp (45 mL) water
» 1 Tbsp (15 mL) + 2 tsp (10 mL) sugar
» 2½ tsp (12 mL) coarse sea salt
» 1 Tbsp (15 mL) caraway seeds, toasted (reserve ½ tsp/2 mL for the tartare)
» ¼ medium white onion, thinly sliced

CARROT–BLOOD ORANGE EMULSION

Simmer the blood orange and carrot juices in a small saucepan over low heat until they have reduced by half, about 10 minutes. Let the reduction cool completely. Once it is cool, slowly whisk in the olive oil. Keep the emulsion at room temperature until you are ready to use it.

» Juice of 1 blood orange (or regular orange)
» 3 Tbsp (45 mL) extra virgin olive oil
» ½ cup (125 mL) carrot juice (or 1 large carrot, juiced)

MACKEREL TARTARE

Gently combine the diced mackerel tails, crème fraîche, dill, shallot, lemon juice, remaining 1 tsp (5 mL) marinade, and remaining caraway seeds in a medium bowl. Fold in the diced beet and season the tartare to taste with sea salt and freshly ground pepper.

» 4 tsp (20 mL) crème fraîche (see page 291)
» 1 tsp (5 mL) finely chopped dill
» 1 tsp (5 mL) finely diced shallot
» 1 Tbsp (15 mL) fresh lemon juice
» ½ tsp (2 mL) caraway seeds, toasted
» 1 tsp (5 mL) marinade
» 1 small red beet, cooked, peeled, and finely diced
» Sea salt and freshly ground black pepper to taste

TO SERVE

Set out four plates. Remove the mackerel fillets from the marinade and pat them dry using paper towel. Place one fillet in the centre of each plate. Top the pieces with equal portions of the mackerel tartare. Drizzle the fish with the carrot–blood orange emulsion. Drain the pickling liquid from the onions, pat them dry with a paper towel, and place a small amount on top of the tartare. Finish the dish with a pinch of coarse sea salt and freshly ground black pepper.

PAIRING SUGGESTION: *Tom Firth:* Hillside Estate Old Vines Gamay Noir or Pentâge Riesling (both Okanagan Valley, BC).

RESTAURANTS
The Mark and The Pacific restaurants,
Hotel Grand Pacific

TYPE
sardines

CHEF
Michael Minshull

LOCATION
Victoria, BC

Black Olive–Grilled Pacific Sardines on Brioche Toast with Nasturtium Greens and Organic Cucumber

The Pacific sardine is one of the most beautiful and under-rated fishes. It has a unique meaty texture and powerful flavour without being fishy. Ask your local fishmonger to fillet the sardines for you. *Serves 8*

NOTE: Black olive oil is an amazing and versatile ingredient; it can be used on just about any fish. Be sure to use good-quality olive oil and olives. Always refrigerate the black olive oil but take it out to soften and shake it well before using. If you do not like black olives, high-quality green ones are also excellent.

BLACK OLIVE OIL

Ensure that there are no pits in the olives. Place all the ingredients in a blender and purée them until the mixture is smooth, about 1 minute. Reserve.

» ½ cup (125 mL) high-quality olives (kalamata, Moroccan, or Cerignola are all good choices), pitted
» ¼ cup (60 mL) high-quality organic extra virgin olive oil
» 1 small sprig tarragon
» Pinch freshly ground black pepper

SARDINES

Brush the flesh side of the sardine fillets with the black olive oil. Squeeze a liberal amount of fresh lemon on the sardines and season them with a pinch of freshly ground black pepper. Refrigerate until ready to barbecue.

» 16 fresh wild Pacific sardine fillets
» ¼ cup (60 mL) black olive oil
» 1 lemon, cut in half
» Pinch freshly ground black pepper

CUCUMBER

Slice the cucumber and onion as thinly as possible. Place both in separate bowls of ice water. This will crisp the cucumber and mellow the strong onion flavours. Let them stand for 10 minutes. Drain off the ice water and combine the cucumber and onion in a medium non-reactive (glass or ceramic) bowl. Toss the slices with the basil, sherry vinegar, and sugar. Season the mixture with sea salt and more freshly ground black pepper, and reserve.

» 1 medium organic English, lemon, or hothouse cucumber
» 1 small Vidalia, Walla Walla, or Italian red onion
» 1½ cups (375 mL) basil, loosely packed
» 2 Tbsp (30 mL) sherry vinegar (or any other wine vinegar)
» 2 tsp (10 mL) sugar
» Sea salt to taste

TO GRILL THE BRIOCHE AND SARDINES

Preheat your barbecue to 400°F (200°C). (Alternatively, an oven broiler may be used.) Toast the brioche slices on the preheated grill, turning them once, until they are golden brown on both sides. In a small bowl, blend the horseradish and the Dijon mustard, and then spread the mixture over the brioche.

Grill the sardines, on the flesh side only, until the skin side is firm to the touch, 3 to 4 minutes. (If you are using an oven broiler, cook the sardines flesh side facing up for about the same time.) Remove the fillets from the heat.

» 8 thick slices fresh brioche (or any other soft bread)
» 2 Tbsp (30 mL) prepared creamy horseradish
» 2 Tbsp (30 mL) Dijon mustard

TO SERVE

Set out eight plates. Place one slice of brioche on each plate and scatter the nasturtium greens around them. Lay the tomatoes on top of the nasturtium greens, followed by the sardines (two per plate), and place the cucumber and onion slices on top. Serve immediately.

PAIRING SUGGESTION: Sake or Pinot Gris. *Tom Firth:* Osake Junmai Nama sake (Granville Island, BC), Poplar Grove Pinot Gris (Okanagan Valley, BC), or Dead Frog Lager (Aldergrove, BC).

» 2 cups (500 mL) fresh nasturtium leaves (or arugula or watercress leaves)
» 2 to 4 large heirloom tomatoes (or organic field or hothouse tomatoes), sliced

RESTAURANT
Manhattan Restaurant,
Delta Vancouver Suites Hotel

TYPE
smelt

CHEF
Michael Viloria

LOCATION
Vancouver, BC

Smelt Fry with Tarragon Mayonnaise

These fish are typically eaten whole—they are so small that everything is edible—but you can always behead them before cooking. Smelts are very addictive (this recipe is no exception) and very affordable. *Serves 4*

TARRAGON MAYONNAISE

Mix the mayonnaise, 1 Tbsp (15 mL) of the parsley, tarragon, and champagne vinegar together in a small bowl and set the mayonnaise aside.

» 1 cup (250 mL) mayonnaise

» 2 Tbsp (30 mL) chopped parsley

» 1 Tbsp (15 mL) chopped tarragon

» 1 Tbsp (15 mL) champagne vinegar

TO MARINATE THE SMELT

Gently toss the smelt in a large, non-reactive (glass or ceramic) bowl with the lemon zest and juice, salt, cayenne pepper, and the remaining parsley until they are well coated. Marinate them, covered, in the refrigerator for 1 hour.

» 12 to 16 whole smelt

» Zest and juice of 1 lemon

» 1 Tbsp (15 mL) sea salt

» 1 tsp (5 mL) cayenne pepper

TO FRY THE SMELT

Heat the canola oil to 325°F (160°C) in a large cast iron frying pan over medium heat. Spread the flour evenly in a large, shallow dish. Working in batches of three or four at a time, dredge the fish in the flour, shake off any excess, and carefully place them in the hot oil for 3 to 4 minutes, or until they are golden brown. Remove the smelt from the oil using tongs and place them on a plate lined with a kitchen or paper towel to drain.

» 2 cups (500 mL) canola oil

» 1 cup (250 mL) all-purpose flour

TO SERVE

Serve immediately, while the smelts are hot, with the tarragon mayonnaise on the side for dipping.

PAIRING SUGGESTION: Sauvignon Blanc. *Tom Firth*: Pentâge Sauvignon Blanc/Semillon (Okanagan Valley, BC) or Magnotta Sauvignon Blanc Special Reserve (Ont).

SOURCE
Little Piggy Catering

CHEFS
*Christabel Padmore
and Patrick Simpson*

TYPE
smoked trout

LOCATION
Victoria, BC

Smoked Trout Mousse

An easy make-ahead item for a dinner party or luncheon, this velvety mousse can be served as a first course with buttered toast points and an endive salad with a lemony vinaigrette. It can also be converted into a canapé topping for cocktail parties.

Little Piggy sources its trout from the Sooke River on Vancouver Island, but there are various sources for sustainable trout throughout Canada, particularly in Ontario, where it is raised in close containment land farms. We smoke the trout ourselves, but specialty fish counters and shops carry it pre-smoked. *Serves 4*

Line a straight-sided 2-cup (500 mL) mold or soufflé dish with parchment paper (or grease it with a small amount of vegetable oil).

Using a food processor or hand blender, purée the smoked trout with ¼ cup (60 mL) of the cream, the butter, lemon juice, and salt until the mixture is smooth. Transfer it to a bowl.

Pour the water into a small saucepan, sprinkle in the gelatin, and let it soften for 1 minute. Over low heat, stir the mixture until the gelatin has dissolved, about 2 minutes. Do not allow the water's heat to pass a simmer. Cool the gelatin mixture to room temperature.

Beat the remaining ½ cup (125 mL) of cream in a medium bowl until stiff peaks form. Gently combine the gelatin mixture with the trout purée in a large bowl, then fold the whipped cream into the mixture until it is well combined. Season the mousse to taste with salt.

Spoon half of the mousse into the prepared mold and smooth the top. Sprinkle it with the chopped dill. Spoon the remaining mousse over the dill, spreading it evenly, but minding the placement of the dill. Gently smooth the top surface. Chill the mousse in the refrigerator, covered, for at least 12 hours or up to two days.

» Two 8 oz (230 g) skinless smoked trout fillets
» ¾ cup (185 mL) whipping cream, chilled
» 1 Tbsp (15 mL) unsalted butter, room temperature
» 2 Tbsp (30 mL) fresh lemon juice
» ½ tsp (2 mL) sea salt
» 2 Tbsp (30 mL) cold water
» 1 package unflavoured gelatin powder (about 1 Tbsp/15 mL)
» ¼ cup (60 mL) chopped dill
» Salt to taste

TO SERVE

Unmold the mousse by running a knife around the edge of the mold. Dip the bottom of the mold into a hot-water bath for a few seconds. Once the mousse has loosened, invert it onto a plate and cut it into portions.

PAIRING SUGGESTION: An Italian Verdicchio, French Sancerre, or Chablis. An Okanagan Chardonnay like the Blasted Church Chardonnay Musque would also be a good pick. *Tom Firth:* Hillebrand Artist Series Sauvignon Blanc (Ont).

RESTAURANT
Mantles Restaurant & Lounge,
Delta Sun Peaks Resort

TYPE
crab

CHEF
David Tombs

LOCATION
Sun Peaks, BC

Spicy Dungeness Crab Cakes

These succulent morsels are "all killer, no filler." We change our menu every eight weeks or so but find it hard not to keep these cakes on it with some sort of seasonal spin. In the summer of 2009 we served them with an organic corn salsa, avocado purée, and roasted pepper coulis. *Serves 4*

NOTE: For an added kick, you can add 1 Tbsp (15 mL) of abodo sauce (reserved liquid from canned chipotle peppers) to the corn salsa.

CORN SALSA

Preheat the oven to 350°F (180°C). Spread the corn kernels on a baking sheet and roast for 10 minutes, or until just starting to turn golden brown. Cool and reserve.

Cut the bacon into ¼-inch (6 mm) strips. In a large frying pan, sauté the strips until almost crisp. Add the zucchini, pepper, onion, garlic, cumin, chili powder, and corn kernels. Sauté for 5 to 7 minutes, until the onion is translucent and the zucchini is medium firm. Cool the mixture and season with the lime juice, cilantro, salt, and pepper.

» 1 cup (250 mL) corn kernels
» 4 slices bacon
» ½ cup (125 mL) finely chopped zucchini
» ½ cup (125 mL) chopped roasted red pepper
» ½ red onion
» 1 clove garlic, minced
» 1 tsp (5 mL) ground cumin
» 1 tsp (5 mL) chili powder
» 1 Tbsp (15 mL) fresh lime juice
» ½ cup (125 mL) chopped cilantro
» Salt and pepper to taste

CRAB CAKES

Drain the crabmeat and reserve. Mix together ¼ cup (60 mL) of the panko, the roasted red pepper, cilantro, mayonnaise, shallot, lime zest and juice, sambal oelek, salt, and freshly ground pepper in a medium bowl. Add the crabmeat and gently toss together until the mixture is well combined.

Divide the mixture into four or eight equal portions and shape each one into a patty. Place the cakes on a parchment-lined baking sheet, cover with plastic wrap, and freeze for 6 to 8 hours, or overnight.

Place the flour and remaining panko into two separate 8- × 16-inch (20 × 40 cm) cake pans. Whisk the eggs together in a mixing bowl with a splash of cold water until the whites and yolks are fully incorporated. Dredge the frozen crab cakes in the flour, immerse in the beaten eggs, then coat liberally with the panko.

Preheat the oven to 350°F (180°C). In a frying pan on the stovetop, heat the canola oil to 340°F (170°C). Fry the cakes, turning them once, until they are light golden brown, about 2 minutes per side. Finish the cakes in the preheated oven for 10 to 12 minutes, or until a paring knife inserted into the middle is warm to the touch. Serve immediately with a bowl of corn salsa.

PAIRING SUGGESTION: A fruit-forward Chardonnay or Gewürztraminer. *Tom Firth*: Unoaked or lightly oaked Chardonnay or high-acid dry wines, such as Flat Rock Cellars Chardonnay (Ont) or Nk'Mip Cellars Riesling (Okanagan Valley, BC).

» 1 lb (500 g) Dungeness crabmeat, picked clean
» 1¼ cups (310 mL) panko (Japanese breadcrumbs)
» ¼ cup (60 mL) diced roasted red pepper (¼-inch/6 mm dice)
» ¼ cup (60 mL) finely chopped cilantro
» ¼ cup (60 mL) mayonnaise (or light mayo)
» 1 shallot, finely minced
» Zest and juice of 1 lime
» 1 Tbsp (15 mL) sambal oelek (Asian chili sauce, or a dash of hot pepper sauce)
» Pinch salt
» Pinch freshly ground black pepper
» 1 cup (250 mL) all-purpose flour (or whole wheat flour)
» 3 large eggs
» 2 cups (500 mL) canola oil

RESTAURANT
Local Lounge & Grille

TYPE
crab

CHEF
Paul Cecconi

LOCATION
Summerland, BC

Dungeness Crab Falafels with Red Pepper Mascarpone Sauce

This versatile dish quickly became one of our favourites at the Local Lounge. Dungeness crab has a sweet, mild, and slightly nutty taste, which pairs well with the chickpeas and spices and the sauce. *Serves 4*

NOTE: You can mold the falafels into any size or shape you like, and you can also bake them in the oven after browning to ensure you heat them all the way through. Falafels can be stored in the freezer for up to one month.

RED PEPPER MASCARPONE SAUCE

Purée all the ingredients except the grapeseed oil in a blender or food processor until smooth. Slowly add the oil to emulsify and season to taste. Refrigerate until ready to serve.

» 2 medium red peppers,
  roasted and peeled
» 2 tsp (10 mL) sambal oelek
  (Asian chili sauce)
» 2 Tbsp (30 mL) honey
» 2 Tbsp (30 mL) mascarpone cheese
» Salt and pepper to taste
» ½ cup (125 mL) grapeseed oil

continued . . .

Soak the chickpeas in enough water to cover by several inches (8–10 cm) for 24 hours.

Drain the soaked chickpeas and rinse them under cold water. Put them in a food processor with all the remaining ingredients except the chickpea flour, baking powder, and crabmeat. Process them until the mixture is well combined and not too coarse. Add the flour, baking powder, and crab and lightly fold them in. Transfer the mixture to a bowl, cover, and refrigerate for 4 hours.

» 2 cups (500 mL) dried chickpeas
» 1 yellow onion, minced
» ⅓ cup (80 mL) finely chopped Italian flat-leaf parsley
» ⅓ cup (80 mL) finely chopped cilantro
» 4 cloves garlic, minced
» 1½ tsp (7 mL) salt
» 1½ tsp (7 mL) red chili pepper flakes
» 1½ tsp (7 mL) ground cumin
» 1 tsp (5 mL) lemon zest
» ½ tsp (2 mL) Old Bay Spice (see page 294)
» ¾ cup (185 mL) chickpea flour (or all-purpose flour)
» 1½ tsp (7 mL) baking powder
» ¾ lb (375 g) Dungeness crabmeat, picked over for any cartilage and dried well between paper towels

TO FRY THE FALAFELS

Preheat a deep fryer to 350°F (180°C). Alternatively, you can use a large frying pan over medium heat with enough oil in it to reach halfway up the falafel.

Roll the falafel into 2-inch (5 cm) balls and fry them until they are golden brown all over, 3 to 6 minutes. Dry on a kitchen or paper towel.

» Oil for deep-frying

TO SERVE

Bring the red pepper mascarpone sauce to room temperature and serve with the hot falafels.

PAIRING SUGGESTION: See Ya Later Ranch Chardonnay (Okanagan Valley, BC). *Tom Firth:* Mistaken Identity Pinot Rosé (BC).

› FALAFEL AMUSE-BOUCHES AT LOCAL LOUNGE
  & GRILLE

RESTAURANT
Le Gavroche

TYPE
crab

CHEF
Manuel Ferreira

LOCATION
Vancouver, BC

Stuffed Dungeness Crab and Sautéed Crab Legs

This recipe was created with the help of my mother. She never writes down a recipe, so when people ask her for it her answer is, "Look, feel, and love." At Le Gavroche, this dish is served family style, with a soup spoon and crusty bread. It could also be called Crab Cooked Two Ways, and nothing is wasted. Happy cracking! *Serves 4*

Place the crabs in boiling, salted water and cover the pot. There should be enough water so that the crab is completely submerged, with an additional 4 or 5 inches (10–12 cm) on top of that. Cook for about 10 minutes. Put the crabs in a bowl of ice water for several minutes and then drain before cleaning (see page 20).

Make sure to keep the crab tomalley (mustard) and the crab livers and set aside. And keep one carapace (the top shell).

Preheat the oven to 350°F (180°C). Heat half the olive oil in a large heavy pot over medium-high. Add half the garlic, half the shallot, and half the ginger, and sauté for 1 minute. Add half the white wine and reduce by half. Add the crab mustard and livers and heat through. Put the hot crab mixture in a large bowl and combine with the panko, eggs, lemon zest, Parmesan cheese, and salt and pepper. Transfer the mixture into the crab shell and bake in the oven for 10 minutes.

While the crabmeat is cooking, slightly crack the crab legs with the back end of a knife. Heat the remaining olive oil in a large frying pan and sauté the rest of the garlic, shallot, and ginger for 1 minute. Add the crab legs and body, lightly sauté, then deglaze with the remaining white wine and the butter. Toss in the cilantro and season with salt and pepper.

- » Two whole Dungeness crabs (about 1½ lb/750 g each)
- » 2 Tbsp (30 mL) olive oil
- » 2 cloves garlic, minced
- » 1 shallot, finely chopped
- » 2 tsp (10 mL) minced fresh ginger (peeled)
- » ½ cup (125 mL) dry white wine
- » 3 Tbsp (45 mL) panko (Japanese breadcrumbs)
- » 2 eggs, beaten
- » 2 Tbsp (30 mL) lemon zest
- » 2 Tbsp (30 mL) grated Parmesan cheese
- » Salt and pepper to taste
- » 1 Tbsp (15 mL) butter
- » 1 Tbsp (30 mL) chopped cilantro

TO SERVE

Place the stuffed crabmeat shell on a platter, arrange the legs and body around it, and serve with country bread.

PAIRING SUGGESTION: Tinhorn Creek Oldfield Series 2Bench White (Okanagan Valley, BC), or white Rhône such as Domaine Gayda L'archet Cuvée Occitane. *Tom Firth:* White Rhône wines such as M. Chapoutier Belleruche Blanc (France).

RESTAURANT
Goldfish Pacific Kitchen

TYPE
shrimp

CHEF
William Tse

LOCATION
Vancouver, BC

Pan-Roasted Northern Shrimp with Lime Butter

At Goldfish Pacific Kitchen we like to enhance the natural sweetness of shrimp with the fragrance of lime and the pungent qualities of red jalapeños. I cook these crustaceans with the shells and heads on to protect the sweet and tender meat. There are a lot of goodies in the head portion of the shrimp. *Serves 4*

LIME BUTTER

Mix the soft butter, ground lime leaves, garlic, and lime juice together in a small bowl. Refrigerate until the butter is hard, about 20 minutes.

» ¼ cup (60 mL) unsalted butter, room temperature
» 2 dried lime leaves, ground to a powder in a clean coffee grinder
» 1 Tbsp (15 mL) chopped garlic
» 1 Tbsp (15 mL) fresh lime juice

TO PAN-ROAST THE SHRIMP

Heat three-quarters of the oil in a wok over high heat until it is just about to smoke. Add the shrimp and sauté them for no more than 2 minutes, giving them a few quick tosses. Remove them from the pan and set them aside.

Add the rest of the oil to the wok, then sauté the onion, garlic, and ginger over high heat for 2 minutes. Add the lemongrass, jalapeño, sambal oelek, and five-spice powder. Add the shrimp to the wok and sauté everything for 2 minutes to incorporate the flavours. Deglaze the pan with the cooking wine and continue stir-frying for another minute. Turn off the heat, add the hardened butter, and toss well—the residual heat from the pan will melt the butter slowly and allow it to coat the shrimp. If the pan is too hot the butter will melt too fast and be runny and oily.

» ½ cup (125 mL) vegetable oil
» 2 lb (1 kg) northern shrimp, heads and shells on (about 72 shrimp)
» ½ cup (125 mL) thinly sliced white onion
» 3 Tbsp (45 mL) thinly sliced garlic
» 3 Tbsp (45 mL) julienned fresh ginger (peeled)
» 3 Tbsp (45 mL) thinly sliced lemongrass
» 2 Tbsp (30 mL) thinly sliced red jalapeños
» 2 tsp (10 mL) sambal oelek
» ½ tsp (2 mL) five-spice powder
» ¼ cup (60 mL) Chinese cooking wine

TO SERVE

Set out four plates. Distribute the shrimps and season to taste with sea salt, freshly ground pepper, and lime wedges.

PAIRING SUGGESTION: A Chardonnay will go really well with this dish. *Tom Firth:* Sandhill Estate Vineyard Chardonnay (Okanagan Valley, BC) or Creekside Estate Reserve Chardonnay (Ont).

» Sea salt and freshly ground black pepper to taste
» Lime wedges, for garnish

RESTAURANT
Chambar

TYPE
spot prawns

CHEF
Nico Schuermans

LOCATION
Vancouver, BC

Lime and Panko–Crusted Prawns with Lemon and Herb Remoulade

These crispy prawns are like popcorn—so addictive you can easily eat a pound apiece. The lime zest with the panko revs up the "wow" factor. Buy the biggest prawns you can find, about 12 to 16 to a pound (500 g). *Serves 4 to 6*

LEMON AND HERB REMOULADE

Mix all the ingredients together in a bowl. Cover the remoulade and refrigerate until you are ready to serve it. You can make it the day before, if you like.

» ½ cup (125 mL) mayonnaise
» 1 Tbsp (15 mL) minced red onion
» 1 Tbsp (15 mL) fresh lemon juice
» 1 tsp (5 mL) sliced chives
» 1 tsp (5 mL) EACH chopped Italian flat-leaf parsley, chervil, and tarragon
» ½ tsp (2 mL) minced garlic
» ½ tsp (2 mL) lemon zest
» ½ tsp (2 mL) chopped capers
» ½ tsp (2 mL) Dijon mustard
» Salt and pepper to taste

LIME AND PANKO–CRUSTED PRAWNS

Preheat the oil to 350°F (180°C) in a large, heavy pot. Mix together the panko, lime zest, salt, and pepper in a shallow bowl. Whisk the egg in a separate bowl. Dip each prawn in the egg, then roll it in the panko seasoning to coat well. Gently place the prawns in the hot oil and deep-fry them for about 2 minutes, or until they are golden brown.

» 4 cups (1 L) vegetable (canola) oil
» 2 cups (500 mL) panko (Japanese breadcrumbs)
» Zest of 2 limes
» Salt and pepper
» 1 large egg
» 1 lb (500 g) BC spot prawns, shelled and deveined (about 4 per person, depending on size of the prawns)

TO SERVE

Remove the prawns from the oil with tongs, drain them on paper towel, and serve them hot, with the lemon and herb remoulade on the side.

PAIRING SUGGESTION: *Tom Firth:* Vineland Estates Chardonnay (Ont), Granville Island Brewery Island Lager, or JoieFarm Un-oaked Chardonnay (Okanagan Valley, BC).

SOURCE
ARAMARK at Rogers Arena
(formerly GM Place)

TYPE
spot prawns

CHEF
David Speight

LOCATION
Vancouver, BC

Beaver Cove Spot Prawns with Citrus Basil Butter

This dish was served to the Vancouver Canucks after they defeated the St. Louis Blues in the first round of the 2008–09 playoffs. During the break between series, the Canucks defenceman Willie Mitchell went fishing near Telegraph Cove and caught some local BC spot prawns and brought them back to the kitchen at GM Place (now called Rogers Arena). With some tips from Willie, we cooked them up for the players using the following recipe with great success. Food does not get any more sustainable than a local boy catching some local spot prawns and having another local boy cook them up for the local hockey team! *Serves 4*

NOTE: Since the fresh season for local BC spot prawns is quite short, using frozen is an option for the rest of the year. However, nothing can compare to the taste of fresh. This recipe can be served as an appetizer or can be made into a main course by serving it over a bed of fresh linguini for a more substantial meal.

First, prepare all ingredients other than the prawns. Set aside. Remove the heads from the spot prawns. Bring a large pot of salted water to a boil, and blanch eight prawns at a time for only 2 seconds. Remove the prawns from the water, place them on a baking sheet, and peel them.

Heat the olive oil in a large saucepan over medium heat. Add the prawns and sauté them for 10 seconds per side. Add the garlic, salt, pepper, and red chili. Continue sautéing for 10 more seconds. Add the white wine, turn the heat up to high, and reduce the liquid by two-thirds. Add the water, tomatoes, and lemon juice. Remove the pan from the heat and quickly whisk in the butter until it is fully incorporated. Add the olives, parsley, and basil. Total cooking time should not exceed 2 to 3 minutes.

» 32 large BC spot prawns
» 5 Tbsp (75 mL) extra virgin olive oil
» 2 cloves garlic, crushed into a paste
» Pinch sea salt
» Pinch freshly ground black pepper
» 1 fresh red chili pepper, seeded and finely diced
» ⅓ cup (80 mL) + 4 tsp (20 mL) dry white wine
» 1 Tbsp (15 mL) water
» 2 vine-ripened tomatoes, seeded and finely diced
» Juice of 1 lemon
» 3 Tbsp (45 mL) cold unsalted butter, thinly sliced
» 1 Tbsp (15 mL) green olives, pitted and finely diced
» 1 bunch Italian flat-leaf parsley, finely chopped
» 1 bunch basil, chopped

TO SERVE

Serve in a medium bowl for family-style service or individually on four small plates.

PAIRING SUGGESTION: A Riesling would be a very good choice. Its high acidity will help cool down the palate, and the complex bouquet can stand up to the spiciness of this dish. *Tom Firth:* Tawse Sketches of Niagara Riesling (Ont) or Quails' Gate Dry Riesling (Okanagan Valley, BC).

Spot Prawns—Sustainable Love

Jane Mundy

Until three years ago, Canadian chefs were frustrated because they couldn't get their hands on West Coast spot prawns. Then Steve Johansen of Organic Ocean Seafood, chef Robert Clark from C restaurant, and the Chefs' Table Society of BC got together and held a spot prawn festival.

"A lot of people who'd lived in BC all their lives didn't know these delectable little gems existed until we held the festival," says Johansen, "because 90 percent of the spot prawn catch in BC was exported to Japan." The festival, held in Vancouver, educated the public—many of whom thought tiger prawns were local—as well as chefs, who became aware of the issues concerning spot prawns and tiger prawns.

"Now we know that tiger prawns are farmed unsustainably in Asia," Johansen says. "Ironically, we were getting prawns imported from Thailand and exporting spot prawns." Talk about a heavy environmental footprint.

Organic Ocean, a group of fishers, was created 10 years ago. Steve Johansen was the first fisher to harvest prawns locally on his boat, *Organic Ocean,* and sell them directly to chefs and the public on the banks of False Creek. "As demand increases we have brought other prawn fishers into the mix to keep up with demand," Steve says. Today, Organic Ocean comprises six fish boats. "We spread the love," he chuckles.

Without a doubt, the spot prawn festival has had the biggest influence on their popularity. "It shed light on how delicious they are and how sustainable the trap-caught fishery is, because it has very little impact on the sea floor and a very limited bycatch," explains Johansen.

The spot prawn season runs for about two months, typically beginning in May. "During the season we leave False Creek Fisherman's Wharf every morning at 6 a.m. and return around 1 p.m. to meet hundreds of people waiting patiently to purchase them," says Johansen.

When it comes to spot prawns, you can't beat the taste of those plucked from the ocean floor just hours before they arrive on your plate. But you don't have to rely on meeting the prawn boat.

"Before we held the first festival, chefs asked if they could use frozen prawns after the season or just serve them when they're fresh," says Johansen. "But after they tried frozen, most chefs serve prawns year round."

The *Organic Ocean* crew freezes spot prawns on the boat so they are designated "frozen at sea" (FAS). The prawns are tailed (meaning the heads are pulled off) and then put into a tub filled with sea water and blast frozen. This method ensures the firmness of the meat and seals in the fresh taste. "When they are frozen in water, the prawns can last for years—like finding the centuries-old guy in the Swiss Alps, frozen in ice," says Johansen with a laugh.

"We also sell frozen prawns to people who venture down to the wharf any time of the year," says Johansen. He hasn't run out of frozen yet, which suggests there are lots of prawns in the waters along Canada's west coast. The 2009 season was a record year, with approximately 8 million lb (3.6 million kg) caught.

"With all the work we have done together, industry as a whole has tried to shift more of [its] marketing toward the North American domestic market," says Johansen, who can now share his spot prawn love throughout Canada.

^ STEVE JOHANSEN

SOURCE
Aquarium du Québec

CHEF
André Roy

LOCATION
Quebec City, QC

TYPE
crayfish, scallops

Crayfish and Scallop Mousse with Wilted Spinach and Orange-Saffron Beurre Blanc

This dish is a delicate blend of textures and flavours. Combining the colourful ingredients with crayfish meat will make you feel like you are on vacation in the tropics. *Serves 4*

ORANGE-SAFFRON BEURRE BLANC

Cook the shallots and white wine in a heavy pot over medium-high heat until the liquid has almost completely evaporated, about 5 minutes. Add ½ cup (125 mL) of the cream and reduce the liquid by half. Gradually add the cold butter, whisking constantly. Stir in the orange juice and saffron. Set the sauce aside and keep warm. (Alternatively, you can make the sauce while the mousse is cooking.)

» 2 Tbsp (30 mL) chopped shallots
» ½ cup (125 mL) dry white wine
» 1 cup (250 mL) + 5 tsp (25 mL) whipping cream
» ¼ cup (60 mL) cold unsalted butter, cubed
» Juice of 1 orange
» 12 saffron threads

CRAYFISH AND SCALLOP MOUSSE

Remove the meat from the crayfish tails and keep it covered in the refrigerator. Place the scallops, egg whites, remaining cream, salt and pepper in the bowl of a food processor equipped with a cutting blade. Process mixture until smooth. Zest the orange and blanch the zest for a few seconds in a small pot of boiling water. Drain the zest and fold half the blanched zest and all the sugar into the scallop mixture.

Preheat the oven to 300°F (150°C). Line four 6 oz (175 g) ramekins with plastic wrap. Place five pieces of the reserved crayfish meat in each ramekin. Add enough scallop mixture to fill each ramekin. Place the ramekins in a *bain-marie* and bake for about 30 minutes, or until set.

» 20 farmed crayfish tails (or you can use frozen)
» ½ lb (250 g) farmed bay scallops or Canadian giant scallops (diver-harvested)
» 6 egg whites
» Salt and white pepper to taste
» Zest of 1 orange
» ¼ cup (60 mL) sugar

TO SERVE

Warm four plates. Blanch the spinach in a large pot of boiling water until it is wilted, about 30 seconds, and drain it. Place one-quarter of the warm spinach onto each of the plates. Remove the mousse with a spatula (carefully, loosening it around the edges first). Place each mousse on top of the spinach and surround it with a drizzle of the orange-saffron beurre blanc. Garnish the dish with the rest of the blanched orange zest and fresh chives.

PAIRING SUGGESTION: *Tom Firth:* Van Westen Viognier, Orlando Vineyard (Okanagan Valley, BC).

» 10 oz (285 g) package washed baby spinach
» Fresh chives, for garnish

SOURCE
Culinary Capers

TYPE
scallops

CHEF
Jonathan Chovancek

LOCATION
Vancouver, BC

Scallops with Sake Gelée, Mango, and Chili-Lime Mayonnaise

This low-fat hors d'oeuvre or appetizer pairs sake with the sweet, nutty flavour of scallops. Enjoy it while it's cold!
Makes 24

NOTE: If fresh sweet mangoes are unavailable, you could substitute roasted and peeled sweet peppers.

SAKE GELÉE

Place the gelatin in about 1 cup (250 mL) cold water (½ cup/125 mL water if using powder) and allow it to soften, about 5 minutes. Bring ¼ cup (60 mL) of the sake to a simmer in a small saucepan over medium-high heat and add the gelatin. Remove the pan from the heat. Stir the mixture until the gelatin is dissolved (drain off the water if you're using sheets), and then add the remaining sake.

Line a 9-inch (23 cm) square plastic or glass container with a single sheet of plastic wrap so that the bottom and sides are covered. Pour the mixture into the lined container and refrigerate it for 6 hours, or overnight.

When the gelée is set, turn it out onto a cutting board. It should be a solid, wobbly square. Cut the gelée into ¼-inch (6 mm) thick slices with a wet knife. With a ¾-inch (2 cm) round cutter (or 1½-inch/4 cm for appetizers), cut out 24 (or 12) circles from the sake slices. Place the gelée circles back onto the tray lined with plastic wrap and set them aside.

» 8 sheets gelatin, softened (or 2 packages [2 Tbsp/30 mL] unflavoured gelatin powder)
» 13 fl oz (375 mL) (1 small bottle) premium sake

TO PREPARE THE MANGO

Peel the mangoes. With a sharp knife, slice each mango lengthwise into ¼-inch (6 mm) slices. With the same round cutter used to cut the jelly circles, cut 24 (12) rounds from the mango slices. Place the mango rounds on a baking sheet and top each one with a gelée round. Cover the tray with plastic wrap and refrigerate.

» 3 ripe mangoes

continued . . .

TO BAKE THE SCALLOPS

Preheat the oven to 350°F (180°C). Dry the scallops with a paper towel and season them with the sea salt. Bake the scallops in the oven for 5 minutes, or until they are medium rare. Cool the scallops quickly in the refrigerator. When they are cold, slice each scallop in half to create two round discs. Cover with plastic wrap and place them in the refrigerator.

» 12 medium sea scallops
» ½ tsp (2 mL) fine sea salt

CHILI-LIME MAYONNAISE

Combine the mayonnaise with the lime zest and chili flakes and refrigerate. (The mayonnaise can be made up to three days in advance.)

» ¼ cup (60 mL) mayonnaise
» 1 tsp (5 mL) lime zest
» ½ tsp (2 mL) red chili pepper flakes

TO SERVE

To assemble the hors d'oeuvres, place a dime-sized dab of chili-lime mayonnaise on a serving spoon (preferably ceramic). Place a scallop on top of each dab. Now, carefully lift each mango/sake gelée stack and place it on top of each scallop. Once the dish is assembled, serve it right away or chill it for up to 2 hours before serving. Top with a grinding of pink peppercorns and shredded micro greens.

» Freshly ground pink peppercorns
» Micro greens

PAIRING SUGGESTION: This dish is best served with a cold premium sake or sherry. *Tom Firth:* Osake Junmai Nama sake or Alvear Fino en Rama (Spain).

SOURCE
Pacific Institute of Culinary Arts

TYPE
scallops

CHEF
Julian Bond

LOCATION
Vancouver, BC

Grilled Scallops with Charred Heirloom Tomato Salad

When it's the height of summer and last-minute guests stop by, this is the easiest and freshest dish you can prepare on the fly. It is best served family style because it is awesome for sharing. And lucky me—Qualicum scallops come from an area close to home. *Serves 4*

TO PREPARE THE SCALLOPS

Clean the scallops (see page 21), dry them on a kitchen or paper towel, and allow them to air-dry further in the refrigerator for at least 30 minutes.

» 4 large scallops

TO PREPARE THE TOMATOES

Core the tomatoes and cut them horizontally in half. Place them in a bowl and sprinkle with good sea salt. Toss with the olive oil, lemon zest and juice, and half of the mixed fresh herbs. Arrange the tomato halves, cut side up, on a baking sheet and let them stand at room temperature for at least 30 minutes.

» 8 medium-sized firm heirloom tomatoes
» Sea salt to taste
» 5 Tbsp (75 mL) extra virgin olive oil (approx)
» Zest and juice of 1 lemon
» ¼ cup (60 mL) mix of torn (not cut) basil, chervil, and thyme

TO GRILL THE TOMATOES AND SCALLOPS

Preheat a barbecue to medium-high heat (Note: The tomatoes and scallops will cook at the same time.) Place the tomatoes, cut side up, on the grill (reserve the juices from tomatoes in the bowl). Cook them until the bottoms are charred, 3 to 4 minutes. Turn the tomatoes over and sear them quickly, about 1 minute.

Meanwhile, drizzle the scallops with a little olive oil and some of the reserved tomato liquid. Grill them on the barbecue for 2 minutes per side—do not overcook them!

TO SERVE

Arrange the tomatoes cut side up on a platter and place the scallops on top of the tomatoes. Drizzle them with a little more olive oil and any remaining tomato juice, garnish with the remaining fresh herbs, and serve the salad warm.

PAIRING SUGGESTION: Foxtrot Vineyards Pinot Noir (Okanagan Valley, BC).
Tom Firth: Van Westen Vineyards Vino Grigio (Okanagan Valley, BC).

RESTAURANT
Goldfish Pacific Kitchen

TYPE
abalone

CHEF
William Tse

LOCATION
Vancouver, BC

Ginger and Star Anise–Braised Abalone with Shiitake Mushroom and Sun-Dried Tomato Ragout

Abalone is one of my favourite foods: its full-bodied flavour and texture are a treat. At Goldfish we braise abalone to infuse it with Pacific Rim flavours, which makes it tender and succulent. Ginger and star anise are a natural complement to this shellfish. *Serves 4*

NOTE: In this recipe the cooking process (braising) is what tenderizes the abalone. If you do not slow-braise it, the abalone will be very tough and hard to eat. Another way to tenderize abalone is to slice it about ⅛-inch (3 mm) thick, place it between some parchment paper, and pound it flat. The pounding process will tenderize the abalone for a quick pan-fry or sauté.

Use dried mushrooms because the drying process really intensifies their flavour. Soak them in water overnight in the refrigerator and, once they are hydrated, squeeze them dry and remove their stems. Then thinly slice them.

RAGOUT

Heat the vegetable oil for 2 to 3 minutes in a medium (8-cup/2 L) heavy-bottomed saucepan over high heat. Add the onion, ginger, and garlic, reduce the heat to medium, and sauté them until they brown slightly, about 5 minutes. Add the rehydrated shiitake mushrooms and the sun-dried tomatoes. Stir in the wine to deglaze the bottom of the pot. Add ½ cup (125 mL) of the chicken stock, 2 Tbsp (30 mL) of the soy sauce, 4 tsp (20 mL) of the oyster sauce, and the mirin and sambal oelek. Reduce the heat to low, letting the mixture cook for 15 minutes. As the ragout cooks, the liquid will evaporate and the flavours will intensify. Season the ragout to taste with salt and freshly ground pepper at the end of cooking. It may already be salty enough.

» 2 Tbsp (30 mL) vegetable oil
» ½ cup (125 mL) finely diced white onion
» 2 Tbsp (30 mL) finely chopped fresh ginger (peeled)
» 2 Tbsp (30 mL) chopped garlic
» 3 cups (750 mL) dried shiitake mushrooms, rehydrated (see recipe intro)
» 1½ cups (375 mL) thinly sliced sun-dried tomatoes
» ¼ cup (60 mL) dry white wine or cooking wine
» 4 cups (1 L) chicken stock
» ⅔ cups (160 mL) soy sauce
» ⅓ cup (80 mL) oyster sauce
» ¼ cup (60 mL) mirin (sweet rice wine)
» 2 tsp (10 mL) sambal oelek (Asian chili sauce)
» Salt and freshly ground black pepper to taste

TO BRAISE THE ABALONE

Wash and clean the abalone (page 21). Place all the remaining ingredients except the abalone (but including the remaining chicken stock, soy sauce, and oyster sauce) in a large, heavy-bottomed stockpot. Bring the mixture to a boil over high heat, and then turn the heat down to medium-low so that the boiling reduces to a rolling simmer. Simmer the mixture for 5 minutes, add the abalone, and then turn the heat to low and cover the pot. Simmer the abalone for about 35 minutes, or until the tip of a paring knife slides easily into it.

» 12 abalone, about 1½ inches (4 cm) long, plum in colour, weighing 4 to 5 oz (125 to 150 g), each with the shell on
» 3 cloves garlic, crushed with the blade of a knife
» 1-inch (2.5 cm) piece fresh ginger, crushed with the blade of a knife
» 2 whole star anise
» 1 fresh Thai bird chili
» 1 bay leaf
» ¼ cup (60 mL) sliced lemongrass

TO SERVE

Serving the abalone in its shell gives you a perspective of the true beauty of this ocean delicacy. Divide the ragout in the centre of each plate, then take the slow-braised abalone—shell side down—and place it on top of the ragout. Garnish with cilantro on top of the abalone meat.

» 2 Tbsp (30 mL) chopped cilantro, for garnish

The shell will give your plate some height and will also give you the option of picking up the abalone with your fingers, spooning some ragout on top, and slurping it back in one bite as if eating an oyster. Or, of course, you can use a knife and fork.

PAIRING SUGGESTION: Sake is a great pairing for this dish. The complexity of sake will enhance the natural flavour of abalone and go well with its velvety texture. *Tom Firth:* Any Fino sherry would also complement the dish.

RESTAURANT
The Cannery Seafood Restaurant
(1971–2010)

TYPE
mussels

CHEFS
Frédéric Couton and
Wayne Sych

LOCATION
Vancouver, BC

Pan-Roasted Mussels with Chorizo and Capers

This is a very simple and delicious way to cook and serve mussels. Any other shellfish can be substituted for the mussels. For the best result, use cast iron frying pans. *Serves 4 as an appetizer or 2 as a main course*

NOTE: Make sure to have a well-ventilated kitchen, with the hood fan on, as the smoke might set off your smoke alarm! To toast pine nuts, spread them on a shallow baking sheet and bake them for 5 minutes in a 350°F (180°C) oven.

Heat the olive oil in two large cast iron frying pans over high heat. Divide the mussels between the two frying pans and arrange them in a single layer. Let them cook for 1 minute. Divide the butter between the two pans. Top each pan of mussels with half each of the chorizo sausage, capers, tomato, and rosemary. Sprinkle each pan with sea salt and the toasted pine nuts. Cook the mussels, covered, for 2 to 3 minutes more or until they open. Discard any mussels that do not open.

» 2 Tbsp (30 mL) olive oil
» 2 lb (1 kg) mussels, scrubbed and de-bearded
» ¼ cup (60 mL) butter, cubed
» ½ cup (125 mL) chorizo sausage, sliced into thin rounds
» 2 Tbsp (30 mL) capers
» 1 Roma tomato, peeled, seeded, and chopped
» 1 Tbsp (15 mL) chopped rosemary
» Sea salt to taste
» 2 Tbsp (30 mL) pine nuts, toasted

TO SERVE

Place each pan on a wooden cutting board and wrap its handle with a thick napkin. Then dive in. Serve the mussels with crusty bread, toasted focaccia, or garlic bread to soak up the butter at the bottom of the pans.

PAIRING SUGGESTION: Mt. Boucherie Chardonnay Summit Reserve (Okanagan Valley, BC). *Tom Firth:* Thirty Bench Wine Makers Small Lot Chardonnay (Ont).

Vinaigrettes and Mignonettes for Oysters on the Half-Shell

by Jane Mundy

Oysters are beautiful *au naturel,* but if you aren't sold on Mother Nature, try serving them with any of the following. Allow two to four oysters per person. World-renowned Fanny Bay oysters, from the east coast of Vancouver Island, are my personal pick and can be purchased in small, medium, or large sizes, but some people prefer the little, sweeter ones, like Kushi or Royal Myagi. All are delicious. *Serves 6*

TO PREPARE OYSTERS

» 24 small or 12 medium beach oysters

Shuck the oysters (see page 22) and place them on a baking sheet in a single layer. Cover with plastic wrap and refrigerate until ready to serve. Discard top shells and rinse bottom shells. Set aside.

WHITE WINE VINAIGRETTE MARINADE AND TOMATO-CUCUMBER RELISH

White wine vinaigrette marinade

» ⅓ cup (80 mL) extra virgin olive oil
» ⅓ cup (80 mL) finely diced fennel
» ⅓ cup (80 mL) finely diced shallots
» ⅓ cup (80 mL) white wine vinegar
» Sea salt and pepper to taste

Remove oysters from shell and place in bowl. Heat the oil in a medium pot over medium heat. Add the fennel and shallots and sauté until softened, about 3 minutes. Add the vinegar and salt and pepper to taste. Bring to a boil and pour over the oysters. Let cool, then refrigerate for 2 hours.

Tomato-cucumber relish

» ¼ cup (60 mL) finely diced tomato
» ½ cup (125 mL) peeled, seeded, and finely diced English cucumber
» 2 Tbsp (30 mL) mirin (sweet rice wine)
» 1 tsp (5 mL) sugar
» 1 tsp (5 mL) lemon zest

Mix all the relish ingredients and refrigerate, covered, for about 2 hours. Drain excess liquid.

To serve

Remove oysters from the marinade and place in their shells. Arrange on a platter and spoon 1 tsp (5 mL) over each oyster. Top with the tomato-cucumber relish.

ROASTED GARLIC AND HERB VINAIGRETTE

» 1 Tbsp (15 mL) cognac or brandy
» 1 Tbsp (15 mL) red wine vinegar
» 1 Tbsp (15 mL) roasted garlic cloves, mashed
» 1 Tbsp (15 mL) mirin (sweet rice wine)
» 1 tsp (5 mL) sugar
» 1 tsp (5 mL) finely chopped thyme
» 1 tsp (5 mL) finely chopped parsley
» 1 tsp (5 mL) finely chopped chives
» ⅓ cup (80 mL) extra virgin olive oil

Combine all the ingredients except the olive oil in a small bowl. Slowly whisk in the olive oil. Top each oyster with a few drops of the vinaigrette.

MIGNONETTES

by Daniel Notkin, Oysterologist, Old Port Fishing Company, Montreal, QC

Though how the term *mignonette* came to be related to oysters is vague, it is most definitely French, stemming from the word *mignon*, which means small, dainty, or lovely. The reference is likely due to the small pieces of shallot that infuse the vinegar. More poetically, one could imagine it defining the subtle, lovely addition the vinaigrette provides to complement each oyster.

CLASSIC MIGNONETTE

» ½ shallot, finely chopped
» 1½ cups (375 mL) red
  wine vinegar
» Freshly ground black pepper
  to taste

Combine the shallot with the vinegar and a few grindings of pepper to taste. Use the same night or, for an interesting experience, let sit for a day or two, tasting it periodically. The first night the balance will be crisp and high on fresh flavours. After a day the mixture will begin to caramelize and impart a beautiful sweetness along with the spice of pepper.

DANNY'S SECRET MIGNONETTE

This is the recipe I use at Restaurant L'Orignal in Montreal. It goes well with the salty, big seaweed flavours and minerality of the French oysters, from the Fines de Clairs to the great Belons, although it is equally amazing with any sustainable world oyster. The key here is to prepare the mignonette just before serving it. While the classic mignonette can improve over time, the slightly higher density and fine dice of the shallots render this mignonette highly "oniony" the following day.

» 1 shallot, finely diced
» 1½ cups (375 mL) champagne or Prosecco

Mix the diced shallot with the champagne or Prosecco. Use immediately or at the latest within 5 hours. People will ask what is in it. Reveal nothing.

PAIRING SUGGESTION FOR OYSTERS ON THE HALF-SHELL: Sauvignon Blanc, chilled vodka, and, of course, champagne.

SOURCE
Edible British Columbia

TYPE
oysters

CHEF
Eric Pateman

LOCATION
Vancouver, BC

Coconut Curry–Poached Oysters with Sautéed Sea Asparagus

What better way to celebrate these delicacies from the West Coast than with a recipe that draws on the Asian flavours so prevalent in the BC dining scene? *Serves 8*

NOTE: Kaffir or makrut limes and their leaves (sometimes called simply "lime leaves") can be found online, or fresh, frozen, or dried at most Asian supermarkets.

OYSTERS

Heat the oil in a heavy-bottomed 12-inch (30 cm) frying pan over medium heat. Add the shallot, lemongrass, garlic, ginger, and the lime zest and leaves. Sauté until the mixture is aromatic and translucent, about 10 minutes. Add the yellow curry paste and sauté for 2 minutes more. Add the fish sauce, white wine, and coconut milk, and stir the mixture well to incorporate the curry paste. Bring the mixture to a boil and reduce the liquid by half. Add the oysters and poach them for 2½ minutes per side.

» ¼ cup (60 mL) vegetable oil
» 1 small shallot, finely diced
» 1 stalk lemongrass, finely diced
» 1 clove garlic, finely diced
» 1-inch (2.5 cm) piece young ginger, peeled and finely diced
» Zest of 2 kaffir limes and their leaves
» 1 tsp (5 mL) yellow curry paste
» 1 tsp (5 mL) fish sauce
» 2 Tbsp (30 mL) white wine
» One 14 oz (398 mL) can coconut milk
» 8 large west coast oysters

SEA ASPARAGUS

While the oysters are poaching, melt the butter in a small pan over medium heat. Add the sea asparagus and sauté it for a few minutes.

» ¼ cup (60 mL) butter
» 2 cups (500 mL) sea asparagus, rinsed

TO SERVE

Set out eight small bowls. Place one oyster in each bowl. Top it with some of the sea asparagus, followed by the coconut curry sauce. Garnish with the chopped Thai basil and serve.

PAIRING SUGGESTION: Any of the off-dry Germanic varietals produced in BC's Okanagan Valley, such as the Lake Breeze Ehrenfelser from Naramata, or a white blend such as Stoneboat Vineyards' Chorus, from Oliver.

» 1 tsp (5 mL) finely chopped Thai basil, for garnish

RESTAURANT
C Restaurant

TYPE
sea urchin

CHEF
Robert Clark

LOCATION
Vancouver, BC

Sea Urchin "Cocktail" with Tomato and Bell Pepper Salad

This is a relatively simple recipe with sensational impact. You can also buy cleaned sea urchin called *uni* in Japanese stores. One sea urchin will yield about five lobes per person. For more information, go to www.oceanwise.ca/seaurchin. *Serves 6*

Clean the urchins. Using a pair of scissors, cut the shells open around the beak (the bottom of the urchin) and drain out the liquid. Gently scoop out the five lobes and rinse them in fresh water. Repeat this for all the remaining urchins. Incorporate all the remaining ingredients together in a large non-reactive (glass or ceramic) bowl. Toss in the urchin lobes and marinate them for 1 hour.

» 6 whole sea urchins (or 30 lobes)
» 2 Tbsp (30 mL) fresh lime juice
» 2 Tbsp (30 mL) extra virgin olive oil
» 1 Tbsp (15 mL) brandy
» ½ cup (125 mL) Clamato juice
» ½ cup (125 mL) parsley leaves
» ½ cup (125 mL) celery leaves

SALAD

For the salad, combine the bell pepper, tomato, rice vinegar, and pepper in a small bowl.

» 1 green, red, or yellow pepper, seeded and diced
» 2 medium tomatoes, diced
» 2 Tbsp (30 mL) rice wine vinegar
» Freshly ground black pepper to taste

GARLIC TOAST

To make the garlic toast, preheat the oven to 350°F (180°C). Slice the bread and toast it in the oven until it is crisp. While the toast is still warm, rub each slice with the garlic cloves, using the crisp toast like a grater.

» 1 whole baguette
» 6 cloves garlic

TO SERVE

To serve, divide the tomato and pepper salad evenly into six martini glasses. Divide the marinated sea urchin into the martini glasses, then garnish it with frisée and watercress. Grate the fresh horseradish on top and serve it with the garlic toast.

PAIRING SUGGESTION: *Tom Firth:* Sumac Ridge Steller's Jay Brut Sparkling Wine (Okanagan Valley, BC) or Marnier Château de Sancerre white (France).

» 1 cup (250 mL) frisée (curly lettuce)
» 1 cup (250 mL) watercress leaves
» ¼ cup (60 mL) finely grated fresh horseradish (or a few tsp/about 10 mL prepared horseradish)

^ BOBBING FOR SEA URCHINS

How to Fish for Sea Urchins

David McRae, BC fisher and director, Pacific Urchin Harvesters Association, New Westminster, BC

When asked where I get my sea urchins, I usually say, "By that island with the green trees and the grey rock."

This is how we get urchins: a mesh bag is tied around a steel ring that holds the bag open, then an orange buoy is tied to the ring. Once underwater, the buoy is filled with air—by the diver's air nozzle from his scuba tank—to counterbalance the weight of the sea urchins as the bag is filled by the diver.

The diver uses a special rake to pry the urchins off the rocks (they stick to the rocks like starfish) and shepherd them into the bag. When the bag is full of urchins, more air is added to the orange buoy—enough to make it float to the surface. At the surface, a hook is lowered to the diver, who attaches it to the ring, and the full bag of sea urchins is hydraulically lifted onto the deck of the *Kuroshio*.

The majority of BC's sea urchin fleet—anywhere from 5 to 20 boats—works along the southern coast, from the bottom of Vancouver Island to Port Hardy, although sea urchin harvesting occurs all along the BC coast, from Victoria to Prince Rupert. (Urchins are also fished in many other countries, from Russia to the United States to China.) The sea urchin population has been co-managed by the Department of Fisheries and Oceans and PUHA for the past 15 years, which has resulted in a sustainable yearly harvest. We are thrilled that Ocean Wise has put us on its sustainable seafood list.

By the way, it's a myth that fishers don't like to eat fish. Believe it or not, I don't just love eating sea urchins; I eat them raw, right out of the shell—the fresher, the better. Don't believe me? Try them yourself!

RESTAURANT
River Café

TYPE
octopus

CHEF
Scott Pohorelic

LOCATION
Calgary, AB

Giant Pacific Octopus with Wild Boar Chorizo

At the River Café we serve this dish as an appetizer on our dinner menu. We purchase whole octopus and they are generally around 15 lb (6.8 kg) but can occasionally be much larger. Our record is a whopping 53 lb (24 kg). Ask your fishmonger for a 1 lb (500 g) piece, preferably from the thick end of the tentacle. *Serves 6*

TO COOK THE OCTOPUS

Place the carrot, celery, and onion in a large pot with the octopus and add enough cold water to cover the octopus. Place the pot over medium heat and bring the water up to 200°F (95°C). If you do not have a thermometer, try to get it up to the same temperature you would steep tea at. Do not let it simmer or boil, for this will make the octopus very tough. Turn the heat down to low to keep the temperature at 200°F (95°C). Cook the octopus, maintaining this temperature, for 3 to 3½ hours, or until the octopus is tender (and a sharp knife easily pierces the tentacle). Remove the octopus from the pot, and discard the water and vegetables. When it has cooled, cut the octopus into bite-sized pieces.

» 1 medium carrot, cut into 1-inch (2.5 cm) lengths
» 1 medium celery stalk, cut into 1-inch (2.5 cm) lengths
» 1 medium onion, cut into 1-inch (2.5 cm) slices
» 1 lb (500 g) giant Pacific octopus tentacle

continued . . .

While the octopus is cooking, combine the wild boar meat, red wine vinegar, red wine, oregano, salt, garlic, and spices in a medium bowl. Mix them together with your hands until they are well combined. Cook the sausage meat in a heavy-bottomed frying pan over medium heat until it starts to brown, about 8 minutes. Add the potatoes and chopped parsley and combine until heated through. Remove from the heat.

» ½ lb (250 g) ground wild boar shoulder (or pork shoulder)
» 1 Tbsp (15 mL) red wine vinegar
» 1 Tbsp (15 mL) red wine (good excuse to open a bottle while cooking)
» 1 Tbsp (15 mL) chopped oregano
» 2 tsp (10 mL) kosher salt (or 1 tsp/5 mL regular table salt)
» 1 tsp (5 mL) minced garlic
» 1 tsp (5 mL) chili powder
» 1 tsp (5 mL) ground chipotle pepper (or cayenne pepper)
» 1 tsp (5 mL) smoked paprika
» Pinch ground cumin
» 1 cup (250 mL) peeled and cooked potatoes, cut into ½-inch (1 cm) dice
» 2 Tbsp (30 mL) chopped parsley

TO SERVE

Set out six plates. Spread a spoonful of yogurt on each plate and spoon some of the sausage mixture onto it. Arrange the octopus over the sausage and garnish with the arugula.

PAIRING SUGGESTION: *Tom Firth:* Wild Rose IPA, Singha Thai beer, or a dry Alsatian Gewürztraminer such as Pierre Sparr (France).

» 6 Tbsp (90 mL) plain yogurt
» Arugula (or any other peppery greens), for garnish

Ginger Squid

This appetizer is on the daily menu at The Lobby. This Balinese squid recipe is lighter than other calamari dishes and has an assertive flavour. It is best left alone—no mayo, just a squeeze of lime. *Serves 4*

TO DEEP-FRY THE SQUID

Cut the squid into 16 large triangle shapes, and score the inside surfaces with diagonal cuts. Heat the canola oil to 350°F (180°C) in a deep, high-sided cast iron pan. Put the cornstarch in a large bowl and dredge the squid pieces thoroughly to ensure an even coating on all sides. Gently drop the squid in the hot oil, three or four pieces at a time, and fry them until they are crispy, about 3 minutes. Keep the heat near high, for the temperature of the oil will decrease during frying. Remove the squid pieces from the oil and drain them on a kitchen towel or paper towels.

» 1½ lb (750 g) cleaned Argentine squid
» 8 cups (2 L) canola oil
» 2 cups (500 mL) cornstarch

TO FINISH THE SQUID

Finely slice four of the green onions and set them aside. Julienne the remaining green onion and set it aside. Heat the ginger and garlic in a large frying pan over medium heat. Do not add any oil to the pan as dry-frying works best. Add the squid and sauté for a couple of minutes, tossing several times to coat the squid evenly. At the very end, add the sliced green onions and sea salt and toss the squid several more times.

» 5 green onions
» 2 Tbsp (30 mL) minced fresh ginger (peeled)
» 1 Tbsp (15 mL) finely chopped garlic
» 1 tsp (5 mL) sea salt (preferably Maldon)

TO SERVE

Heap the squid onto a large serving plate and garnish with the julienned green onion and lime halves.

PAIRING SUGGESTION: Pinot Gris or Sauvignon Blanc. *Tom Firth:* Thornhaven Estates Pinot Gris (Okanagan Valley, BC) or Hillebrand Artist Series Sauvignon Blanc (Ont).

» 2 limes, cut in half crosswise, for garnish

SOURCE
Barbecue Secrets DELUXE!
(Whitecap Books, 2009)

TYPE
squid

CHEF
*Rockin' Ronnie
Shewchuk*

LOCATION
Victoria, BC

Seared Calamari with Fresh Tomato Basil Salsa

The secret to great grilled squid is to use the freshest and smallest you can find, and to cook it over high heat for no more than one minute per side—any longer and it turns rubbery. In this recipe, the tomato salsa provides a cool, tangy, herbal complement to the hot, garlicky calamari. You also can cook this dish on a plank to give it some extra smoky flavour, but you won't get the nice charring that happens when you grill it over direct heat. *Serves 4*

TO MARINATE THE SQUID

Coat the squid in the salt, then rinse it thoroughly with cold water. Pat dry with paper towels. Slit the bodies and score the inside surfaces with diagonal cuts. Cut each squid into large, bite-sized pieces. Place them in a bowl with ¼ cup (60 mL) of the olive oil, the red pepper flakes, and garlic. Toss to coat and marinate in the refrigerator for about 1 hour.

» 1 lb (500 g) cleaned squid, equal parts bodies and tentacles
» ¼ cup (60 mL) kosher salt
» ½ cup (125 mL) extra virgin olive oil
» ½ tsp (2 mL) red pepper flakes
» 2 cloves garlic, finely chopped

TOMATO BASIL SALSA

Preheat your grill on high. While the grill is heating, coarsely chop the tomatoes (halves or quarters are fine), slice the basil leaves into fine shreds, and toss them together in a bowl with the vinegar and the remainder (¼ cup/60 mL) of the olive oil. Distribute the salsa between four plates.

» 2 cups (500 mL) small ripe cherry or grape tomatoes
» 1 Tbsp (15 mL) basil leaves
» 1 Tbsp (15 mL) rice wine vinegar (or white wine vinegar)

When the grill is hot, open it up and gently place the calamari on the cooking grill, taking care not to let the pieces slip through the cracks. (You may even want to use a grill-topper with small holes, designed for this kind of task.) Don't walk away! Stand at the open grill and tend the squid with a good pair of tongs, turning the pieces often so they are cooked quickly and evenly, no more than 1 minute per side. Remove the squid from the grill and transfer to the plates.

TO SERVE

Sprinkle each serving with just a pinch of kosher salt and a light grinding of pepper. Drizzle the calamari with a little more olive oil and serve it immediately.

PAIRING SUGGESTION: A crisp, fruity white. *Tom Firth:* Sandhill Small Lots Viognier or Burrowing Owl Pinot Gris (both Okanagan Valley, BC)

» Kosher salt and freshly ground black pepper to taste

RESTAURANT
Strathcona Hotel

TYPE
squid

CHEF
Peter DeBruyn

LOCATION
Victoria, BC

Lemon Coconut Calamari

We've taken the traditional pub-style calamari and infused it with wonderful citrus and garlic flavours to make this calamari a standout. Calamari is typically breaded and deep-fried, but you can omit the breading step—still delicious and also easier. We serve calamari with a tzatziki sauce at the Strathcona Hotel. Other sauces will complement this dish very well, including a chipotle mayonnaise, lemon and caper mayonnaise, or even a warm spiced tomato sauce. *Serves 6*

NOTE: Squid cooks quickly at a high heat. If the heat is too low, the squid will soak up the oil and you will have a product that is somewhat greasy.

TO MARINATE THE SQUID

Mix the coconut milk, garlic, and lemon zest and juice together in an airtight container. Add the squid, toss it with the marinade, and refrigerate, covered, for 24 hours.

» ¼ cup (60 mL) coconut milk
» 4 cloves garlic, minced
» Zest and juice of 1 lemon
» 1½ lb (750 g) cleaned squid, cut into ¼-inch (6 mm) pieces

TO TOAST THE COCONUT FLAKES

Preheat the oven to 325°F (160°C). Place the coconut flakes on a baking sheet and toast in the oven until golden brown, 5 to 8 minutes. Remove from the oven, let the coconut cool, and store in an airtight container until you are ready to use it.

» ¼ cup (60 mL) coconut flakes

TO DEEP-FRY THE SQUID

Heat the oil to 450°F (230°C) in a deep-sided pan (or a home deep fryer to medium-high). Combine the flour, cornstarch, and salt in a shallow dish. Strain the marinade from the squid, then dredge the squid pieces in the flour mixture, shaking off any excess coating. Carefully place the squid in the hot oil and cook for about 1 minute, or until golden brown. Remove the squid from the oil using a shallow mesh sieve (or tongs) and dry them on a sheet lined with a kitchen or paper towel to soak up any excess oil.

» ½ cup (125 mL) vegetable oil
» ¾ cup (185 mL) all-purpose flour
» ¾ cup (185 mL) cornstarch
» Pinch salt

TO SERVE

Heap the squid on a serving dish, sprinkle with the toasted coconut flakes and sliced red onion, and then garnish it with the parsley.

PAIRING SUGGESTION: Pinot Blanc. *Tom Firth:* Red Rooster Pinot Blanc (Okanagan Valley, BC) or 13th Street Gamay Noir (Ont).

» 1 medium red onion, sliced in 1½-inch (4 cm) strips
» 1 sprig parsley

SOUPS *and* CHOWDERS

RESTAURANT
Aura Restaurant, Inn at Laurel Point

CHEF
Patrick Gayler

TYPE
scallops, spot prawns

LOCATION
Victoria, BC

Coconut Scallop Bisque with Spot Prawn Escabeche, Chili Oil, Mango Fennel Purée, and Seared Diver Scallops

This soup is rich but not too heavy, because we use rice to thicken it rather than a roux. Escabeche is an excellent way to control the delicate texture and sweet flavour of the prawns. Diver scallops are also used in the bisque and seared just before serving. Everything except the seared scallops can be made ahead, making this a great dish for entertaining. *Serves 10 to 12*

NOTE: Escabeche is a type of Mediterranean cuisine in which fish is typically poached or fried, then covered with a spicy marinade and refrigerated for at least 24 hours. It is a popular dish in Spain and Southern France, where it is usually served cold as an appetizer.

SPOT PRAWN ESCABECHE

Combine all the ingredients except the prawns in a large saucepan and bring to a simmer over medium-high heat. Add the prawns and stir to ensure they are completely submerged. Allow the liquid to come back to a simmer and then quickly remove the pan from the heat. Allow the prawns to steep for 2 to 3 minutes, and then remove the prawns from the liquid and cool immediately. Cool the cooking liquid. Once both the prawns and liquid are cold, add ½ cup (125 mL) of the liquid to the prawns and marinate overnight.

» 2 cups (500 mL) water
» ½ cup (125 mL) dry white wine
» 3 Tbsp (45 mL) olive oil
» 1 lemon, thinly sliced
» 1 lime, thinly sliced
» 1 orange, thinly sliced
» 1 clove garlic, minced
» Pinch red chili pepper flakes
» Pinch salt
» 12 BC spot prawns, shelled
  and cleaned

continued . . .

COCONUT SCALLOP BISQUE

Heat the grapeseed oil in a large pan over medium heat. Add the mirepoix, pineapple, garlic, ginger, lemongrass, and lime leaves. Sauté the mixture until everything has softened, about 2 minutes, then add the rice and toast it until it is light brown. Deglaze the pan with the wine, then add the stock. Bring the mixture to a simmer and reduce the liquid by one-third (this should take about 10 minutes). Add the scallops and simmer them until they are cooked, 5 to 7 minutes. Slowly stir in the cream and then the coconut milk. Simmer the bisque for 15 minutes to develop the flavours. Season to taste, then purée the mixture and strain it through a fine-mesh sieve or cheesecloth.

» 2 Tbsp (30 mL) grapeseed oil
» 2 cups (500 mL) white mirepoix (equal parts roughly chopped white onion, white leek, and celery)
» ¼ pineapple, peeled, cored, and chopped into ¼-inch (6 mm) pieces
» 5 cloves garlic, minced
» 1-inch (2.5 cm) piece fresh ginger, peeled and minced
» 3 stalks lemongrass, chopped
» 3 lime leaves (see Note page 88)
» ⅓ cup (80 mL) + 4 tsp (20 mL) jasmine rice
» 1 cup (250 mL) dry white wine
» 1 gallon (4 L) chicken stock
» 1 lb (500 g) diver scallops (just for the bisque)
» 2 cups (500 mL) whipping cream
» 1 to 2 cups (250 to 500 mL) coconut milk, depending on how thick you want the soup
» Salt and pepper to taste

MANGO-FENNEL PURÉE

Combine all the ingredients in a medium saucepan and simmer very lightly until the fennel is extremely soft and the liquid has thickened. (Additional water may be required to ensure there is enough liquid to cook the fennel.) Purée in a blender until completely smooth and cool, with the consistency of applesauce.

» 4 fennel bulbs, sliced
» 2 cups (500 mL) mango purée
» 1 cup (250 mL) orange juice
» 1 cup (250 mL) dry white wine

continued . . .

CHILI OIL

Combine the oil and spices in a small saucepan and cook over low heat until the oil is slightly reddened and has the desired spice, about 8 minutes. Remove from the heat, add the garlic, and cool.

» ⅓ cup (80 mL) grapeseed oil
» 1 Tbsp (15 mL) red chili pepper flakes
» 1 Tbsp (15 mL) Szechuan peppercorns, freshly ground
» 1 clove garlic, minced

SEARED DIVER SCALLOPS

Heat the oil in a large frying pan over medium-high heat. Season the scallops and then place them in the pan, making sure not to overcrowd the pan. Sear for 1 minute, and then flip the scallops over and lower the heat to medium. Sear for another minute. Remove the pan from the heat and allow the scallops to finish cooking in the pan for a further 1 to 2 minutes.

» 2 Tbsp (30 mL) grapeseed oil
» Salt and pepper to taste
» 12 large diver scallops, patted dry with paper towel

TO SERVE

Heat the soup while the scallops are searing. Divide the escabeche between 10 to 12 bowls, place a dollop of the purée by the side, and place the scallops on top. We pour the soup tableside for an elegant presentation. Alternatively, you can remove the centres from the hearts of palm and slice them thinly on an angle. Marinate the slices briefly in lemon juice and then stuff the scallops and/or escabeche inside them to serve. Pass the chili oil around the table.

PAIRING SUGGESTION: *Tom Firth:* Dirty Laundry Unoaked Chardonnay (Okanagan Valley, BC) or Jackson Triggs Niagara Estate White Meritage (Ont).

» One 14 oz (398 mL) can hearts of palm (optional)

RESTAURANT
*Wilfrid's Restaurant,
Fairmont Château Laurier*

TYPE
lobster

CHEF
Geoffrey Morden

LOCATION
Ottawa, ON

Spicy Lobster Soup with Coconut Essence, Lime, and Toasted Local Corn

This soup blends the exotic flavours of Southeast Asia with spiny or Maine lobster and farm-fresh local corn. Late summer is the best time to make it, when lobsters are plentiful and summer corn is at its peak. This is our most popular soup at Wilfrid's Restaurant. *Serves 8*

NOTE: As its name suggests, coconut cream is thicker than coconut milk, with a paste-like consistency. Its mild, not-too-sweet taste lends itself to savoury dishes such as this soup.

Heat the canola oil in a large, heavy-bottomed stockpot over medium heat. Add the minced shallots and ginger-garlic paste and sauté the mixture for 2 minutes. Add the ground cumin and coriander, green chilies, lime zest, lemongrass, and red curry paste, and sauté the mixture for an additional 3 minutes. Add the chicken stock and simmer the broth for 30 minutes. Strain the broth through a fine-mesh sieve.

Return the broth to the same pot and bring it back up to a simmer over medium heat. Add the coconut cream, lime juice, brown sugar, torn basil, chopped cilantro, green onion, lobster meat, and corn, and simmer the soup for 1 minute. Add a few dashes of fish sauce.

TO SERVE

Ladle the piping hot soup into warm bowls and sprinkle with cilantro leaves.

PAIRING SUGGESTION: This spicy broth lends itself well to a chilled crisp Canadian Sauvignon Blanc or Gewürztraminer. *Tom Firth:* CedarCreek Gewürztraminer or Sandhill Small Lots Viognier (both BC).

» ¼ cup (60 mL) canola oil
» 3 medium shallots, minced
» ¼ cup (60 mL) ginger-garlic paste
» 2 Tbsp (30 mL) ground cumin
» 1 Tbsp (15 mL) ground coriander
» 3 fresh medium green chilies, seeded and minced
» 1 Tbsp (15 mL) lime zest
» 1 stalk lemongrass, minced
» 1 Tbsp (15 mL) red curry paste
» 8 cups (2 L) chicken stock
» 1 cup (250 mL) unsweetened coconut cream
» 1 Tbsp (15 mL) fresh lime juice
» ¼ cup (60 mL) brown sugar
» ¼ cup (60 mL) basil leaves, torn
» ½ cup (125 mL) chopped cilantro
» ¼ cup (60 mL) chopped green onion
» ½ cup (125 mL) cooked and chopped lobster meat (precooked lobster [from the fishmonger or by following instructions on page 226] or canned sustainable lobster)
» ½ cup (125 mL) cooked corn kernels
» 2 to 3 dashes fish sauce
» Cilantro leaves, for garnish

RESTAURANT
Manhattan Restaurant,
Delta Vancouver Suites Hotel

TYPE
clams

CHEF
Michael Viloria

LOCATION
Vancouver, BC

Manhattan Clam Chowder

This hearty dish is a combination of two classic chowders.
Serves 4

Heat the butter in a large stockpot over medium heat and sauté the onion, fennel, celery, carrot, and garlic for 5 minutes, stirring the mixture so it does not stick. Add the potatoes, tomatoes, and tomato juice. Simmer the mixture for 10 to 15 minutes, reducing its volume by one-third. Once the potatoes are tender, add the cream and the clams to the pot and bring the liquid to a boil. The chowder will be ready once the clamshells have opened. Discard any clams that are not open and season the chowder to taste.

» ¼ cup (60 mL) butter
» 1 medium onion, diced
» 1 medium fennel bulb, cored and diced (reserve the fronds)
» 2 celery stalks, diced
» 1 medium carrot, diced
» 1 clove garlic, sliced
» 3 medium potatoes, peeled and diced
» One 28 oz (796 mL) can diced plum tomatoes
» 2 cups (500 mL) tomato juice
» 1 cup (250 mL) whipping cream
» 2 lb (1 kg) clams, scrubbed
» Salt and pepper to taste

TO SERVE

Divide the chowder into four bowls, garnish it with the chopped fennel fronds and parsley, and serve it with Goldfish crackers or some fresh sourdough bread.

PAIRING SUGGESTION: Riesling or Chardonnay. *Tom Firth*: Pentâge Gamay (Okanagan Valley, BC), Magnotta Chardonnay (Ont), or Tawse Sketches of Niagara Riesling (Ont).

Grilled Spot Prawn Bisque with Parisienne Gnocchi

In Vancouver, spot prawn season is limited to six to eight weeks in the summer to control overfishing. Buy these prawns only from a reputable fishmonger or, if you're fortunate enough to live on the West Coast, go directly to the fishers' wharf. Spot prawns are firm, plump, and sweet, and the shells and heads make an excellent bisque. They are best grilled with a little garlic-herb butter, kosher salt, and lemon. And they are, of course, terrific with gnocchi. *Serves 4*

NOTE: If you cannot get garlic ramps, use roasted garlic, shallots, or leeks.

TO MAKE THE GNOCCHI

Combine the water, butter, and salt in a large saucepan and bring to a simmer over medium heat. Add the flour all at once and stir with a wooden spoon until the dough pulls away from the sides of the pot and the bottom of the pot has no dough sticking to it. The dough should be glossy but still moist. Continue to stir for 3 minutes to allow more moisture to evaporate from the dough, making sure the dough does not colour. You will notice the aroma of cooked flour.

Immediately transfer the dough to the bowl of a mixer fitted with a paddle, then add the mustard and herbs. Mix for a few seconds, then add the cheese.

With the mixer at its lowest speed, add three of the eggs, one at a time, until each egg is completely incorporated. Increase the speed to medium and add another two eggs, one at a time until completely incorporated (you might need one more egg). Turn off the machine. Take a small amount of dough between your thumb and forefinger, and stretch it out slowly. If the dough does not break when your fingers are about 2 inches (5 cm) apart, then it is ready. If it breaks, let it mix a little longer. Add another egg if necessary.

Place the dough in a piping bag and cut the end so the hole is ½-inch (1 cm) round. Let it rest at room temperature for 30 minutes.

Drop the gnocchi in 1-inch (2.5 cm) increments from the piping bag into simmering salted water. Once the gnocchi float to the top, poach them for 1 minute longer and then drain on paper towels.

» 1½ cups (375 mL) water
» 12 Tbsp (180 mL) unsalted butter
» 1 Tbsp (15 mL) kosher salt
» 2 cups (500 mL) all-purpose flour, sifted
» 2 Tbsp (30 mL) strong Dijon mustard
» 1 Tbsp (15 mL) chopped tarragon
» 1 Tbsp (15 mL) chopped chives
» 1 Tbsp (15 mL) chopped parsley
» 1 cup (250 mL) grated Emmenthal
» 5 or 6 large eggs

continued . . .

TO GRILL THE PRAWNS

Salt the spot prawns and brush with 2 Tbsp (30 mL) of the garlic butter. Grill the prawns over high heat (preferably on a barbecue) for 1 minute per side, or until they turn pink and opaque. Leave them in a warm spot, with the remaining garlic butter and the lemon juice brushed over. Cut the spot prawns in half lengthwise.

» Kosher salt to taste
» 8 BC spot prawns, tailed, shells on
» 3 Tbsp (45 mL) garlic butter
» 1 Tbsp (15 mL) fresh lemon juice

TO SAUTÉ THE GNOCCHI

Heat the butter and oil in a large frying pan over medium heat. Add the gnocchi and season with salt and pepper. Toss and fry until they are golden and slightly puffed. Add the cherry tomatoes, pre-steamed zucchini, garlic ramps, and bok choy. Toss until coated with butter and heated through.

» 1 tsp (5 mL) butter
» 1 tsp (5 mL) olive oil
» Salt and pepper to taste
» 1 cup (250 mL) cherry tomatoes, halved
» 1 medium zucchini, julienned and blanched
» 8 garlic ramps, roasted
» 1 medium bok choy, chopped and blanched

TO SERVE

Reheat the prawn bisque and carefully froth with a hand blender. Divide the spot prawns and gnocchi into serving bowls. Pour the bisque over the prawns and gnocchi, top with the black olives, and serve.

PAIRING SUGGESTION: *Tom Firth:* Mission Hill s.l.c. Chardonnay (Okanagan Valley, BC) or Thirty Bench Wine Makers Small Lot Chardonnay (Ont).

» Prawn Bisque Sauce (see page 289)
» 12 black olives (not canned), for garnish

RESTAURANT
Blue Water Café and Raw Bar

TYPE
sea urchin, oysters

CHEF
Frank Pabst

LOCATION
Vancouver, BC

Red Sea Urchin in a Cucumber Vichyssoise with Kushi Oysters and Lemon Cream

Vichyssoise is a creamy French-style soup made with puréed leeks, onions, and potatoes and traditionally served cold. Red sea urchins are larger than the smaller and sweeter green urchins. Preparing the urchins for this dish can be a bit messy—don an apron and work over a baking sheet with a generous lip to catch all the juices that run out. *Serves 4*

NOTE: The hole in a sea urchin is its mouth.

VICHYSSOISE

Melt the butter over medium-high heat in a medium pot and sweat the leeks and the onion with a good pinch of salt and several grindings of pepper for about 5 minutes, until they are tender but not browned.

Add the potatoes and chicken stock and simmer the soup for 35 minutes, until the potatoes are tender. Add the cream, then transfer the soup to a food processor and purée it while gradually adding the raw cucumber slices.

Strain the purée through a medium-mesh sieve into a clean bowl. Season the soup to taste, then refrigerate it until it is chilled, about 1 hour.

» 3 Tbsp (45 mL) unsalted butter
» 1½ cups (375 mL) thinly sliced leeks, white part only
» ½ small onion, thinly sliced
» Salt and freshly ground black pepper
» ½ cup (125 mL) thinly sliced potatoes
» 2 cups (500 mL) chicken stock
» ¾ cup (185 mL) table cream (18%) or half-and-half
» 1 English cucumber, peeled, seeded, and sliced

LEMON CREAM

Combine the whipped cream, lemon zest, tarragon, lemon juice, cayenne pepper, and a pinch of salt in a small bowl.

» 1 cup (250 mL) whipped cream
» Zest of ½ lemon
» 1 tsp (5 mL) chopped tarragon
» 1 tsp (5 mL) fresh lemon juice
» Pinch cayenne pepper
» Pinch salt

SEA URCHIN

Place a small cutting board in the centre of a baking sheet. Place each sea urchin, mouth side up, on the cutting board, and crack it open with a heavy chef's knife without smashing completely through the urchin. Alternatively, with sharp, pointy scissors, cut a 1-inch (2.5 cm) circle around the mouth of each sea urchin. With a teaspoon, carefully remove the roe from each sea urchin and wash it in a bowl of cold salted water to remove any grit. Discard the remainder of the urchin.

» 4 medium red sea urchins

TO SERVE

Ladle ¾ cup (185 mL) of the vichyssoise into four soup bowls, and then garnish with the sea urchin and the oysters. Scoop a spoonful of lemon cream into the centre of each bowl and sprinkle it with chives, cucumber, and watercress.

PAIRING SUGGESTION: Roero Arneis (Piedmont, Italy). *Tom Firth:* Van Westen Vivacious (Okanagan Valley, BC).

» 12 Kushi oysters, shucked
» 1 Tbsp (15 mL) finely chopped chives
» 1 Tbsp (15 mL) finely diced English cucumber
» 4 to 8 sprigs watercress

By the end of the day we had about 1,500 lb of live urchins on board.

Hitching a Ride on a Boat Full of Prickles

Quang Dang, Diva at the Met (previously at C Restaurant), Vancouver, BC

Are you itchin' for urchin? Thanks to BC fishers and the Pacific Urchin Harvesters Association, sea urchins are appearing not only in sushi bars. They are also fast becoming the foie gras of seafood in many restaurants across Canada. Why not try this delicacy at home?

When I worked at C Restaurant, I would get my sea urchins delivered to the restaurant within eight hours of harvesting—that's fresh. I always wanted to know where the urchins came from, barring actually harvesting them myself, since I'm not a diver. So David McRae, a director of the Pacific Urchin Harvesters Association (PUHA), invited me aboard his boat, the *Kuroshio*.

I boarded the ferry to Vancouver Island just after 5 a.m. and met David in Sidney, just as the boat was heading out to the bull kelp beds—a sea urchin's favourite haunt. Tom Mulhall, Dave's diver on board the *Kuroshio*, donned his scuba gear while I relaxed, enjoyed the scenery, and helped ready urchin bags for the diver.

One dive takes 20 to 30 minutes, and with each dive, Tom brought up about 100 urchins. We moved around and fished in different locations—each fisher has their own secret spots. I think fishers are always looking over their shoulder to make sure no one's following them. David reminded me of that old saying: if a fisher is asked where they made their catch—in this case, sea urchins—they answer, "If I told you, I would have to kill you, so do you want me to lie or tell you the truth?"

By the end of the day we had about 1,500 lb (680 kg) of live urchins on board. To tell you the truth, I didn't do much more to help than crack open a few urchins for a quality check—to see how they were faring, coming out of that specific area.

That evening I brought back to the restaurant about 30 urchins just five hours out of the water. The kitchen staff started cleaning them right away, which meant cracking each spiny shell and pulling out the gonads. On the fly I made a little urchin salad with bull kelp, cucumber, and ponzu sauce (a Japanese citrus-based sauce). With the rest of the urchins I made a chowder with all things that should be in a white chowder: potato, cream, bacon, carrots, celery. Both dishes were wonderful—like a bite of the ocean.

I love urchin, especially when it's chewy fresh. It has a custard-like texture and tastes like an ocean breeze. I urge you to try it. It's a wonderful and sustainable seafood item from BC's coastal waters that is underappreciated—but not by me or the diners at C!

‹ (ABOVE LEFT) QUANG DANG OGLES AN URCHIN

SALADS

RESTAURANT
Refuel Restaurant

TYPE
tuna

CHEF
Ted Anderson

LOCATION
Vancouver, BC

Ultra-Rare Albacore BLT Salad

The rich flavour of albacore tuna works well with ripe summer tomatoes. Find the best tomatoes you can—heirlooms, hybrids, or from your garden. Hothouse or imported just will not do. We only use tomatoes from Stoney Paradise Farm in Kelowna, BC. Wrap the fish in thinly sliced bread instead of using breadcrumbs for more of a "sandwich." *Serves 4*

BACON EMULSION

Combine the white wine vinegar, Dijon mustard, and egg yolk in a medium mixing bowl. Slowly add ¾ cup (185 mL) of the canola oil in a thin, steady stream while whisking the egg mixture constantly. Whisk in half of the rendered bacon fat using the same technique. The sauce should have the appearance of mayonnaise. If it becomes too thick, whisk in some cold water, one dash at a time. Add salt to taste. (The bacon emulsion will keep for 3 days in the refrigerator and is amazing on sandwiches.)

» 4 tsp (20 mL) white wine vinegar
» 2 tsp (10 mL) Dijon mustard
» 1 large egg yolk
» ¾ cup (185 mL) + 2 Tbsp (30 mL) canola oil
» ½ cup (125 mL) rendered bacon fat (reserve half for the breadcrumbs)
» Sea salt

TO FRY THE BREADCRUMBS

Heat the remaining bacon fat in a medium, heavy-bottomed cast iron frying pan over medium heat. Add the breadcrumbs and fry, stirring gently, until golden brown, about 5 minutes. Drain them on a paper towel.

» 1 cup (250 mL) fresh breadcrumbs

continued . . .

SALAD

Season the tomatoes with sea salt and freshly ground black pepper. Smear some bacon emulsion in the centre of each plate. Top each smear with one-quarter of the iceberg lettuce. Evenly divide the seasoned tomato slices onto the lettuce and set the plates aside.

Season the tuna loins with salt and set them aside. Heat the same cast iron pan used to fry the breadcrumbs over high heat until it just starts to smoke. Add the remaining 2 Tbsp (30 mL) canola oil. Sear the tuna loins, one at a time, for about 15 seconds on all sides. Drain them on a paper towel.

» 2 lb (1 kg) firm, ripe tomatoes, cut into thick slices
» Sea salt
» Freshly ground black pepper
» 1½ cups (375 mL) very thinly sliced crisp iceberg lettuce
» Four 6 oz (175 g) boneless albacore tuna loins, trimmed into an even shape (ask your fishmonger to do this for you)

TO SERVE

Slice each seared tuna loin into 1-inch (2.5 cm) medallions and place on the tomatoes. Finish with a sprinkling of the fried breadcrumbs and serve.

PAIRING SUGGESTION: *Tom Firth:* Pentâge Chenin Blanc or Road 13 Honest John's White (both Okanagan Valley, BC).

RESTAURANT
The Velvet Glove, Fairmont Winnipeg Hotel

TYPE
tuna, crab

CHEF
Luc Jean

LOCATION
Winnipeg, MB

Seared Albacore Tuna with Dungeness Crab, Beet and Fennel Salad, and Spicy Passion Fruit Sauce

This recipe is so fresh and also has zing to it—great for a summer barbecue. *Serves 6 as a main course*

NOTE: Frozen crab claws are already cooked; once thawed, just crack and remove shell.

SPECIAL EQUIPMENT: Ideally, use a mandoline to get the beet and fennel paper thin, but feel free to use a knife if you have good knife skills.

SPICY PASSION FRUIT SAUCE

Place the mirin, passion fruit purée, ginger, lemon juice, and turmeric in a medium, heavy saucepan over high heat. Boil the mixture for about 6 minutes, or until it is reduced to ¼ cup (60 mL). Add the cream and coconut milk, bring the sauce back up to a boil, then reduce the heat to medium and simmer for about 12 minutes, or until it has thickened slightly. Stir in the curry paste. Season the sauce to taste with sea salt and freshly ground pepper. Set aside.

» ½ cup (125 mL) mirin (sweet rice wine)
» ½ cup (125 mL) passion fruit purée
» 1 tsp (5 mL) chopped fresh ginger (peeled)
» 1 Tbsp (15 mL) fresh lemon juice
» 1 tsp (5 mL) ground turmeric
» 2 cups (500 mL) whipping cream
» 1 cup (250 mL) coconut milk
» ½ tsp (2 mL) red curry paste
» Sea salt and freshly ground black pepper to taste

BEET AND FENNEL SALAD

Shave the fennel bulbs crosswise into paper-thin slices using a mandoline. (Halve the bulbs lengthwise if they are too large for the slicer.) Peel the beet and julienne it using a mandoline (alternatively, slice thinly with a sharp knife). Place the julienned beet in ice water for a few minutes. Strain the beet and combine it with the fennel in a medium bowl. Add ¼ cup (60 mL) of the passion fruit sauce to the fennel and beets and toss them until they are evenly coated. Add the baby lettuces just before serving. Season to taste with sea salt and pepper.

» 2 medium fennel bulbs
» 1 large beet
» 3 cups (750 mL) baby lettuces
» Sea salt and freshly ground black pepper to taste

continued . . .

ALBACORE TUNA AND DUNGENESS CRAB

Cut the tuna loins into 1½-inch (4 cm) thick medallions. Season the medallions with salt and pepper. Heat a large frying pan over high heat. Once the pan is hot, add the olive oil and pan-fry the tuna medallions until they are medium rare, 1 to 2 minutes per side.

In a medium saucepan melt the butter over medium heat. Add the crab claws and warm them through, 3 to 5 minutes. Season the butter to taste with salt and pepper. Add the chopped parsley.

» Two 1 lb (500 g) albacore tuna loins
» 2 Tbsp (30 mL) olive oil
» 2 Tbsp (30 mL) salted butter
» 1 lb (500 g) frozen Dungeness or stone crab claws, shelled
» 2 Tbsp (30 mL) chopped parsley
» Salt and pepper to taste

TO SERVE

Place one-quarter of the beet and fennel salad on each of six plates. Mound the seared tuna and crab claws atop the salad. Pour some of the extra sauce on the tuna and crab and drizzle it around each plate.

PAIRING SUGGESTION: Zenato Lugana (Lugana, Italy). It is well balanced and crisp, with a long, citrus finish. *Tom Firth:* Fielding Estate Pinot Gris (Ont).

RESTAURANT
Elixir Bistro, Opus Hotel

TYPE
tuna, anchovies

CHEF
Don Letendre

LOCATION
Vancouver, BC

Albacore Tuna Niçoise Salad

Salade Niçoise is a dish typical of the region of Nice in Southern France. Its most common ingredients are garlic, anchovies, tomatoes, and green beans. In this recipe we add seared albacore tuna, olive tapenade, nugget potatoes, and boiled quail's eggs. Grilled salmon or mackerel can be used instead of tuna, and hen's eggs can be substituted for quail's eggs. This dish is low-fat and healthy, and can be eaten as a light dinner or lunch. *Serves 4*

NOTE: White anchovies and caperberries can be found at reputable Italian grocers. If you cannot find caperberries, substitute capers. I prefer to use white anchovies for the tapenade; they are less salty than regular salt-cured anchovies, but you can use anchovy paste instead.

DIJON AIOLI

Put the egg yolks, Dijon mustard, white wine vinegar, and minced garlic clove in a chilled, medium metal bowl. (The chilled bowl helps the yolk and oil to emulsify.) Whisk the yolk mixture until it doubles in volume. Add the olive oil in a slow, steady stream until it is fully incorporated and the mixture has emulsified into a mayonnaise. Season the aioli to taste with lemon juice and salt. Refrigerate until ready to serve.

- » 3 large egg yolks
- » 2 Tbsp (30 mL) Dijon mustard
- » 1 Tbsp (15 mL) white wine vinegar
- » 1 clove garlic, minced
- » 2 cups (500 mL) olive oil
- » 1 tsp (5 mL) fresh lemon juice, or to taste
- » Salt to taste

PISTOU

Set aside 12 of the basil leaves for the salad. Pound the remainder of the basil and the three garlic cloves together in a mortar and pestle or food processor to make a paste. Transfer the mixture to a medium bowl. Slowly whisk in the olive oil and fold in the Parmesan cheese. Season to taste with lemon juice, salt, and pepper.

- » 2 cups (500 mL) basil leaves
- » 3 cloves garlic
- » ¼ cup (60 mL) olive oil
- » ¼ cup (60 mL) grated Parmesan cheese
- » Fresh lemon juice to taste
- » Salt and black pepper to taste

continued . . .

NIÇOISE SALAD

Cook the quail eggs in boiling water for 2 minutes and 20 seconds, and then submerge them in an ice bath. Peel once they are cool.

Heat the olive oil in a large frying pan over medium-high heat until just smoking. Sear the tuna on both sides, 1 minute per side.

Toss the basil, parsley, and arugula in a medium mixing bowl.

» 8 quail eggs
» 1 Tbsp (15 mL) olive oil
» 1 lb (500 g) albacore tuna loin, cut into 4 equal pieces
» ¼ cup (60 mL) chopped basil
» ½ cup (125 mL) Italian flat-leaf parsley leaves
» 2 cups (500 mL) arugula

TO SERVE

Divide the green beans, potatoes, cherry tomatoes, and caperberries onto four chilled plates. Top them with the herb and arugula mix. Dollop three quenelles of tapenade (use two spoons to mold the mixture into an oval), three pools of the Dijon aioli, and three pools of the pistou around each salad.

Top each salad with a piece of seared tuna, two quail eggs, two anchovy fillets, and the reserved basil leaves. Season with kosher salt, freshly ground black pepper, and a drizzle of balsamic vinegar.

PAIRING SUGGESTION: Poplar Grove Pinot Gris (Okanagan Valley, BC). *Tom Firth:* Pillitteri Estates Pinot Grigio (Ont).

» 4 cups (1 L) small green beans, blanched
» 12 Yukon Gold nugget potatoes, cooked
» 12 cherry tomatoes
» 12 caperberries, rinsed
» ½ cup (125 mL) tapenade (see page 291)
» 8 anchovy fillets
» Kosher salt
» Freshly ground black pepper
» 2 Tbsp (30 mL) aged balsamic vinegar

RESTAURANT
Barley Station Brew Pub

TYPE
salmon

CHEF
Walter Bonn

LOCATION
Salmon Arm, BC

Wild Salmon Spinach Salad with Strawberries and Spiced Pecans

This is one of our most popular salads; it gets jazzed up with spicy pecans, which you can toast ahead of time and store in an airtight container. We make a big batch—they are great for snacking. *Serves 4*

SPICED PECANS

Preheat the oven to 350°F (180°C). Combine the honey, paprika, cayenne pepper, and cumin in a small bowl. Add the pecans and toss them until they are well coated. Distribute them evenly onto a baking sheet in a single layer and bake for about 5 minutes. Allow the pecans to cool completely before using.

» 2 Tbsp (30 mL) honey
» 1 tsp (5 mL) paprika
» 1 tsp (5 mL) cayenne pepper
» ½ tsp (2 mL) ground cumin
» 2 cups (500 mL) pecan halves

CREAMY CHIVE DRESSING

Whisk together the buttermilk, lemon juice, cider vinegar, sour cream, mayonnaise, salt, pepper, and cayenne pepper in a medium bowl until smooth. Stir in the chives and refrigerate until ready to use.

» ¼ cup (60 mL) buttermilk
» 2 tsp (10 mL) fresh lemon juice
» 1 tsp (5 mL) apple cider vinegar
» 1 cup (250 mL) sour cream
» ½ cup (125 mL) mayonnaise
» Salt and pepper to taste
» Pinch cayenne pepper
» ¼ cup (60 mL) chopped chives

continued . . .

SALAD

To assemble the salad, pile the spinach onto four plates, and then layer on the sunflower sprouts, sliced red onion and spiced pecans. Sprinkle with the feta cheese and strawberries and set aside.

» 1 lb (500 g) baby spinach leaves, washed and dried
» ⅓ cup (80 mL) sunflower sprouts (or pea sprouts)
» ⅓ cup (80 mL) thinly sliced red onion
» ⅓ cup (80 mL) feta cheese
» ¾ cup (185 mL) fresh strawberries, halved

SALMON

Preheat the oven to 350°F (180°C). Heat the oil in a heavy cast iron pan over medium-high heat. Sprinkle the salmon generously with the Cajun spice. Sear the salmon fillets for 1 minute per side. Transfer the pan to the oven and bake for 5 minutes, or until the salmon is medium rare.

» 1 Tbsp (15 mL) grapeseed oil
» 1 lb (500 g) skinless wild salmon fillet, cut into 4 pieces
» Cajun spice (or salt and pepper) to taste

TO SERVE

Place the salmon on top of the prepared salad and drizzle it with the creamy chive dressing.

PAIRING SUGGESTION: We prefer to serve a light Belgium wheat ale, such as Löwenbräu, which pairs nicely with seafood. Its light, refreshing citrus flavour complements the salad beautifully. If you prefer wine, try either the Recline Ridge Ortega or Larch Hills Siegerrebe (both Okanagan Valley, BC) for a light, flavourful finish.

RESTAURANT
Glowbal Grill Steaks & Satay

TYPE
mahi mahi, crab

CHEF
Erik Heck

LOCATION
Vancouver, BC

Olive Oil–Poached Mahi Mahi with Mango-Malibu Purée and a Dungeness Crab, White Peach, and Avocado Salad

Mahi mahi is a beautiful, dense fish. This recipe reminds me of the week I spent in Maui. All I ate the whole time I was there was mahi mahi, tuna, and fresh fruit. All the ingredients work together so well and leave you with a fresh, healthy, tropical feeling. *Serves 4*

NOTE: The amount of oil is only an estimate because it depends on the size and depth of your pan. The olive oil must cover the fish, and the fish fillets should not touch each other. A large, deep frying pan should do the trick.

PURÉE

Place the diced mango and rum in a food processor and purée until smooth. (Use a blender or hand blender if you do not have a food processor.) Add honey to taste if you feel the purée is not sweet enough.

» 2 cups (500 mL) skinned and diced fresh mango
» ½ cup (125 mL) coconut-flavoured rum
» Honey to taste (optional)

MAHI MAHI

Heat the extra virgin olive oil to 200°F (95°C) in a large, deep frying pan. Place the mahi mahi in the hot oil and cook it for 12 to 15 minutes, or until it is cooked through. Make sure not to deep-fry the fish. If the fish is bubbling, the oil is too hot. Remove the fillets from the pan and drain them on a kitchen or paper towel.

» 4 to 6 cups (1 to 1.5 L) extra virgin olive oil
» Four 6 oz (175 g) skinless mahi mahi fillets

SALAD

While the fish is cooking, combine the avocado, peach, Dungeness crabmeat, onion, and watercress (reserve a few leaves for garnish) in a small bowl. Add the orange juice and zest, extra virgin olive oil, sambal oelek, and salt and pepper, and toss gently to mix the salad well.

» 1 cup (250 mL) peeled, pitted, and diced avocado

» 1 cup (250 mL) peeled, pitted, and diced white peach (or any peach if white is not available)

» 1 lb (500 g) Dungeness crabmeat

» ¼ medium red onion, thinly shaved

» 1 cup (250 mL) watercress leaves

» 1 tsp (5 mL) orange juice

» 1 tsp (5 mL) orange zest

» ¼ cup (60 mL) extra virgin olive oil

» Dash sambal oelek (Asian chili sauce)

» Pinch salt and pepper

TO SERVE

Place the salad on four plates and top it with the mahi mahi. Garnish with the reserved watercress leaves.

PAIRING SUGGESTION: Sauvignon or Chenin Blanc. *Tom Firth:* Arrowleaf White Feather (Okanagan Valley, BC) or Cave Spring Chenin Blanc Estate Bottled (Ont).

RESTAURANT
Ryan Duffy's

TYPE
mackerel

CHEF
Chris Velden

LOCATION
Halifax, NS

Pan-Seared Atlantic Mackerel with Seven-Herb Cream and Warm Potato Salad

You can grill mackerel, sauté it, pickle it, fry it, or eat it raw. Mackerel works very well with bacon and sour cream, and this recipe reflects my German heritage: the seven herbs with potatoes is a tradition in Frankfurt. At Ryan Duffy's we serve mackerel in July and August while it is fresh. *Serves 4*

NOTE: If mackerel is hard to come by, use arctic char, wild salmon, or albacore tuna instead.

POTATO SALAD

Boil the potatoes in a large pot of water until they are cooked, about 15 minutes. Drain the water and peel the potatoes while they are still hot. Set aside. Once they are cool, slice them into a large bowl.

Heat the grapeseed oil in a frying pan over medium-high heat. Add the bacon and fry it until crispy. Add the onion and sauté the mixture for 1 or 2 minutes, or until the onion is translucent. Add the stock and vinegar and bring everything to a boil. Add salt and pepper to taste. Reduce the heat to medium-low and simmer the mixture for 5 minutes. Pour it over the sliced potatoes.

Add the cucumber and the Dijon mustard and mix the salad well. Fold in the parsley, diced egg, and tomato. Taste and add more salt and pepper if needed. Keep the salad warm (either in a *bain-marie* or place above a pot of simmering water on the back burner) until you're ready to serve the dish.

» 1½ lb (750 g) fingerling or new potatoes, washed and left whole
» 2 Tbsp (30 mL) grapeseed oil
» 4 slices bacon, diced
» ½ medium onion, diced
» ½ cup (125 mL) chicken stock
» ⅓ cup (80 mL) vinegar (white, balsamic, or tarragon)
» Salt and pepper to taste
» 1 English cucumber, peeled and diced
» 1 Tbsp (15 mL) Dijon mustard
» 2 Tbsp (30 mL) chopped parsley
» 2 large hard-boiled eggs, peeled and diced
» 1 medium tomato, seeded and diced

continued . . .

SEVEN-HERB CREAM

Set a few sprigs of each of the herbs aside for garnish before chopping them for the seven-herb cream. Place all the ingredients in a food processor and mix them together until they are well combined. Add more salt and pepper to taste if needed.

» 3 Tbsp (45 mL) chopped parsley
» 2 Tbsp (30 mL) chopped chives
» 2 Tbsp (30 mL) chopped dill
» 2 Tbsp (30 mL) chopped chervil
» 2 Tbsp (30 mL) chopped basil
» 1 Tbsp (15 mL) chopped mint
» 1 Tbsp (15 mL) chopped cilantro
» 2 cups (500 mL) sour cream
» 1 Tbsp (15 mL) fresh lemon juice
» 1 clove garlic, chopped
» Salt and pepper to taste

MACKEREL

Preheat the oven to 375°F (190°C). Line a baking sheet with parchment paper. Score the skin of the mackerel fillets diagonally with a sharp knife and season them with salt and pepper. Heat the olive oil in a medium frying pan over medium-high heat. Place the fillets, skin side down, in the pan and fry them for about 2 minutes to crisp up the skin, then flip them and cook them another minute, until they are golden brown. Remove the fillets from the pan, place them on the parchment paper–lined baking sheet, and bake for about 5 minutes. Once the fish is cooked, remove any remaining bones. (It is easier to remove the bones after cooking, so you do not tear the fillets.)

» Eight 3 to 5 oz (90 to 150 g) mackerel fillets (from 4 medium fish), skin on and scaled
» Salt and pepper to taste
» 2 Tbsp (30 mL) olive oil (approx)

TO SERVE

Scoop the warm potato salad onto four plates and lay the mackerel on top of the potato salad. Spoon the seven-herb cream sauce onto the fish and around the plate. Garnish the plate with herb sprigs.

PAIRING SUGGESTION: A German Riesling or a Chardonnay. Try Peter Lehmann Weighbridge Unwooded Chardonnay. *Tom Firth:* Dr. Loosen Riesling (Germany).

Poached BC Spot Prawns with Beetroot Salad and Basil Mayonnaise

Serves 4

BEETROOT SALAD

Combine all the ingredients in a glass bowl. Toss together evenly and season to taste. Let the salad sit for at least 2 hours to allow the flavours to blend.

» 3 lb (1.5 kg) beets, boiled, peeled, and diced into large chunks
» 1 English cucumber, peeled, seeded, and diced into large chunks
» 1 medium red onion, minced
» 3 cloves garlic, minced
» 2 Tbsp (30 mL) extra virgin olive oil
» ½ cup (125 mL) fresh lemon juice
» 3 Tbsp (45 mL) chopped Italian flat-leaf parsley
» Salt and freshly ground black pepper to taste

TO COOK THE PRAWNS

Bring a large pot of water to a boil, and add the salt. Place prawns into boiling water for 15 seconds. Remove them from the water and plunge into ice until chilled.

» 1 lb (500 g) BC spot prawn tails, shell on
» ½ tsp (2 mL) salt

TO SERVE

Arrange the beetroot salad on four plates and place the prawns on top. Drizzle with basil mayonnaise.

PAIRING SUGGESTION: *Tom Firth:* Tawse 17th Street Pinot Noir (Ont) or Marqués de Cáceres Rioja Reserva (Spain).

» Mayonnaise (see page 292) combined with fresh basil

RESTAURANT
Aubergine Grille, Westin Resort & Spa

TYPE
octopus

CHEF
Jeffery Young

LOCATION
Whistler, BC

Octopus Carpaccio with Warm Spinach, Frisée, and Sea Lettuce Salad

Cooking the octopus for this elegant salad takes a bit of time, but it is well worth the effort. You can also serve the octopus slices as part of an Italian antipasto platter. *Serves 4*

NOTE: You might be able to purchase octopus that has already been tenderized—ask your fishmonger. Partially freezing the octopus just before slicing will make it easier to cut into very thin rounds.

OCTOPUS

Put the octopus in a large stockpot and cover with the vegetable stock, adding water if necessary. Bring to a boil over high heat and then reduce the heat to simmer for about 3 hours, or until the octopus is tender.

Allow the octopus to cool in the stock. Gently remove the octopus from the stock and drain well in a colander. Lay the tentacle or legs on a sheet of plastic wrap and roll up tightly. Place the octopus "rolls" on a baking sheet and chill overnight, or 4 to 6 hours. Using a very sharp knife, slice the octopus thinly on a bit of an angle.

» One 12 oz (340 g) octopus tentacle (or 1 whole octopus, trimmed, beak and stomach removed [page 21]), suckers removed
» 8 cups (2 L) vegetable stock

DRESSING

Combine all the ingredients in a small saucepan and warm over low heat until the shallots and chilies soften, about 2 minutes.

» ¾ cup (185 mL) extra virgin olive oil
» ½ cup (125 mL) fresh lemon juice
» 1 Tbsp (15 mL) finely diced shallot
» 1 Tbsp (15 mL) capers, finely chopped
» 1 tsp (5 mL) sugar
» 1 tsp (5 tsp) finely chopped chives
» Pinch finely chopped tarragon
» Pinch finely chopped thyme
» Pinch finely chopped fresh green chili
» Pinch kosher salt
» Pinch freshly ground black pepper

SALAD

Place the spinach, frisée, and sea lettuce leaves in a medium bowl. Pour half of the warm dressing over them and toss the salad to coat it evenly.

» 2 cups (500 mL) baby spinach leaves, washed and trimmed
» 2 cups (500 mL) frisée lettuce, washed and trimmed
» ¼ cup (60 mL) sea lettuce leaves (or 3 nori sheets, cut into thin strips)

TO SERVE

Set out four plates. Lay the octopus slices in a circular pattern in the centre of each plate. Pile the salad around the octopus. Spoon some of the remaining dressing over the octopus.

PAIRING SUGGESTION: Sumac Ridge Private Reserve Sauvignon Blanc. *Tom Firth*: Lake Breeze Seven Poplars Sauvignon Blanc. (Both wines from Okanagan Valley, BC.)

Sesame-Marinated Jellyfish with Cucumber and Daikon

Few people think of adding jellyfish to their culinary repertoire, but it is a great flavour carrier with a crunchy texture. Dried jellyfish is available at specialty Asian markets. For more information about preparing jellyfish, go to www.oceanwise.ca/jellyfish. *Serves 4*

TO COOK THE JELLYFISH

Rinse the shredded jellyfish under cold water and drain. Cover with boiling water and allow it to stand for 10 minutes, then drain it and rinse it again under a slow stream of cold running water for 30 minutes. Drain the jellyfish and pat it dry with a kitchen towel.

» 1¼ cups (310 mL) dried shredded jellyfish

MARINADE

Mix together all the marinade ingredients in a small bowl. Combine the jellyfish and the marinade in a resealable Ziploc bag and refrigerate overnight.

» ¼ cup (60 mL) sesame oil
» 2 tsp (10 mL) rice wine vinegar (unseasoned)
» 2 tsp (10 mL) sugar
» 2 tsp (10 mL) soy sauce
» 1 tsp (5 mL) shichimi togarashi (Japanese seven-spice, page 295)
» 1 Tbsp (15 mL) toasted sesame seeds

TO SERVE

Rinse the julienned daikon under cold running water for 10 minutes. Strain in a colander.

Line the inside of four wide-mouth or martini glasses with the cucumber slices. Cover them with a layer of daikon and top the daikon with one-quarter of the marinated jellyfish. Garnish the glasses with black sesame seeds and a pinch of shichimi togarashi.

PAIRING SUGGESTION: This dish would come alive with a refreshing bubbly, such as Prosecco di Conegliano from Veneto (Italy). *Tom Firth:* Mission Hill Five Vineyards Pinot Blanc (Okanagan Valley, BC).

» 1 cup (250 mL) julienned daikon (white radish)
» 1 English cucumber, thinly sliced
» 1 tsp (5 mL) black sesame seeds
» Pinch shichimi togarashi

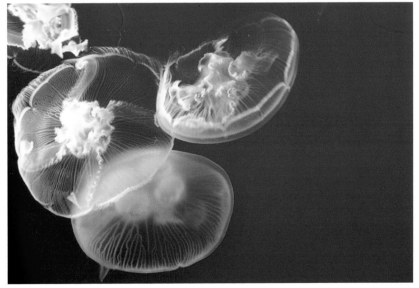

MAINS

Smoked Paprika and Citrus–Crusted BC Albacore Tuna

At O'Doul's we serve this dish with a tomato and white bean ragout. The combination of tuna with the smoked paprika makes it a versatile dish any time of the year. *Serves 4*

TO COOK THE BEANS

Rinse and drain the beans and place them in a large saucepan with the vegetable stock and bay leaves. Bring the stock to a boil, then turn the heat down to low and allow the beans to simmer for about 1 hour. Remove them from the heat and drain. Set aside to cool.

» 1 cup (250 mL) dried white navy beans, soaked overnight
» 4 cups (1 L) vegetable stock
» 2 bay leaves

TO COOK THE RAGOUT

Heat a large heavy-bottomed saucepan over medium heat and add the olive oil. Add the onion, celery, carrot, and garlic and sauté until the onion and garlic are translucent. Stir in the tomato paste and cook the mixture for about 3 minutes. Deglaze the pan with the red wine and allow the liquid to reduce by half (this should take about 5 minutes). Reduce the heat to medium-low and add the tomatoes. Stir in the cooked beans and simmer for 1½ to 2 hours, or until the liquid has reduced by half. Add the chopped thyme and 1 tsp (5 mL) of the parsley. Season the ragout to taste with salt and pepper and keep it warm over low heat until you are ready to serve it.

» 2 Tbsp (30 mL) extra virgin olive oil
» ½ cup (125 mL) diced white onion
» ¼ cup (60 mL) diced celery
» ¼ cup (60 mL) diced carrot
» 2 cloves garlic, minced
» 2 Tbsp (30 mL) tomato paste
» ½ cup (125 mL) red wine
» One 28 oz (796 mL) can tomatoes, drained and diced
» 1 tsp (5 mL) finely chopped thyme
» 3 Tbsp (45 mL) finely chopped Italian flat-leaf parsley
» Salt and pepper to taste

TO COAT AND SEAR THE TUNA

Mix the two types of paprika, lemon and orange zest, kosher salt, and the remaining parsley together in a small bowl. Pour the spice mixture onto a flat surface and roll the tuna portions in seasoning until they are well coated.

Preheat a non-stick frying pan over medium-high heat and then add the vegetable oil. Place the seasoned tuna pieces in the pan and sear for about 45 seconds per side. Drain the tuna on a kitchen or paper towel.

» ¼ cup (60 mL) hot smoked paprika
» ¼ cup (60 mL) sweet smoked paprika
» Zest of 3 lemons
» Zest of 2 oranges
» 2 tsp (10 mL) kosher salt
» Four 6 oz (175 g) albacore tuna fillets
» 3 Tbsp (45 mL) vegetable oil

TO SERVE

Distribute the tomato and bean ragout onto four plates. Cut each tuna portion into four or five slices, and mound on top of the ragout. Sprinkle the plates with a handful of the reserved chopped parsley.

» Chopped parsley for garnish

PAIRING SUGGESTION: Garry Oaks Zeta (Zweigelt) from Salt Spring Island, BC. Its soft fruitiness would work with the sweet tuna meat. It is also slightly spicy, so it pairs well with the smoked paprika. *Tom Firth*: Sandbanks Baco Noir Reserve (Ont).

RESTAURANT		TYPE
Epic Restaurant, Fairmont Royal York		arctic char
CHEF	LOCATION	
Ryan Gustafson	Toronto, ON	

Arctic Char with Butternut Squash, Lentils, and Artichoke Emulsion

The earthiness of the lentils and squash with the acidity of the artichoke to finish the dish create a perfect harmony with this type of fish. At Epic, we serve this dish with rainbow chard and baby turnips. *Serves 4*

NOTE: French lentils, or lentils du Puy, are smaller and darker than regular green lentils. They are preferred by most chefs because du Puy lentils remain firm after cooking and have a rich flavour. If you cannot find them, substitute brown lentils.

SPECIAL EQUIPMENT: Enough cheesecloth to make 2 spice bags.

DU PUY LENTILS

Place the first six ingredients in a stockpot and bring the mixture to a simmer over medium-high heat. Using cheesecloth, make a spice bag containing the remaining four ingredients and place it in the pot. Cook the lentils until they are al dente—firm, but chewable—about 30 minutes. Remove them from the heat, strain the lentils in a colander, and air-dry them on a baking sheet in the refrigerator.

» ¾ lb (375 g) du Puy lentils
» 8 cups (2 L) chicken stock
» 1 large onion, chopped
» 1 large carrot, chopped
» ½ celery stalk, chopped
» 4 cloves garlic
» 25 whole black peppercorns
» 4 sprigs rosemary
» 4 sprigs thyme
» 2 bay leaves

continued . . .

^ FISHERMAN'S WHARF
IN VANCOUVER

ARTICHOKE FOAM

Using cheesecloth, make a spice bag containing the bay leaf, thyme, and peppercorns. Set the bag aside. Heat the olive oil in a saucepan over medium heat. Add the shallots and sweat them for 1 minute, making sure not to brown them. Add the artichoke hearts and the garlic and cook them in the oil for another minute. Deglaze the saucepan with the white wine and add the spice bag. Allow the liquid to reduce by half before adding the cream.

Let the ingredients simmer for 7 minutes (still on medium heat), and then remove the pan from the heat, discarding the spice bag. Blend the mixture with a handheld blender or food processor until the foam is smooth. Put the foam through a fine-mesh sieve and season it with salt. Refrigerate until you need it.

» 1 bay leaf
» 3 sprigs thyme
» 10 whole black peppercorns
» 1 Tbsp (15 mL) olive oil
» 2 shallots, chopped
» 12 oz (355 mL) artichoke hearts, roughly chopped
» 1 clove garlic, minced
» 1 cup (250 mL) dry white wine
» 2 cups (500 mL) whipping cream
» Salt

BUTTERNUT SQUASH AND LENTILS

Heat the butter in another large pan over medium-high heat. Add the shallot and all the diced squash and sauté for 1 minute. Add the garlic, all the cooked lentils, and the chicken stock. Let the mixture simmer until the stock is absorbed. Finish the squash with more salt and pepper to taste and add a pinch of herbs.

» 2 Tbsp (30 mL) butter
» 1 shallot, chopped
» 1 cup (250 mL) butternut squash, cut into small dice
» 1 clove garlic, minced
» 2 cups (500 mL) cooked du Puy lentils (recipe on page 144)
» ½ cup (125 mL) chicken stock
» Pinch finely chopped parsley and thyme

ARCTIC CHAR

Pat the char pieces dry with a kitchen or paper towel and season them with salt and pepper. Heat the butter and olive oil in a large frying pan over medium-high heat until it bubbles. Place the portions of char in the pan, being sure not to crowd them, and sear until they are golden brown. Gently flip the char over, remove the pan from the heat, and place it in the oven for 3 to 4 minutes, or until the fish is almost firm. Remove the pan from the oven and sprinkle the herbs on top. Set the fish aside and keep warm.

» Four 6 oz (175 g) pieces arctic char
» Salt and pepper to taste
» 2 Tbsp (30 mL) butter
» 2 Tbsp (30 mL) olive oil
» 1 Tbsp (15 mL) finely chopped parsley
» 1 Tbsp (15 mL) finely chopped thyme

ARTICHOKE EMULSION

Bring the artichoke foam and milk to a low simmer in a small saucepan over medium-low heat. Season it with salt and pepper to taste. Swirl the butter into the pot and foam the artichoke emulsion with a handheld blender.

» 2 cups (500 mL) artichoke foam (recipe on facing page)
» ¼ cup (60 mL) skim milk
» Kosher salt and freshly ground black pepper to taste
» 1 Tbsp (15 mL) butter

TO SERVE

Set out four plates. Spoon the squash and lentils into the middle of the plates. Place the arctic char on top, surround with the artichoke foam, and finish with a sprinkle of parsley and thyme.

PAIRING SUGGESTION: 13th Street Sandstone Old Vines Chardonnay (Ont). *Tom Firth:* Hidden Bench Felseck Vineyard Pinot Noir (Ont).

» Finely chopped parsley and thyme, for garnish

RESTAURANT
L'Orignal

TYPE
arctic char

CHEF
Marco Santos

LOCATION
Montreal, QC

Arctic Char with Tomato Confit and Dried Black Olive Crust

This dish is a rich Mediterranean combination of flavours and styles. With a light but complex fish and a rich flavour to the crust and tomato confit, this dish satisfies on both a warm evening and a cold winter's night. Despite the number of steps and seeming complexity, you cannot go wrong with this recipe; the taste of each bite will transport you. *Serves 4*

TO PREPARE THE OLIVES

Start the day before by drying the olives for the crust. To do this, turn the oven on to the lowest possible setting—ideally 150°F (75°C). Place the olives on a baking sheet and let them dry in the oven overnight. The following day, crumble them in a food processor.

» 1 cup (250 mL) black olives, pitted

TOMATO CONFIT

Preheat the oven to 300°F (150°C). Blanch the whole tomatoes in boiling water for 30 seconds. This will cause the skin to loosen, which will allow you to remove it more easily. Remove the tomatoes from the boiling water and place into an ice-water bath. This will help the skins separate from the meat. Peel the skins off the tomatoes, cut them in half, and remove the seeds and liquid. Roughly chop the tomatoes. Mix with the olive oil, garlic, salt, and pepper. Place the mixture in an ovenproof metal dish and cook for about 2 hours. Let cool. Mix the tomato confit with the lemon zest, parsley, chives, salt, pepper, and olive oil to taste. Set aside.

» 2 cups (500 mL) Roma tomatoes (about 8 tomatoes)
» 2 Tbsp (30 mL) olive oil + extra to taste
» 4 cloves garlic, minced
» ½ tsp (2 mL) salt
» ½ tsp (2 mL) pepper
» Zest of 2 lemons
» ¼ cup (60 mL) chopped parsley
» ¼ cup (60 mL) chopped chives
» Salt and pepper to taste

continued . . .

TO ROAST THE RED PEPPERS

Preheat or adjust the oven to 450°F (230°C). Roast the red peppers for 8 to 10 minutes in the oven until the skin is blackened. (Or, using metal tongs you can char the peppers directly over the flame of a burner.) Remove from the oven and place them in a bowl covered with plastic wrap. The steam will cause the skin to separate more easily from the flesh. After 15 minutes, remove the wrap and peel the skin from the peppers. Cut into a rough chop.

» 3 large red peppers

POTATO CASSEROLE

Meanwhile, place the potatoes in a pot of cold water over high heat until the water boils, then reduce to a simmer. Continue to cook until they are al dente, about 10 minutes. Drain the potatoes in a colander and slice them in half lengthwise. Coat the potatoes with the olive oil in a large ovenproof frying pan and roast them in the oven for about 10 minutes, or until they begin to brown. Remove the potatoes from the oven. Add the cubed chorizo, blood sausage (if using), roasted red peppers, and shallots and sauté over medium heat for 3 to 5 minutes.

Heat the water in a small pan, and sauté the green beans until they are soft. Drain in a colander. Add salt and pepper to taste. Add the beans to the potato mixture.

» 2 lb (1 kg) fingerling or new potatoes
» 2 Tbsp (30 mL) olive oil
» 1 cup (250 mL) Portuguese chorizo sausage
» 1 cup (250 mL) coarsely chopped blood sausage or blood pudding (optional)
» 3 shallots, finely diced
» 2 Tbsp (30 mL) water
» 2 cups (500 mL) extra fine green beans
» Salt and pepper to taste

SAUCE

Heat the oil in a medium pot over medium heat and add the onion. Cook until caramelized, about 10 minutes. Deglaze the pan with the white wine, allowing the mixture to continue to simmer and reduce almost completely. Add the cream and let it reduce by half. Stir in the lemon zest (if desired). Remove from the stove and strain through a fine-mesh sieve into a container that is deep enough and suitable for blending with a hand blender without splattering (or use a food processor). Add the parsley and cilantro and blend until smooth.

» 1 Tbsp (15 mL) olive oil
» ½ cup (125 mL) diced white onion
» 1 cup (250 mL) dry white wine
» 2 cups (500 mL) whipping cream
» 1 cup (250 mL) chopped parsley
» 1 cup (250 mL) chopped cilantro
» Zest of 1 lemon (optional)

ARCTIC CHAR

Adjust the oven to 350°F (180°C). In a large frying pan, heat the olive oil over medium high. When the oil is almost smoking, place the arctic char skin side down and fry until crisp, about 3 minutes. Flip the fish skin side up, and cover with half the tomato confit and all of the crumbled olives. Remove from the stove and finish in the oven for 5 minutes.

TO SERVE

Centre the potato casserole on warm plates and top with arctic char and the remaining tomato confit. Pool the sauce around the plates and drizzle a few drops over the fish.

PAIRING SUGGESTION: *Tom Firth:* Boutari Moschofilero (Greece) or Sandhill Small Lots Barbera (Okanagan Valley, BC).

» 2 Tbsp (30 mL) olive oil
» Four 6 oz (175 g) arctic char fillets, skin on

RESTAURANT
Goldfish Pacific Kitchen

TYPE
barramundi

CHEF
William Tse

LOCATION
Vancouver, BC

Steamed Sake-Marinated Barramundi with Ginger and Scallion Julienne

This is an easy-to-prepare dish with full-bodied flavour. Barramundi belongs to the perch family and has exceptional nutritional value and exceptional taste—somewhere between sablefish, walleye, swordfish, and bass. At Goldfish we like to enhance barramundi's natural flavours by simply steaming it with a few ingredients, letting the natural flavour of the fish to come through.

Steaming with ginger and scallions is a traditional Chinese way to prepare fish, something my mom taught me as a child. Remember to peel the ginger as the peel will add bitterness.

Serve with steamed jasmine rice. *Serves 4*

SPECIAL EQUIPMENT: You will need a large bamboo steamer basket with a lid or two smaller ones (which you stack) with one lid. Two may work better if you need more room for all the fillets. The bamboo from the steamer baskets will add to the flavour.

MARINADE

In a bowl add the sake, soy sauce, and water. Bruise the thyme with your hands to release the natural oils, and crush the chili with the heel of your knife. Add the thyme, chili, ginger, and garlic to the bowl. Mix well.

For best results let the marinade steep for at least an hour before adding the fish.

» ½ cup (125 mL) sake
» ¼ cup (60 mL) light soy sauce
» 1 cup (125 mL) cold water
» 3 sprigs thyme
» ½ Thai bird chili
» 2 Tbsp (30 mL) finely sliced ginger (peeled)
» 2 Tbsp (30 mL) finely sliced garlic

continued . . .

Pat the fish dry with a paper towel. Place the fish into the marinade, making sure it is fully submerged. Marinate for 20 minutes. Be careful not to marinate for too long as this will start to negatively affect the flavour and colour.

Remove the fish from the marinade and pat dry once again with paper towel. Season with sea salt and white pepper.

Oil the steamer basket, or spray with nonstick spray. (Or a good trick is to line the bottom of the steamer basket with lettuce, if you have it—iceberg or romaine works best.) In a pot or very large skillet add a sufficient amount of water for steaming. Place the fish in the basket, making sure that the fillets are not touching one another.

Cover the steamer baskets and steam for about 8 minutes, or until the fish is firm but still moist inside.

» Four 6 oz (175 g) barramundi fillets, preferably skin on
» Sea salt and freshly ground white pepper to taste

TO FINISH

Prepare the rest of the ingredients while the fish is steaming—once the fish is cooked you will be serving it immediately.

Transfer the fish onto serving dishes. Divide the green onion and ginger julienne on top. In a small pot or fry pan, heat the oil until it barely starts to smoke. Be very careful—if the oil gets too hot it will catch on fire. Pour an even amount of the oil on each piece of fish. The heat from the oil will slightly crisp up the ginger and green onion. (I call this flashing with hot oil.)

To finish add 1 Tbsp (15 mL) of soy sauce on top of each dish.

PAIRING SUGGESTION: The solid flavours, good acidity, and fine balance of Pinot Noir really enhance barramundi and all the other flavours of this dish. *Tom Firth:* Spy Valley Pinot Noir (New Zealand) or MacMurray Ranch Sonoma Coast Pinot Noir (California).

» ¼ cup (60 mL) julienned green onion (cut green onion into 2-inch/5 cm lengths then slice lengthwise)
» ¼ cup (60 mL) julienned fresh ginger (peeled)
» ½ cup (125 mL) vegetable oil
» 4 Tbsp (60 mL) light soy sauce

RESTAURANT
The District Social House

TYPE
Pacific cod

CHEF
Paul Mon-Kau

LOCATION
North Vancouver, BC

The District Battered Cod

This is a classic fish-and-chips recipe. Only the ocean is different—Atlantic cod is no longer sustainable. In the UK, Stella Artois beer, or Stella for short, is also known as "The Wife Beater" in dubious honour of Marlon Brando's character Stanley Kowalski in *A Streetcar Named Desire*. Since our beater, er, batter, is made with Stella, using it seemed curiously apt as well as marginally offensive. *Serves 4*

NOTE: To make this at home you will need a deep fryer and a case of your favourite lager. You can substitute lingcod for the Pacific cod if desired.

TARTAR SAUCE

Mix the mayonnaise, lemon juice, onion, pickle, capers, dill, tarragon, and a pinch of salt together in a small bowl and set it aside.

» 1 cup (250 mL) mayonnaise
» 2 Tbsp (30 mL) fresh lemon juice
» 1 Tbsp (15 mL) finely minced white onion
» 1 Tbsp (15 mL) finely diced pickle
» 1 Tbsp (15 mL) chopped capers
» 1 Tbsp (15 mL) finely chopped dill
» 1½ tsp (7 mL) finely chopped tarragon
» Pinch salt

BATTER

Combine 3 cups (750 mL) of the flour, the cornstarch, salt and pepper in a large mixing bowl. Slowly add the lager while beating the mixture with a fork to work out all the lumps.

» 5 cups (1.25 L) all-purpose flour
» 1 cup (250 mL) cornstarch
» Pinch salt
» Pinch pepper
» Two 12 fl oz (330 mL) bottles Stella, or your favourite lager

TO COOK THE POTATOES

Add the oil to a deep fryer and preheat to 375°F (190°C). Preheat the oven to 150°F (66°C). Cut the potatoes into strips about ½ inch (1 cm) wide and ½ inch (1 cm) thick. Carefully place the potatoes in the deep fryer and cook them for 3 to 4 minutes, or until they are golden brown and crispy. Remove from the hot oil using tongs, drain on paper towel, and keep them warm in the oven.

» 6 to 8 cups (1.5 to 2 L) canola oil
» 2 lb (1 kg) russet potatoes

TO COOK THE FISH

Dredge the pieces of fish in the remaining 2 cups (500 mL) of flour, dip in the batter, and carefully place them in the deep fryer, using the same oil as for the potatoes. Immediately shake the fryer basket to prevent the fish from sticking together. If necessary, separate with tongs any pieces that have stuck together after 30 seconds of cooking. Cook the fish for 4 to 6 minutes, or until it is golden brown.

» Eight 6 to 7 oz (175 to 200 g) pieces Pacific cod

TO SERVE

Mound the fries on a large dish and top with the pieces of fish. Tuck in with the lemon wedges on the side and the tartar sauce for dipping.

PAIRING SUGGESTION: I'd prefer to match this dish with its obvious natural companion, a cold glass of Stella Artois. But if it was a huge concern, and wine *had* to come to dinner, I would suggest the See Ya Later Ranch Non Vintage SYL Brut Sparkling Wine (Okanagan Valley, BC). *Tom Firth:* Any fresh European-style lager.

» 4 lemon wedges, for garnish

Tapenade-Crusted Lingcod with Roasted Red Pepper and Fennel

Unique to the West Coast, lingcod aren't the prettiest-looking fish. However, their mild flavour and dense white flesh lend themselves very well to the saltiness of the tapenade. *Serves 4*

TO ROAST THE PEPPERS

Preheat the oven to 450°F (230°C). Place the peppers on a baking sheet and roast, turning occasionally to roast evenly, for about 25 minutes, or until they are blackened. Remove them from the oven and place in a paper bag to cool completely. Remove the skins (they should come off easily), discard the seeds, and slice the peppers lengthwise into strips. These can be done one day ahead and stored in the refrigerator.

» 3 medium red peppers

TO BAKE THE FISH

Preheat the oven to 425°F (220°C). Heat ¼ cup (60 mL) of the olive oil in a frying pan over high heat. Season the lingcod fillets with half of the salt and sear the skin side only for about 3 minutes, or until the skin is crispy and brown (this may need to be done in batches). Transfer the fish to a baking sheet. Spread one-quarter of the tapenade on each fillet and bake them for 6 to 8 minutes, or until the flesh separates from the bones easily. While the fish is cooking, bring water to a boil in a medium saucepan and boil the new potatoes until barely tender, about 8 minutes. Drain and keep warm.

» ½ cup (125 mL) olive oil
» Four 6 oz (175 g) lingcod fillets
» 1 tsp (5 mL) salt
» ¼ cup (60 mL) tapenade (see page 291)
» 6 new potatoes, halved

TO FINISH THE PEPPERS

Heat the remaining ¼ cup (60 mL) of olive oil in a separate frying pan over medium-high heat. Add the fennel and sauté for about 5 minutes, or until soft (reduce the heat if necessary). Add the roasted peppers and remaining salt and sauté for 1 to 2 minutes, or until the peppers are heated through.

» 2 medium fennel bulbs, cored and thinly sliced

TO SERVE

Set out four plates. Place three potato halves on each plate, spoon 2 Tbsp (30 mL) of the fennel-pepper mixture beside them, and place a tapenade-crusted lingcod fillet on top. Garnish with the fresh herbs.

PAIRING SUGGESTION: *Tom Firth:* Banrock Station Unwooded Chardonnay (Australia) or Jackson Triggs Okanagan SunRock Vineyard Chardonnay.

» ½ cup (125 mL) mixed chopped herbs (chives, basil, and parsley), for garnish

SOURCE
Ramada Plaza & Conference Centre

CHEF
Michael Traquair

TYPE
king croaker

LOCATION
Abbotsford, BC

Pan-Seared King Croaker with Roasted Squash Purée, Chanterelles, and Creamed Watercress

King croaker is a pearl-white fish, very buttery in flavour, light and flaky—delicious! We served this dish at a local wine-maker's dinner held in the Fraser Valley. *Serves 4 as a main or 8 as an appetizer*

NOTE: If king croaker is not available, you could substitute halibut or Pacific cod.

SQUASH PURÉE

Preheat the oven to 350°F (180°C). Cut the squash into 1- × 1-inch (2.5 × 2.5 cm) pieces. Place the squash in a medium bowl and toss it with the honey. Add 2 Tbsp (30 mL) of the oil and toss it again. Transfer the squash to a 9- × 13-inch (3.5 L) casserole dish, add the water, and cover the dish tightly with aluminum foil. Bake the squash for 45 minutes, or until it is soft enough to be mashed. Mash it with a fork, then bake it again, uncovered, for another 5 minutes, or until the edges are golden brown. (There should be very little liquid left in the dish, if any.)

Scrape the squash into a food processor and add 2 Tbsp (30 mL) of the butter. Blend the mixture until the squash is very smooth, for 30 seconds to 1 minute, making sure to scrape down the sides of the bowl halfway through. (You can use a potato masher instead; the squash just won't be as smooth.) Add salt to taste. Keep the purée warm in a covered pot in the oven until you're ready to serve it. The purée can be cooled down and kept, refrigerated, for up to three days or frozen using a food saver vacuum seal and kept in the freezer for up to six months.

» 4 cups (1 L) peeled and seeded butternut or acorn squash
» 2 tsp (10 mL) honey
» 4 Tbsp (60 mL) vegetable oil
» ½ cup (125 mL) water
» 5 Tbsp (75 mL) butter
» Salt

continued . . .

CREAMED WATERCRESS

While the squash is baking, rinse the watercress leaves in cold water to remove any dirt. Pat them dry with a kitchen or paper towel. Heat a medium saucepan over medium heat and add 1 Tbsp (15 mL) of the remaining butter to the pan. When the butter is completely melted, add ¼ cup (60 mL) of the diced shallots. Cook them, stirring them occasionally, for 1 to 2 minutes, or until they are translucent. Add the white wine while stirring constantly. Reduce the liquid by half, about 5 minutes. Add the whipping cream to the pan and bring it to a simmer. Turn the heat down to low and simmer the mixture for 8 to 10 minutes, until it thickens.

Remove the pan from the heat and stir in the watercress. Pour the wilted watercress and all the cooking liquid into a blender and purée until it is smooth. Season the sauce to taste with salt and pepper. Pour the sauce back into the saucepan and keep it warm until you are ready to serve it. (The sauce can be cooled down and refrigerated for up to three days.)

» 1½ cups (325 mL) watercress leaves (approx)
» 5 Tbsp (75 mL) finely diced shallots (reserve 1 Tbsp/15 mL for the chanterelles)
» ½ cup (125 mL) dry white wine
» 1 cup (250 mL) whipping cream
» Salt and freshly ground black pepper

TO SEAR THE FISH

Preheat the oven to 375°F (190°C). Heat the remaining 2 Tbsp (30 mL) of oil in a large ovenproof frying pan over medium-high heat. Lightly season both sides of the fish with salt and pepper. Place it in the hot pan and sear it over medium-high heat, turning it once, until it is golden brown, about 2 minutes per side. Place the pan in the oven and roast the fish until it is cooked through, 4 to 6 minutes.

» 1½ lb (750 g) skinless king croaker fillet, cut into four 6 oz (175 g) pieces for a main course or eight 3 oz (90 g) pieces for an appetizer

Heat a medium frying pan over medium-high heat and then add the remaining 2 Tbsp (30 mL) of butter. When it is melted, add the remaining 1 Tbsp (15 mL) of shallots and the chanterelles. Toss them until the mushrooms are evenly coated. Sauté the mixture until the chanterelles are tender, about 4 minutes. Season the mushrooms to taste with salt and stir in the chopped chives.

» 1½ cups (375 mL) chanterelle mushrooms, thoroughly cleaned with a soft, dry brush (not washed in water) and cut into quarters
» Salt to taste
» 2 tsp (10 mL) chopped chives

TO SERVE

Place one-quarter of the warm squash purée in the centre of each plate. Add 1 to 2 Tbsp (15 to 30 mL) of the creamed watercress next to the squash. Place a piece of fish on top of the squash purée. Spoon the mushrooms over the fish. Garnish with more watercress leaves or chopped chives.

PAIRING SUGGESTION: Township 7 Viognier (BC). *Tom Firth:* Black Prince Melon de Bourgogne (Ont).

» Watercress leaves or chopped chives, for garnish

FISHBOATS AT REST AT VANCOUVER'S FISHERMAN'S WHARF

TV SERIES
Chef at Home

CHEF
Michael Smith

TYPE
*haddock (or
any white fish)*

LOCATION
PEI

Pan-Fried Haddock

This is one of the easiest ways to cook any type of white fish. It is also one of the tastiest and fastest. Perhaps more than any other technique, this is how I choose to get fish on the table in a hurry. *White fish* is a generic term that refers to many different types of fish, all of them easy to find and cook. This method is excellent for any white fish: halibut, hake, haddock, cod, or tilapia. *Serves 4 to 6*

NOTE: You can add lots of personalized flavour to the seasoned flour. Try replacing half or more of the flour with fine cornmeal. Dill, thyme, tarragon, and oregano all work well as fresh herbs, while chili powder, curry powder, ground cumin, and red pepper flakes all make excellent spices. My all-time favourite addition is Old Bay Spice (see page 294).

Whisk together the flour, paprika, Old Bay Spice, lemon zest, salt, and pepper. Pour the seasoned flour into a shallow dish that is large enough to hold one or two fish fillets.

Depending on the size of the fillets, and your guests' inclination to share, cut the fish into individual portions or leave them whole. Dredge the fillets in the seasoned flour until they are evenly coated. Rest them on a pan or plate but do not stack them on top of one another.

Preheat your largest, heaviest frying pan over medium-high heat. Pour the vegetable oil into the hot pan. Add the butter to the centre of the oil. The oil will protect the delicate butter from burning, and the butter will add a nutty flavour. When the butter begins to brown and sizzle, swirl it around the pan and, working in batches, quickly add the fish fillets. Turn up the heat, adjusting it as needed to keep the pan sizzling hot. Sear the fillets, turning them once, until they are cooked through and golden brown on both sides, 3 to 4 minutes per side. You may want to add a bit more butter after you flip the fish over. Remove fish from the pan and keep warm.

Add the lemon juice to the pan and swirl to form a quick sauce. Coat the fillets with the sauce and serve them immediately.

PAIRING SUGGESTION: *Tom Firth:* Mission Hill S.L.C. Sauvignon Blanc/Semillon (BC) or Blomidon Estate Winery L'Acadie Blanc (Nova Scotia).

SEASONED FLOUR
» 1 cup (250 mL) whole wheat flour (or any other flour)
» 1 Tbsp (15 mL) paprika
» 1 Tbsp (15 mL) Old Bay Spice (see page 294)
» Zest of 1 lemon
» Pinch sea salt
» Pinch freshly ground black pepper

» 2 lb (1 kg) skinless haddock (or any white fish) fillets (4 to 6 fillets)
» 2 Tbsp (30 mL) vegetable oil
» 2 Tbsp (30 mL) butter
» Juice of 1 lemon

SOURCE
*Everyone Can Cook Seafood
(Whitecap Books, 2004)*

TYPE
haddock

CHEF
Eric Akis

LOCATION
Victoria, BC

Haddock and Winter Vegetable Casserole

Here is a complete meal that is inexpensive to make and can be baked in one pan. Try it for a winter Sunday dinner.
Serves 4

Preheat the oven to 450°F (230°C). Brush a 9- × 13-inch (23 × 33 cm) casserole dish with 1 Tbsp (15 mL) of the melted butter. Place the carrots and potatoes in a large pot and cover them with cold water. Bring the water to a boil over medium-high heat and cook the vegetables until they are tender when poked with a knife but still firm. Add the cabbage and continue cooking the vegetables until the cabbage brightens in colour, about 2 minutes. Drain the vegetables well and place them in the casserole dish.

Set the haddock fillets on top of the vegetables and season them with salt and pepper.

Combine the remaining 2 Tbsp (30 mL) of melted butter, the white wine, stock, and garlic in a small mixing bowl. Pour the mixture over the haddock and vegetables. Sprinkle in the frozen peas. Cover the casserole and bake it for 20 minutes, or until the haddock is cooked through. Sprinkle the dish with parsley and serve.

PAIRING SUGGESTION: I like to serve the fish with a dry BC Gewürztraminer. It is spicy and earthy and goes well with the brothy fish, root vegetables, and cabbage. *Tom Firth:* CedarCreek Gewürztraminer or See Ya Later Ranch Gewürztraminer (both Okanagan Valley, BC).

» 3 Tbsp (45 mL) melted butter
» 2 medium carrots, halved lengthwise and sliced diagonally
» 4 medium red-skinned potatoes, cut into wedges
» 2 cups (500 mL) chopped green cabbage
» Four 5 oz (150 g) haddock fillets
» Salt and pepper to taste
» ½ cup (125 mL) dry white wine
» ½ cup (125 mL) fish, chicken, or vegetable stock
» 2 cloves garlic, minced
» ½ cup (125 mL) frozen peas
» 1 Tbsp (15 mL) chopped parsley, for garnish

RESTAURANT
Tomato Fresh Food Café

TYPE
halibut

CHEFS
*Christian Gaudreault
and Star Spilos*

LOCATION
Vancouver, BC

Lemon Pepper Pacific Halibut

This dish is on the daily fresh sheet at the Tomato Fresh Food Café when halibut is in season. It is a mild, firm-textured fish that is delicious and versatile. *Serves 4*

NOTE: You can make a larger quantity of the lemon crust and store it in the refrigerator for up to two weeks.

LEMON PEPPER CRUST

Preheat the oven to 425°F (220°C). Combine the zest, salt, pepper, and parsley in a food processor and process the mixture until it is well blended. Spread about 2 tsp (10 mL) of the lemon pepper mixture on one side of each fillet.

» Zest of 4 lemons
» 1 Tbsp (15 mL) coarse salt
» 1 Tbsp (15 mL) freshly ground black pepper
» 1 Tbsp (15 mL) chopped parsley

HALIBUT

Heat the oil in a large ovenproof frying pan over medium-high heat. Place the halibut fillets in the pan, lemon pepper side down, and sear them for about 2 minutes, until they start to brown. Flip the halibut over, remove the pan from the heat, and place it in the oven for about 6 minutes, or until the fish is firm but still moist inside. Remove the pan from the oven and serve the halibut with a lemon wedge.

PAIRING SUGGESTION: Wild Goose Gewürztraminer or CedarCreek Merlot (both from the Okanagan Valley, BC).

» 2 Tbsp (30 mL) canola oil (approx)
» Four 5 oz (150 g) halibut fillets
» Salt and freshly ground pepper to taste
» 1 lemon, cut into wedges, for garnish

SOURCE
Indishpensable

TYPE
halibut,
anchovies

CHEF
Damian Connolly

LOCATION
Vancouver, BC

Prosciutto and Rosemary–Wrapped Halibut with Truffled New Potatoes and Vegetable Confit

Fresh tastes best. With halibut in season from May to September, this dish was designed for late summer. That is when these herbs, tomatoes, zucchini, and baby potatoes are also in season and available in abundance. The dish is balanced perfectly with the natural salt from the prosciutto and the delicate, silky halibut combined with sweet tomatoes, zucchini, and basil. The new potatoes work wonderfully with the sour dill and bold truffle oil. *Serves 4*

TRUFFLED NEW POTATOES

Place the potatoes in a medium pot, barely cover with cold water, and add about 1 tsp (5 mL) of salt. Cover and bring the water to a boil. Reduce the heat to medium-low and lightly simmer the potatoes for another 15 minutes, or until they are tender when poked with a knife. Strain off the water, transfer the potatoes to a large bowl, and smash them roughly with a fork or a heavy whisk. Add half the parsley, dill, green onion, ¼ cup (60 mL) of the olive oil, 2 Tbsp (30 mL) of the truffle oil, and the butter. Season the potatoes well with salt and pepper. Cover to keep them warm.

» 1½ lb (750 g) Yukon Gold nugget potatoes, washed
» 1 tsp (5 mL) salt (approx)
» ½ cup (125 mL) chopped parsley
» ½ cup (125 mL) chopped dill
» ½ cup (125 mL) chopped green onion
» ½ cup (125 mL) olive oil (reserve half for the vegetable confit)
» 3 Tbsp (45 mL) truffle oil (reserve 1 Tbsp/15 mL for garnish)
» 2 Tbsp (30 mL) butter
» Salt and pepper

PROSCIUTTO AND ROSEMARY–WRAPPED HALIBUT

Preheat the oven to 350°F (180°C). Place the halibut on a plate and pat it dry with a kitchen or paper towel. Season both sides of the fish with black pepper. Place a sprig of rosemary on top of each fillet and gently wrap the prosciutto around the halibut and rosemary. Set the wrapped fillets aside and begin making the confit vegetables. At the appropriate time (see next page), cook the halibut fillets in the preheated oven for 7 to 8 minutes.

» Four 6 oz (175 g) skinless halibut fillets
» Freshly ground black pepper
» 4 large sprigs rosemary
» 4 large prosciutto slices

VEGETABLE CONFIT

Heat the remaining ¼ cup (60 mL) olive oil in a large frying pan over medium-low heat. Add the onion, garlic, and oregano and sweat everything for 4 to 5 minutes. Add the zucchini and turn the heat up to medium. Cook the zucchini and onion mixture for 2 to 3 minutes. (At this point, place the fish in the oven.) Add the cherry tomatoes, capers, anchovies, basil, the remaining parsley, and white wine. Reduce the heat to medium-low again and cook the confit for 3 to 5 minutes, covered.

» ½ cup (125 mL) finely diced yellow onion

» 2 Tbsp (30 mL) finely diced garlic

» 2 tsp (10 mL) fresh oregano leaves picked off the stem

» 2 cups (500 mL) thickly diced zucchini

» 2 cups (500 mL) halved cherry tomatoes

» 2 Tbsp (30 mL) roughly chopped capers

» 4 finely diced fresh anchovies (canned, oil-packed anchovies can be substituted)

» ¼ cup (60 mL) chopped basil

» ½ cup (125 mL) dry white wine

TO SERVE

Set out four plates. Place a piece of fish in the centre of each plate. Spoon the confit vegetables around the fish, and surround them with the potatoes. Using a small spoon, gently drizzle the remaining truffle oil over the confit vegetables.

PAIRING SUGGESTION: Le Rocher des Violettes Cuvée Touche-Mitaine (Domaine Xavier Weisskopf) (Loire Valley, France). This is a dish with some strong flavours that will require a wine with personality. Instead of a red, try this Chenin that is full and dense, showing minerals and white tree fruits with a full mouthfeel and snappy acidity. It is a complex wine for a dish with complex flavours. *Tom Firth:* Vineland Estates Chardonnay (Ont).

SOURCE
Fresh Off The Boat Ocean Foods

CHEF
Mary-Anne Charles

LOCATION
South Surrey, BC

TYPE
halibut

Halibut Cheeks and Leeks

Halibut cheeks have a similar texture to scallops and need to be cooked quickly. This recipe is delightfully simple to make, but at the same time brings out the true, delicate flavour of the halibut. *Serves 2*

NOTE: Do not overcook the cheeks. The texture will change and they will become stringy and tough.

Heat the olive oil in a large frying pan over medium-high heat. Add the leeks to the pan and sauté them until they are soft but not limp, just a few minutes. Add the butter.

Season the halibut cheeks with salt and pepper and add them to the leeks in the frying pan. Cook them until they are opaque, 2 to 3 minutes per side.

» 2 Tbsp (30 mL) olive oil
» 2 medium leeks, roughly chopped
» 1 Tbsp (15 mL) butter
» 1 lb (500 g) halibut cheeks
» Salt and pepper to taste

TO SERVE

Set out two plates. Divide the halibut cheeks and leeks between the plates. You have plenty of sauce options, including a squeeze of fresh lemon juice, a splash of white wine, your favourite salad dressing, lime zest and coconut milk, Chinese black bean sauce and pure maple syrup, or whatever is in your refrigerator. A wee bit of any of these works great. The halibut cheeks are also marvellous without embellishment. A nice accompaniment to this dish is cooked basmati rice and asparagus.

PAIRING SUGGESTION: A nice Sauvignon Blanc or unoaked Chardonnay. *Tom Firth:* Joseph Drouhin Saint-Véran (France) or Oyster Bay Marlborough Sauvignon Blanc (New Zealand).

RESTAURANT
Wild Rice

TYPE
halibut

CHEF
Rob Erickson

LOCATION
Vancouver, BC

Seared Halibut Cheeks with Asian Risotto and Bamboo Shoot Tempura

This dish reminds me of the time I spent in Haida Gwaii (the Queen Charlotte Islands). Halibut cheeks are one of my favourite items from the West Coast. All of the ingredients in this recipe should be easy to find at any Asian market or higher-end grocery store with a good import section. When preparing this dish make sure to keep the cheeks moist and tender. A rubbery or overly firm texture means they have been overcooked, so next time cook them less. Also, the rice should still have a little bite to it, like a good risotto. Do not cook it too long or it will become mushy. *Serves 4*

GINGER BEET REDUCTION

Place the beets in a small saucepan with 2 Tbsp (30 mL) of the rice wine vinegar, a pinch of salt and enough water to cover them. Bring to a boil, uncovered, over high heat and cook until a fork easily pierces the beets. Drain the beets and let cool. Peel off the skin and place the peeled beets in a blender with ½ cup (125 mL) of the vegetable stock, the sliced ginger, the remaining 3 Tbsp (45 mL) of rice wine vinegar, and the coconut milk. Purée until smooth. Season to taste with salt and set aside.

» 3 beets, stems and tops removed
» 5 Tbsp (75 mL) rice wine vinegar
» Salt
» 3½ cups (125 mL) vegetable stock, room temperature (reserve 3 cups/ 750 mL for the rice)
» 2 thumb-sized pieces fresh ginger, peeled and sliced
» ¼ cup (60 mL) coconut milk

TEMPURA BAMBOO SHOOTS

Combine the rice flour, shichimi togarashi, baking soda, cornstarch, and a pinch of salt in a medium bowl. Slowly whisk in the club soda until the mixture reaches a smooth consistency, like pancake batter. Set aside to rest for a few minutes. Drain the bamboo shoots and pat them dry on paper towels. Heat 1 cup (250 mL) of the vegetable oil to 350°F (180°C) in a small saucepan. Dip the bamboo shoots in the tempura batter to coat them and quickly fry (about 1½ minutes) in the hot oil. Drain on a kitchen towel or paper towels.

» ½ cup (125 mL) rice flour
» 1 Tbsp (15 mL) shichimi togarashi (Japanese seven-spice, page 295)
» 1½ tsp (7 mL) baking soda
» 1 tsp (5 mL) cornstarch
» One 12 oz (355 mL) can club soda
» One 19 oz (540 mL) can shredded bamboo shoots
» 1 cup (250 mL) + 2 Tbsp (30 mL) vegetable oil

JADE PEARL AND LOTUS RICE RISOTTO

Add 1 Tbsp (15 mL) of the remaining vegetable oil to a large pot and gently sauté the lotus root until tender. Remove from the oil, drain on a kitchen or paper towel, and set aside. Add the onion to the same pan with a little more oil if needed and sauté until it is translucent. Add the jade pearl rice and stir to coat each grain with oil. Cook over medium heat, stirring for 1 minute. Add 1 cup (250 mL) of the hot stock and cook, stirring constantly, until the stock is reduced. Continue to add the remaining stock ladle by ladle, stirring all the time, until the rice is cooked through. Fold in the lotus root, brown sugar, soy sauce, and sesame oil. Season with a pinch of salt and freshly ground pepper. Set aside.

» 1 fresh lotus root, peeled and finely diced
» ½ white onion, finely diced
» 1 cup (250 mL) jade pearl rice
» Remaining vegetable stock, hot (see facing page)
» 1 Tbsp (15 mL) brown sugar
» 1 tsp (5 mL) light soy sauce
» 1 tsp (5 mL) sesame oil
» Salt and freshly ground black pepper to taste

HALIBUT CHEEKS

Season the halibut cheeks with salt and pepper. Heat a frying pan over high heat. Add in the remaining 1 Tbsp (15 mL) of vegetable oil. Place the halibut cheeks in the pan and sear quickly, about 1½ minutes per side.

» 1 lb (500 g) halibut cheeks
» Salt and freshly ground black pepper

TO SERVE

Spread one-quarter of the beet reduction on each of four plates. Divide the risotto into four servings, and mound it on top of the beet reduction. Place the halibut cheeks on top of the risotto. Arrange the tempura bamboo shoots over the halibut.

PAIRING SUGGESTION: JoieFarm A Noble Blend (Okanagan Valley, BC). *Tom Firth:* Pacific Rim Chenin Blanc (California).

RESTAURANT
Mangia E Bevi Ristorante

TYPE
sablefish

CHEF
Rob Parrott

LOCATION
West Vancouver, BC

Pistachio-Crusted Sablefish with Roasted Red Pepper Sauce

Merluzzo alla Crosta, a classic Italian dish, has been on the menu since our doors opened. Sablefish is also known as Alaskan black cod. *Serves 4*

Preheat the oven to 400°F (200°C).

ROASTED RED PEPPER SAUCE

Heat the butter in a medium saucepan and sauté the onion over medium-high heat for 2 minutes. Add the roasted peppers and sauté for another 3 minutes. Add the chicken stock and reduce by half (this should take about 8 minutes). Add the cream and honey and further reduce to a sauce consistency (another few minutes). Purée the sauce in a food processor or blender until smooth and transfer it back to the pan. Add the basil, salt, and pepper. Keep it warm while the sablefish cooks.

» 2 Tbsp (30 mL) butter
» ½ large white onion, diced
» 4 red peppers, roasted and peeled (see page 158)
» 2 cups (500 mL) chicken stock
» 2 cups (500 mL) whipping cream
» 2 Tbsp (30 mL) honey
» 2 Tbsp (30 mL) chopped basil (reserve a few leaves for garnish)
» Salt and pepper to taste

SABLEFISH

Season the sablefish with salt and pepper, the garlic, and olive oil. Roll the fillets in the ground pistachios. Bake in the oven for 10 minutes.

» Four 6 oz (175 g) sablefish fillets
» Salt and pepper to taste
» 2 tsp (10 mL) minced garlic
» 1 Tbsp (15 mL) olive oil
» 1 cup (250 mL) ground pistachios

TO SERVE

Set out four plates. Pool the sauce into the middle of each plate and place the sablefish fillets on top. Garnish with a few fresh basil leaves.

PAIRING SUGGESTION: *Tom Firth:* Pentâge Chardonnay Musque, Sandhill Chardonnay (both from the Okanagan Valley, BC), or Bollini Chardonnay Trentino "Barricato 40" (Italy).

RESTAURANT
Cioppino's Mediterranean Grill & Enoteca

TYPE
sablefish

CHEF
Pino Posteraro

LOCATION
Vancouver, BC

Roasted Sablefish with Soy Sabayon and Chinese Salad

The Asian influences in this dish come from two years working in Singapore. It is one of Cioppino's most popular fish dishes and is always on our menu. Serve it with green asparagus, green peas, and snow peas. *Serves 4*

NOTE: Make the soy sabayon ahead of time or while the fish is marinating. You will need only about one-quarter of this recipe, but the sabayon will keep refrigerated in an airtight container or a glass jar for up to two weeks.

SOY SABAYON

Place the white wine, white wine vinegar, black peppercorns, shallots, bay leaves, tarragon, ginger, thyme, and lemon and lime zests in a medium saucepan over high heat. Season the mixture to taste with salt. Cook the mixture until it has reduced by three-quarters, about 25 minutes. While the sauce is reducing, place the whipping cream in a medium saucepan over low heat. Reduce it by half, about 20 minutes.

Pour the cream reduction into the reduced sauce (gastrique). Stir the mixture to combine the cream and the gastrique. Strain the mixture through a fine-mesh sieve into a bowl and discard the solids.

Stir the soy sauce and mirin into the cream sauce, and then transfer it to a blender and add the cayenne pepper and lemon and lime juice and zest. With the motor running, slowly add the clarified butter in a thin, steady stream, until the sauce emulsifies to the consistency of a hollandaise sauce. Use it immediately. (Alternatively, cool and refrigerate the sabayon, then warm it in a bowl over a pot of simmering water before using it.)

» ½ cup (125 mL) dry white wine
» 2 tsp (10 mL) aromatic white wine
» 3½ Tbsp (52.5 mL) white wine vinegar
» 8 whole black peppercorns
» 3 shallots, sliced
» 2 bay leaves
» 1 sprig tarragon
» 5 Tbsp (75 mL) minced fresh ginger (peeled)
» 1 Tbsp (15 mL) thyme leaves
» 1 Tbsp (15 mL) lemon zest
» 1 Tbsp (15 mL) lime zest
» Pinch salt, or to taste
» ⅔ cup (160 mL) whipping cream
» 3½ Tbsp (52.5 mL) soy sauce
» 3½ Tbsp (52.5 mL) mirin (sweet rice wine)
» Pinch cayenne pepper
» Zest and juice of 1 lemon
» Zest and juice of 1 lime
» 1 cup (250 mL) clarified butter (see page 290)

GINGER SOY MARINADE

Combine the soy sauce, maple syrup, lemon and lime zests, ginger, fennel seeds, demerara sugar, molasses, and white miso paste in a large bowl. Add the sablefish fillets and marinate them, refrigerated, for 45 minutes to 1 hour.

» 2½ Tbsp (37 mL) soy sauce
» 2 Tbsp (30 mL) maple syrup
» Zest of 1 lemon
» Zest of 1 lime
» 1 Tbsp (15 mL) grated fresh ginger (peeled)
» 1 Tbsp (15 mL) fennel seeds, toasted
» 2 tsp (10 mL) demerara sugar
» 2 tsp (10 mL) molasses
» 2 tsp (10 mL) white miso paste
» Four 5 oz (150 g) sablefish fillets, skin on (about 1½ inches/ 4 cm thick)

TO ROAST THE SABLEFISH

Preheat the oven to 500°F (260°C). Remove the fish from the marinade and pat it dry with kitchen or paper towels. Season it lightly with salt and pepper. Heat the olive oil in a large ovenproof non-stick frying pan over medium heat. Place all the fish in the pan at once, skin side down, and cook it for 2 minutes. Place the pan in the preheated oven and, depending on the thickness of the fillets, roast them for 4 to 6 minutes, or until their flesh flakes when poked with a fork.

» Salt and freshly ground black pepper
» 1 Tbsp (15 mL) extra virgin olive oil

TO SERVE

Set out four plates. Place a sablefish fillet on each plate. Drizzle it with soy sabayon (about 2 to 3 Tbsp/30 to 45 mL per plate) and garnish it with the green onions and mixed herbs—the "Chinese salad."

PAIRING SUGGESTION: Poderi Aldo Conterno Bussiador Chardonnay (Langhe, Piedmont, Italy). *Tom Firth:* Beni di Batasiolo Roero Arneis (Italy).

» 4 green onions, chopped
» Handful mixed herbs (cilantro, arugula, Italian flat-leaf parsley)

RESTAURANT
Hoodoos at Sun Rivers

TYPE
sablefish, spot prawns

CHEF
Willie Petz

LOCATION
Kamloops, BC

Seared Sablefish with Spot Prawns and Jalapeño Basil Butter Sauce

We serve this dish with potato pancakes, and then layer seared baby bok choy, acorn squash, and steamed white asparagus atop the potato. *Serves 4*

JALAPEÑO BASIL BUTTER SAUCE

Heat one cube of the butter in a medium saucepan over medium-low heat. Add the onion and half of the julienned jalapeños and sauté them until they are translucent, about 3 minutes. Add the wine and reduce the liquid by half, a few more minutes. Add the whipping cream and reduce the liquid by half again.

Remove the saucepan from the heat and whisk in the remaining butter, a few cubes at a time. When you have finished whisking in the butter, the sauce should have a smooth, creamy texture. Season the sauce with salt and pepper to taste and then strain it through a fine-mesh sieve into a stainless steel bowl. Stir in the remaining julienned red jalapeños and the basil leaves and set the bowl aside in a warm area on the stove.

» ½ cup (125 mL) cold butter, cut into about 8 cubes
» ⅓ cup (80 mL) diced white onion
» 3 red (or green) jalapeños, seeded and julienned
» ⅓ cup (80 mL) Chenin Blanc (or any other dry white wine)
» ⅔ cup (160 mL) whipping cream
» Salt and pepper to taste
» 2 Tbsp (30 mL) julienned basil leaves

TO SEAR THE FISH

Crush the peppercorns in a mortar and pestle and blend well with Hungarian paprika. Coat both sides of the sablefish evenly with the spices. Heat the olive oil in a large frying pan over medium-high heat. Sear the sablefish, turning once, until it is medium-rare, 1 to 2 minutes per side. Remove the fillets from the pan. Add the spot prawns and sauté them, turning once, for 30 seconds per side.

» 3 Tbsp (45 mL) crushed black peppercorns
» 1 tsp (5 mL) Hungarian paprika
» Four 5 oz (150 g) pieces sablefish, skin on
» 2 Tbsp (30 mL) olive oil
» 4 whole BC spot prawns, shell on

TO SERVE

Set out four plates. Place one fish fillet on each plate. Ladle butter sauce around the fish and then add the spot prawn as garnish.

PAIRING SUGGESTION: *Tom Firth:* Tawse Quarry Road Vineyard Estate Bottled Chardonnay (Ont) or Mission Hill s.l.c. Chardonnay (Okanagan Valley, BC).

SOURCE
Pacific Institute of Culinary Arts

TYPE
sablefish

CHEF
David Cymet,
Student

LOCATION
Vancouver, BC

Steamed Asian Sablefish

This simple, easy-to-make dish combines silky sablefish (formerly known as black cod) with Asian flavours. If sablefish is not available, you may substitute any white fish, such as pollock or Pacific halibut. *Serves 4*

SPECIAL EQUIPMENT: Wok and steamer stand

TO COOK THE RICE

Combine the washed rice, water, butter or oil, and salt in a rice cooker—it will take 30 to 40 minutes to cook. Alternatively, bring the water to boil in a medium saucepan over medium-high heat, and then add the washed rice, butter or oil, and salt. Stir, cover, and reduce heat to simmer for 25 minutes. Remove pan from the heat and let stand 5 more minutes before uncovering.

» 1 cup (250 mL) basmati rice, washed
» 2 cups (500 mL) water
» 1 Tbsp (15 mL) butter or olive oil
» ¼ tsp (1 mL) salt

TO STEAM THE FISH

Heat the olive oil in a deep pan with a well-fitting lid on medium-high. Add the minced white onion, julienned green onions, and ginger. Stir often until the onions are browned, 3 to 5 minutes. Transfer to a round ovenproof dish that is just smaller in diameter than the steamer stand.

While the onions are cooking, place the sablefish fillets on a baking sheet and brush them evenly with the sambal oelek and soy sauce. Sprinkle with the ground pepper and kosher salt.

Bring a wok of water to boil over high heat. Place the steamer stand in the wok. Transfer the fillets from the baking sheet to the dish with the onions. Add the wine. Cover the fillets with the reserved green onions and ginger and cover immediately. Place the fish on top of the steamer stand, tightly covered.

When steam appears from the edges of the lid, reduce the heat to medium, ensuring steam vapour continues to escape from the covered pan. Steam for 10 minutes. Remove from the heat and let stand 5 minutes longer, covered.

» ⅓ cup (80 mL) olive oil
» 1 medium white onion, minced
» 1 bunch green onions, julienned (reserve a small amount)
» 1 thumb-sized piece ginger, peeled and julienned (reserve a small amount)
» 1½ lb (750 g) sablefish fillets
» 1 Tbsp (15 mL) sambal olek (Asian chili sauce)
» 1 Tbsp (15 mL) dark soy sauce (preferably Kikkoman)
» ½ tsp (2 mL) EACH freshly ground black pepper and kosher salt
» 5 Tbsp (75 mL) Chinese cooking wine, mirin, sake, or any white wine

TO SERVE

Set out four plates. Mound a bed of rice on each plate and place a fillet on top, ensuring generous amounts of onion and the resulting broth are used.

PAIRING SUGGESTION: *Tom Firth:* 13th Street Gamay Noir (Ont) or Desert Hills Gewürztraminer (Okanagan Valley, BC).

RESTAURANTS
Refuel Restaurant and Campagnolo Restaurant

TYPE
salmon

CHEF
Robert Belcham

LOCATION
Vancouver, BC

Slow-Roasted Wild Spring Salmon with New Potatoes, Spinach, and Grainy Mustard

Spring menus cry out for salmon. The perfect pairing of this glorious fish with new potatoes and tender spinach is as suitable for festive occasions as it is for every day. *Serves 4*

TO BOIL THE POTATOES

Simmer the new potatoes in a medium pot of water over medium-high heat until they are tender when poked with a knife. Drain and cool. When they are cool enough to handle, cut them into slices ¼ inch (6 mm) thick.

» 3 cups (750 mL) whole new potatoes

TO BAKE THE SALMON

Preheat the oven to 225°F (105°C). Lightly butter a baking dish that will hold the salmon fillets without crowding them. Season the salmon with salt and pepper. Place the baking dish in the oven and bake the salmon until it is done, about 20 minutes. The flesh should still be pink, easily flake apart, and be very moist.

» Butter
» Four 6 oz (175 g) wild spring salmon fillets, skin on
» Salt and pepper to taste

TO MAKE THE SAUCE

While the salmon is cooking, melt 2 Tbsp (30 mL) of the butter in a large frying pan over medium heat. When the butter has stopped foaming, add the sliced potatoes, and season them with salt and pepper. Sauté, turning the slices as needed, until they are brown on both sides, about 8 minutes. Add the shallots and continue cooking the mixture until the shallots are translucent, about 5 minutes. Add the wine and shake the pan to loosen any brown bits from the bottom. Reduce the liquid by half, about 1 minute.

Add the remaining butter and swirl the pan until the butter is melted and incorporated. If the butter sauce starts to separate, add a few drops of water to the pan and whisk it into the sauce to bring it back together. Finally, add the mustard and season the sauce to taste with salt and pepper. Add the spinach to the pan and very lightly fold it into the sauce to wilt it.

» ½ cup (125 mL) unsalted butter
» Salt and pepper
» ¼ cup (60 mL) minced shallots
» ¼ cup (60 mL) dry white wine
» 3 Tbsp (45 mL) grainy mustard
» 2 cups (500 mL) baby spinach, washed and dried

TO SERVE

Place the salmon fillets on four warm plates and top them with the potato, spinach, and grainy mustard sauce.

PAIRING SUGGESTION: Chardonnay. *Tom Firth:* Mike Weir Chardonnay or Closson Chase Vineyard Pinot Noir (both Ont).

RESTAURANT
C Restaurant

TYPE
salmon

CHEF
Robert Clark

LOCATION
Vancouver, BC

Orange-Baked Wild Pink Salmon with New Potato and Bean Salad

One of my favourite fish, pinks have yet to receive the credit they deserve. Because they are abundant, many of them wind up in cans, but fresh pink salmon is also deliciously versatile. *Serves 6*

SALMON

Place the pink salmon fillet, skin side down, on a piece of aluminum foil large enough to completely wrap the fish. With a sharp knife, cut the fillet into six equal pieces, cutting the flesh but not through the skin. Season it with the kosher salt and the orange zest. Let the fish sit, wrapped and refrigerated, for 20 minutes or up to 1 hour.

Preheat oven to 400°F (200°C). Sauté the butter and diced onion in a large pan over medium heat until the onion is translucent. Add 2 Tbsp (30 mL) of the orange juice, the white wine, and tarragon vinegar and reduce the mixture until the liquid has completely evaporated, about 5 minutes. Remove the pan from the heat and stir in the parsley. Add salt and pepper to taste. Spread this mixture over the fish fillet. Seal the aluminum foil around the fish and place the packet on a baking sheet. Place the pan in the preheated oven for 12 to 15 minutes, or until the fish is just slightly undercooked and still moist.

» 2 lb (1 kg) wild pink salmon fillet
» 2 tsp (10 mL) kosher salt
» Zest and juice of 1 orange
» 2 Tbsp (30 mL) butter
» 1 cup (250 mL) diced white onion
» ½ cup (125 mL) dry white wine
» 2 Tbsp (30 mL) tarragon vinegar
» ½ cup (125 mL) chopped parsley
» Salt and pepper to taste

TARRAGON MAYONNAISE

Place the egg yolks, orange juice, tarragon vinegar, mustard, sugar, and a pinch of salt in a medium bowl. Slowly add the oil and the hot water to the mixture, whisking in a slow, steady stream until it has all been emulsified. Add the chopped tarragon and season to taste with salt and pepper.

» 2 large egg yolks
» Juice of 1 orange
» 1 Tbsp (15 mL) tarragon vinegar
» 2 tsp (10 mL) Dijon mustard
» Pinch sugar
» Pinch salt
» 1 cup (250 mL) grapeseed oil
» 1 Tbsp (15 mL) hot water
» 2 Tbsp (30 mL) chopped tarragon

continued . . .

Toss the beans, potatoes, and pickles with the tarragon mayonnaise.

» 4 cups (1 L) green beans, blanched in salted water

» 1½ lb (750 g) cooked nugget potatoes, cut in halves

» ¼ cup (60 mL) chopped dill pickles

TO SERVE

Divide the salad evenly onto six plates and garnish it with the tomato wedges. Place the cooked pink salmon on top.

PAIRING SUGGESTION: *Tom Firth:* Georges Duboeuf Beaujolais-Villages (France) or Thornhaven Estates Gewürztraminer (Okanagan Valley, BC).

» 2 cups (500 mL) heirloom (or vine-ripened) tomatoes, cut into wedges, for garnish

The State of Salmon and the Case for Pink

Robert Clark, C Restaurant, Vancouver, BC

As with other salmon species, the state of wild pink salmon stocks should be a concern. But at the same time, our current worries about the salmon supply provide us with an opportunity to see the true value and strength of this seafood. In 2009, the supply of pink salmon outstripped demand, so now is the time to consider pink. We just need to be conscientious about preserving the habitat of this delicious fish to be able to keep fishing them.

The collapse of the Fraser River sockeye salmon supply in the summer of 2009 was a catastrophe, and the reasons for it remain mysterious. But public energy seems focused on the negative aspects of this situation rather than seizing on it as an opportunity to demonstrate the importance of salmon. Sockeye is one of five species and the Fraser is one of many rivers. Natural disasters and human error happen. We should figure out what happened in the Fraser River, learn from our mistakes there, and fix them to ensure a healthy environment for fish.

Sockeye salmon is like the canary in the coal mine—a harbinger of the decline of the salmon stock overall. Our natural knee-jerk reaction is to stop the fishing of salmon in general and ask chefs not to support or buy wild Pacific salmon. However, if we succumb to the pressure of not buying wild Pacific salmon and create an environment where there is no demand for wild salmon, I believe the species will suffer greatly without a vested economic interest in keeping it healthy.

It was encouraging to see how upset people were about the sockeye collapse, but there doesn't seem to be a similar appreciation for pinks. I'm probably the only chef on the planet who thinks we should pay more for pink salmon.

If the pink run collapses, it won't hit the headlines—few consumers would care. But I would. Not only do we need to create a demand for pinks, we need to increase its value because we will then worry about it and protect it, as we do with sockeye. And it will bring more economic value to many communities.

The disadvantage with pink salmon is its shelf life. A sockeye that is 12 to 14 days old can still be sold as "fresh" and is still edible. But a pink lasts only 3 to 4 days. It doesn't travel or store well and historically, most of it winds up canned.

There are many advantages to eating it, however. The great thing about the pink is its two-year life cycle, as opposed to the four- to five-year life cycles of sockeye and spring. A mature pink has only been eating smaller fish for a few years, so its environmental footprint is only half that of sockeye or spring.

As for the taste of pink, it is the mildest of the salmon and twice as flavourful as brook trout. Don't compare it to sockeye. Pink is a perfect introductory fish for someone who isn't crazy about fish or who finds other salmon "too fishy." I suggest the home cook seek out frozen pink fillets when they aren't in season (any months except August to September, when they are typically available fresh). In BC, pinks are sold at farmers' markets or at fishers' wharves, right off the boat. I buy my pinks from Finest at Sea, a fisher-owned retail outlet in Vancouver and Victoria.

The easiest way to cook pink is on the barbecue. Take a whole side, put it on a piece of aluminum foil, sprinkle it with salt and pepper, citrus zest, and a few shallots, cook it for 7 minutes, and voila! It's not only delicious, it also won't fall apart or mess up your grill.

As a diner, the most important thing to do when it comes to salmon sustainability is learn to appreciate the five wild species. We need to understand and respect salmon enough that we manage it well. That way we'll leave enough fish in our oceans to feed generations to come.

RESTAURANT
Chutney Villa

TYPE
salmon

CHEF
Chindi Varadarajulu

LOCATION
Vancouver, BC

Masala Salmon Wrapped in Banana Leaf

This recipe from Kerala, on the southwestern tip of India, features marinated, masala-fried fish wrapped in banana leaf. It's known as *meen pollichadu*, which literally means "fish seared or grilled." A neighbour of mine used to make this recipe when I was a child. On a recent culinary tour to South India, I was lucky enough to rediscover it. It is a popular dish that had humble beginnings—in villages and roadside coffee stalls—but has now moved up the ranks to fine dining establishments. *Serves 4*

NOTE: Oily fish are better with this dish, but if you do not want to use salmon, choose a white fish such as halibut, sablefish, or lingcod.

TO SEAR THE FISH

Dry-rub the salmon with the pepper, 1 tsp (5 mL) of the salt, and 1 tsp (5 mL) of the chili powder. Heat the canola or grapeseed oil in a large frying pan over high heat. Place the salmon fillets in the pan and sear them for 1 minute per side. Set them aside.

» 2 tsp (10 mL) freshly ground black pepper
» 3 tsp (15 mL) salt
» 1¼ tsp (6 mL) chili powder
» 2 tsp (10 mL) canola or grapeseed oil
» Four 6 oz (175 g) wild salmon fillets

MASALA

Heat the vegetable oil in a wok or medium deep-sided pan over medium heat. When the oil is hot, add the fennel, cumin, and fenugreek seeds. Stir them constantly for 2 minutes. Add the curry leaves and shallots. Cook the spice mixture until the shallots turn brown, 3 to 5 minutes. Add the chopped tomatoes, ginger, and garlic. When the tomatoes start to soften, add the coriander, fennel seed, cumin, turmeric, and the remaining ¼ tsp (1 mL) of the chili powder. Simmer the mixture until the tomatoes get very soft, about 8 minutes. Turn the heat down to low and stir in the coconut milk. Season the masala to taste with salt and cook it for a further 5 minutes, or until the sauce becomes quite thick.

» 2 Tbsp (30 mL) vegetable oil
» 1 tsp (5 mL) fennel seeds
» 1 tsp (5 mL) cumin seeds
» 1 tsp (5 mL) fenugreek seeds
» 5 dried curry leaves (or 5 dried bay leaves)
» 6 shallots, thinly sliced
» 1 cup (250 mL) chopped tomatoes
» 1 tsp (5 mL) ground ginger
» 1 tsp (5 mL) minced garlic
» 2 Tbsp (30 mL) ground coriander
» 2 tsp (10 mL) ground fennel seed
» 2 tsp (10 mL) ground cumin
» ½ tsp (2 mL) ground turmeric
» ½ cup (125 mL) coconut milk

TO GRILL THE FISH

Preheat the barbecue to 350°F to 400°F (180°C to 200°C). Spread a heaping tablespoon (>15 mL) of the masala onto each banana leaf. Place the fish on it. Add another spoon of masala and spread it over the fish. Fold the banana leaf around the fish and secure it with a toothpick.

Place the wrapped fish on the preheated grill and barbecue it for 3 to 5 minutes per side. (You can also bake the fish in an oven preheated to 350°F/180°C for 15 minutes.)

» 8 pieces banana leaf (available at Asian supermarkets, or use aluminum foil)

TO SERVE

Set out four plates. Serve the salmon in the banana leaves with a lime wedge, rice, and a dollop of yogurt.

PAIRING SUGGESTION: *Tom Firth:* Dirty Laundry Hush rosé (Okanagan Valley, BC) or Michel Torino Cuma Torrontes (Argentina).

» 2 limes, cut into wedges
» 1 cup (250 mL) plain yogurt

SOURCE
Chef at Home (series on Food Network Canada)

TYPE
salmon

CHEF
Michael Smith

LOCATION
PEI

Grilled Salmon Burgers

You can fill your grill with more than just beefy burgers! Try a batch of these salmon burgers—they're healthy, super simple to make, and fun to eat. *Serves 4*

Preheat your barbecue to its highest setting. Place all the ingredients in a food processor and pulse the mixture until everything just comes together in a coarse mixture. Do not purée it; a rough chop is all it needs. Form the mixture into four large patties (it will seem loose but as it cooks it will firm up). Carefully place the patties on the grill and sear them until they are cooked through, about 4 minutes per side.

» 1 lb (500 g) skinless wild salmon fillet, cubed
» ½ cup (125 mL) cilantro
» ¼ cup (60 mL) minced red onion
» 2 Tbsp (30 mL) grated fresh ginger (peeled)
» 2 tsp (10 mL) soy sauce

TO SERVE

Cut four warmed or toasted soft hamburger buns in half. Slide each burger onto a bun and serve them alongside the toppings.

PAIRING SUGGESTION: *Tom Firth:* Creemore Springs Premium Lager, Rosehall Run Pinot Noir Rosehall Vineyard (Ont), or Nk'Mip Qwam Qwmt Pinot Noir (Okanagan Valley, BC).

» 4 hamburger buns
» Your favourite hamburger toppings

RESTAURANT
Breakers Fresh Food Café

TYPE
salmon

CHEF
Trish Dixon

LOCATION
Tofino, BC

West Coast Burrito

Here's a Tofino must-have after a day out in the surf and sunshine! *Serves 4*

Preheat the oven to 400°F (200°C).

GARLIC AIOLI

Whisk 1 tsp (5 mL) of the minced garlic, the sour cream, lemon juice, 2 Tbsp (30 mL) of the chopped parsley, and the Dijon mustard together in a small bowl until they are well blended. Set the garlic aioli aside and refrigerate until ready to use.

» 2 tsp (10 mL) minced garlic
» ½ cup (125 mL) sour cream
» 2 Tbsp (30 mL) fresh lemon juice
» ¼ cup (60 mL) chopped parsley (2 Tbsp/30 mL) for garnish)
» 1 Tbsp (15 mL) grainy Dijon mustard

BURRITO VEGETABLES

In a medium frying pan, heat 2 Tbsp (30 mL) of the oil over medium heat. Add the celery, green pepper, corn, onion, zucchini, remaining 1 tsp (5 mL) of minced garlic, and the salt and pepper. Sauté until the vegetables are just starting to brown. Cover the pan with a lid and set aside.

» 4 Tbsp (60 mL) vegetable oil, divided
» ½ cup (125 mL) finely diced celery
» ½ cup (125 mL) finely diced green pepper
» ½ cup (125 mL) corn kernels (frozen can be used, well thawed and drained)
» ½ cup (125 mL) finely chopped white onion
» 1 small zucchini, finely diced
» Pinch salt and pepper

SALMON

Heat the remaining 2 Tbsp (30 mL) of vegetable oil in a large frying pan over medium-high heat. Lightly salt and pepper the salmon, and then sear it for 2 minutes per side.

» 1 lb (500 g) wild BC salmon fillets

TO ASSEMBLE AND BAKE THE BURRITOS

Lay out four tortillas across the countertop. In the centre of each tortilla, in the following order, distribute equal portions of rice, sautéed vegetables, salmon, feta, mozzarella, garlic aioli, and organic greens. Roll the two shorter sides of the tortilla toward the centre, then roll the side that is closest to you over and tuck the tortilla so that all sides are secure.

Place the four burritos on a greased baking sheet and bake in the preheated oven for 5 to 8 minutes. Remove them from the oven and let sit 1 minute.

» Four 12-inch (30 cm) whole wheat tortillas
» 2 cups (500 mL) cooked basmati rice, cooled
» 1 cup (250 mL) crumbled feta cheese
» ½ cup (125 mL) shredded mozzarella
» 3 cups (750 mL) organic greens, washed and dried

TO SERVE

Set out four plates. Cut each burrito in half. Lay one half on each plate and stack the corresponding half on it. Top with salsa and garnish with the remaining chopped parsley. To make a full meal of it, serve with a tossed green salad.

PAIRING SUGGESTION: Soaring Eagle Pinot Meunier (Okanagan Valley, BC). *Tom Firth:* See Ya Later Ranch Pinot Noir (Okanagan Valley, BC).

» ¾ cup (185 mL) tomato salsa of your choice

RESTAURANT
Restaurant 62

TYPE
striped bass

CHEF
Jeff Massey

LOCATION
Abbotsford, BC

Pan-Seared Striped Bass with White Asparagus and Warm Tomato-Shallot Vinaigrette

This dish is a variation on one of the most memorable meals I had while dining in Vancouver. I love the firm texture of the striped bass as well as the sweet acidity of the tomato vinaigrette. *Serves 6*

TOMATO-SHALLOT VINAIGRETTE

Warm the olive oil gently in a small, heavy-bottomed saucepan over medium-low heat. Add the shallots and cook until they soften, about 3 minutes. Add the garlic, basil, and chili and cook the mixture for 1 minute more, stirring occasionally. Add the honey, stir in the tomatoes to coat them, and cook for 2 minutes. Deglaze the pan with the sherry vinegar and white wine and simmer the vinaigrette for 5 to 6 minutes, or until the tomatoes soften and release their juices. Season to taste with sea salt and pepper. Set the vinaigrette aside.

» ¼ cup (60 mL) extra virgin olive oil
» 3 medium shallots, sliced lengthwise
» 2 cloves garlic, minced
» 2 Tbsp (30 mL) basil chiffonade (finely sliced)
» ½ small fresh red chili, seeded and minced
» 1 Tbsp (15 mL) honey
» 2 cups (500 mL) organic tomatoes, cut in half (or grape, cherry, or Roma tomatoes)
» 3 Tbsp (45 mL) sherry vinegar
» 3 Tbsp (45 mL) dry white wine
» Sea salt and freshly ground black pepper to taste

ASPARAGUS AND FISH

Bring a large pot of salted water to a boil for the asparagus. Meanwhile, heat a large, heavy-bottomed frying pan over medium-high heat and add the vegetable oil. Season the striped bass liberally with sea salt and pepper. Place the fish in the pan, flesh side down, and sear until it is an even golden brown colour, about 3 minutes.

While the fish is cooking, place the asparagus in the boiling water and blanch it for 2 minutes. Drain and place in a serving dish and toss with the butter. Season to taste with sea salt and keep warm until you are ready to serve.

Turn the fish, reduce the heat to low, and allow it to cook for another 3 to 5 minutes, or until it is firm and opaque.

» 2 Tbsp (30 mL) vegetable oil
» Six 6 oz (175 g) skinless striped bass fillets
» 1 bunch white asparagus, bottoms trimmed, stalks peeled
» 2 Tbsp (30 mL) unsalted butter
» Sea salt

TO SERVE

Divide the warm asparagus among the centres of six plates and top with a piece of fish. Distribute the warm tomato-shallot vinaigrette evenly over the fish. The dish can be finished with an optional drizzle of extra virgin olive oil and a fresh basil leaf.

PAIRING SUGGESTION: Try this dish with Pacific Breeze Pinot Blanc (BC). *Tom Firth:* St Hallet Poacher's Blend Semillon Sauvignon Blanc (South Australia).

» Extra virgin olive oil and 6 basil leaves, for garnish

SOURCE
UBC *Food Services*

TYPE
striped bass

CHEF
Andy Chan

LOCATION
Vancouver, BC

Seared Wild Striped Bass with Fennel and Lemon Risotto, Summer Zucchini and Carrot Ribbons, and Champagne Butter Emulsion

Striped bass is a good low-fat, high-protein source of vitamin B and omega-3 fatty acids, which lower blood cholesterol, have anti-inflammatory effects, and enhance brain function, among other health benefits. With all that going for you, don't feel an instant of guilt over the butter and champagne . . .
Serves 4

FENNEL AND LEMON RISOTTO

Bring the stock to a simmer in a medium saucepan, and then reduce the heat to low. Heat one-third of the olive oil (2 Tbsp/30 mL) in a medium frying pan over medium heat. Sauté the fennel and ⅓ cup (80 mL) of the shallots until they are soft and translucent, 2 to 3 minutes. Add the rice and stir it for 2 to 3 minutes, or until it is well coated and glossy.

Add the wine and bay leaf and continue stirring the rice until the wine has been absorbed, 2 to 3 minutes. Add two ladles of stock and simmer the rice, stirring it occasionally, until it has absorbed all the liquid. Continue adding stock in this manner until all of it has been used and the rice is al dente. If the rice is not quite done, you can add a little more stock or water. Season the risotto to taste with salt and pepper. Just before serving it, stir the butter and the lemon zest and juice into the risotto.

» 2 cups (500 mL) low-sodium vegetable stock
» 6 Tbsp (90 mL) olive oil
» 1 medium fennel bulb, diced
» ⅓ cup (80 mL) + 4 tsp (20 mL) minced shallots
» ⅔ cup (160 mL) arborio rice
» 5 Tbsp (75 mL) white wine
» 1 bay leaf
» Salt and freshly ground black pepper to taste
» 2 Tbsp (30 mL) cold butter, cubed
» Zest and juice of 1 lemon

CHAMPAGNE BUTTER EMULSION

While the risotto is cooking, combine the champagne and the remaining 4 tsp (20 mL) of shallots in a small saucepan. Reduce the mixture by half, or until it has the consistency of a glaze. Using a whisk, stir in the butter a few cubes at a time. Once all the butter has been added and the sauce has thickened, strain it through a fine-mesh sieve into a clean saucepan and season it with salt and pepper. Keep the sauce warm.

» 2 cups (500 mL) champagne (or sparkling wine)
» 1 cup (250 mL) cold butter, cubed

TO SEAR THE FISH

Heat 2 Tbsp (30 mL) of the olive oil in a large frying pan until it is almost smoking. Season the fish with salt and pepper and place it in the pan, skin side down. Sear the fillets, turning them once, until both sides are golden brown, about 4 minutes per side.

» Four 5 oz (150 g) striped bass fillets

ZUCCHINI AND CARROT RIBBONS

Heat the remaining 2 Tbsp (30 mL) of olive oil in a frying pan over medium to medium-high heat. Add the carrot ribbons and sauté them for 1 to 2 minutes. Add the zucchini ribbons and continue sautéing until the vegetables are soft. Season the vegetables to taste with salt and pepper.

» 2 large carrots, sliced lengthwise into thin ribbons
» 1 large green zucchini, sliced lengthwise into thin ribbons

TO SERVE

Divide the risotto between four pre-warmed plates. Place the striped bass on top and pour the sauce over the fish. Top the bass with a tangle of carrot and zucchini ribbons.

PAIRING SUGGESTION: *Tom Firth:* Hillebrand N/V Trius Brut (Ont) or JoieFarm Un-Oaked Chardonnay (Okanagan Valley, BC).

RESTAURANT *Ryan Duffy's*	**TYPE** *swordfish*
CHEF *Chris Velden*	**LOCATION** *Halifax, NS*

Grilled Swordfish with Summer Vegetables and Salsa Verde

I love swordfish because it is easy to handle and does not have a fishy taste. It's also meaty, making it a great dish for carnivores. Harpoon-caught swordfish—the sustainable option—is typically available in the summer months. Unfortunately the harpoon-swordfish fishers here on the East Coast are a dying breed. There are only about 100 boats left because the longliners are scooping 90 percent of the quota.

I paired this dish with salsa verde (you must use fresh herbs) because a local farmer here in Halifax sold me five pounds of his tomatillos, and I had to come up with something. *Serves 4*

NOTE: When working with hot peppers like habaneros or jalapeños, wear gloves or wash your hands thoroughly immediately after handling them. If harpoon-caught swordfish is not available, use sablefish, catfish, or Pacific halibut.

SALSA VERDE

Husk and wash the fresh tomatillos and cut them in half. Place them in a medium saucepan with all the other ingredients and bring the mixture to a hard boil. Turn down the heat to low and simmer the salsa for 15 minutes. (If you are using canned tomatillos simmer for about 5 minutes.) Pour the salsa into a blender or food processor and blend it until it is smooth. Set aside (the salsa should be served at room temperature).

» ½ lb (250 g) tomatillos (or 16 oz [500 mL] canned tomatillos, rinsed)
» ¼ cup (60 mL) finely chopped onion
» 1 Tbsp (15 mL) chopped cilantro
» 1½ tsp (7 mL) chopped oregano
» ½ jalapeño, chopped (half the seeds removed)
» Juice of ½ lemon
» 1 cup (250 mL) water
» Salt and pepper to taste

continued . . .

TO BAKE THE POTATOES

Preheat the oven to 375°F (190°C). Place the sweet potatoes in a large bowl and drizzle them with 2 Tbsp (30 mL) of the olive oil. Season with salt and pepper and toss them until they are evenly coated with oil. Place the potatoes on a large baking tray and bake in the oven for about 15 minutes, or until they are just tender. Turn the oven off and keep the potatoes warm.

» 4 medium-sized sweet potatoes, peeled and cut into wedges
» 6 Tbsp (90 mL) olive oil (approx)

TO GRILL THE FISH

Preheat the grill to medium-high. Lightly oil the grill if it is not non-stick. Rub the fish with 2 Tbsp (30 mL) of the olive oil, season it with salt and pepper, and grill the fillets for 3 to 4 minutes, or until just cooked through. (The cooking time depends on the thickness of the fish.)

» Four 7 oz (200 g) swordfish fillets
» Salt and freshly ground black pepper to taste

VEGETABLES

While the fish is grilling, heat the remaining 2 Tbsp (30 mL) of olive oil in a frying pan over medium heat. Add the shallot and garlic. Sauté the mixture until it is light brown. Add the peppers and sauté the mixture for 1 minute, then add the tomatoes and the green onions. Toss the ingredients together lightly. Season the vegetables to taste with the salt and pepper and remove from the heat.

» 1 shallot, minced
» 1 clove garlic, minced
» 2 red, green, or yellow peppers, seeded and cut into 1-inch (2.5 cm) strips
» 4 medium tomatoes, cut into wedges
» 1 bunch green onions, sliced

TO SERVE

Stack the potatoes and the vegetables in the middle of four plates. Place a piece of fish on each stack and spoon the salsa verde over the fish. Garnish the plate with fresh herbs.

PAIRING SUGGESTION: Grand Pré L'Acadie Blanc "Reserve" (Nova Scotia), or Robert Mondavi Woodbridge White Zinfandel (California).

» 4 sprigs each oregano and cilantro, for garnish

RESTAURANT
Blue Water Café and Raw Bar

TYPE
mackerel

CHEF
Frank Pabst

LOCATION
Vancouver, BC

Grilled Mackerel with Chunky Romesco Sauce

Every year, Blue Water hosts an Unsung Heroes Festival to introduce diners to unusual seafood varieties (see page 41), which for many people include mackerel. The romesco sauce is best made the day before you plan to serve it. *Serves 4*

NOTE: Make the breadcrumbs from a stale piece of focaccia. The breadcrumbs bind the liquids together so the sauce doesn't have water edges when you plate the dish. Espelette pepper comes from Spain's Basque region and is made from a dried mildly hot chili. If you cannot find it, replace it with a mix of sweet paprika and cayenne pepper.

ROMESCO SAUCE

Preheat the grill to high. Place the red peppers directly on the grill and cook them, turning them occasionally, until the skins are lightly charred on all sides. Remove them from the heat, place them in a covered bowl, and allow them to cool. Using a sharp knife, remove and discard the peel and seeds, then finely chop the peppers.

Fill a bowl with ice water. Bring a small pot of water to a boil on high heat. Add the tomatoes and submerge them for 10 seconds, then plunge them into the ice bath. Peel the tomatoes, cut them in half, discard the seeds, then cut them into a small dice.

Preheat the oven to 375°F (190°C). Place the almonds and hazelnuts on a baking sheet and toast the nuts for 4 minutes. Remove them from the oven, allow them to cool, then rub them with a kitchen towel to remove the loose skins. Roughly chop the nuts.

Heat the olive oil in a small frying pan over medium heat. Add the breadcrumbs and the garlic and toast the mixture until it is golden and crispy, about 2 minutes. Add the chopped nuts, red peppers, tomatoes, shallot, and vinegar. Season the sauce with paprika, salt, and espelette pepper, and then cook it for 10 more minutes, stirring it frequently. Remove it from the heat and allow it to cool slightly.

In a blender or a food processor, purée one-third of this mixture. Stir this purée back into the sauce. Add the parsley and set the sauce aside to cool.

» 4 red peppers
» 2 ripe Roma tomatoes
» 2 Tbsp (30 mL) raw almonds
» 2 Tbsp (30 mL) raw hazelnuts
» 2 Tbsp (30 mL) extra virgin olive oil
» 2 Tbsp (30 mL) focaccia breadcrumbs
» 3 cloves garlic, minced
» 1 shallot, minced
» 3 Tbsp (45 mL) aged sherry vinegar
» 1 Tbsp (15 mL) Spanish paprika
» Salt to taste
» 1 tsp (5 mL) espelette pepper
» ½ cup (125 mL) roughly chopped Italian flat-leaf parsley

continued . . .

GRILLED MACKEREL

Preheat a grill to high. Brush the mackerel with 1½ tsp (7 mL) of the olive oil, season it with salt and pepper, and grill it, skin side down, for 2 minutes. Turn the fish over and grill it for 30 seconds more. Transfer the fish to a plate and squeeze fresh lemon juice over it.

Brush the green onions with 1½ tsp (7 mL) of the olive oil and grill them until they're lightly browned. Season with salt and pepper.

Heat the remaining 2 Tbsp (30 mL) of olive oil in a frying pan over medium heat. Add the focaccia slices and pan-fry them on both sides until they are golden brown and crunchy, about 2 minutes. Drain them on a kitchen towel or paper towels to absorb the excess oil, then rub the focaccia slices with the garlic.

» Four 5 oz (150 g) mackerel fillets, skin on

» 3 Tbsp (45 mL) olive oil

» Salt and pepper

» 1 lemon, cut into wedges

» 8 green onions

» 4 thin slices focaccia bread

» 1 clove garlic

TO SERVE

Set out four plates. Place a mackerel fillet on each plate. Arrange a slice of focaccia beside the fish. Top the focaccia with 2 Tbsp (30 mL) of romesco sauce and two grilled green onions.

PAIRING SUGGESTION: Try a light and fresh Grüner Veltliner from Austria. *Tom Firth*: Gobelsburger Grüner Veltliner (Austria) or Alois Lageder Pinot Bianco (Italy).

RESTAURANT		TYPE
Wilfrid's Restaurant,		yellow perch
Fairmont Château Laurier		
CHEF	LOCATION	
Geoffrey Morden	Ottawa, ON	

Pan-Fried Yellow Perch with Bacon-Thyme Hash and Red Onion–Peach Compote

This dish is an upscale variation of the classic "shore lunch"— a meal of freshly caught fish devoured near the body of water from whence it came. Yellow perch are delicious when they are prepared simply. *Serves 2*

RED ONION–PEACH COMPOTE

Heat a medium, heavy-bottomed frying pan over medium heat. Add half (2 Tbsp/30 mL) of the canola oil and half (2 Tbsp/30 mL) of the butter to the pan. Allow the butter to melt and start to bubble. Add the sliced red onion and sauté for 5 minutes, stirring frequently. Reduce the heat to low and add the ginger and garlic. Allow the onion, garlic, and ginger mixture to cook for an additional 5 minutes.

Add the red wine vinegar, brown sugar, and pepper. Stir the mixture, increase the heat to medium, and simmer it for 5 minutes, or until it has thickened slightly. Remove the compote from the heat and allow it to cool for 2 minutes.

Add the peach dice, a pinch of salt, and the chopped chives. Set the compote aside and let it cool to room temperature before serving it.

» ¼ cup (60 mL) canola oil
» ¼ cup (60 mL) unsalted butter
» 1 cup (250 mL) thinly sliced red onion
» 1 tsp (5 mL) minced fresh ginger (peeled)
» 1 tsp (5 mL) minced garlic
» ½ cup (125 mL) red wine vinegar
» 2 Tbsp (30 mL) brown sugar
» Freshly ground black pepper to taste
» 1 medium peach, cut into ½-inch (1 cm) dice
» Pinch salt (approx)
» 1 Tbsp (15 mL) chopped chives, cut into 1-inch (2.5 cm) pieces

BACON-THYME HASH

Heat a medium heavy-bottomed frying pan over medium heat. Add the sliced bacon to the pan and sauté it for 5 minutes, or until it is golden brown but not yet crisp. Add the potatoes and 1 Tbsp (15 mL) of the remaining butter to the pan. Stir them and then season them to taste with more salt and freshly ground pepper. Sauté the bacon-potato mixture until the potatoes begin to caramelize, about 7 minutes. Stir in the thyme. Remove the pan from the heat and keep warm while you cook the fish.

» 1 slice bacon, cut into 1-inch (2.5 cm) slices
» 1 cup (250 mL) peeled and finely diced sweet potato
» 1 cup (250 mL) peeled and finely diced Yukon Gold potato
» Salt and pepper
» 1 Tbsp (15 mL) chopped fresh thyme

continued . . .

Combine the all-purpose flour, lemon zest, cumin, cayenne pepper, and paprika in a medium-sized shallow dish. Heat the remaining 2 Tbsp (30 mL) of canola oil and 1 Tbsp (15 mL) of butter in a large heavy-bottomed frying pan over medium heat. One at a time, lightly dredge the perch fillets in the flour mixture. Add them to the hot butter and oil, flesh side down, three to four fillets at a time. Do not overcrowd the pan or the fish will not crisp up nicely. Pan-fry the perch, turning it once, until it is golden brown on both sides, 3 to 4 minutes in total. Remove the fish from the pan and allow it to drain on a plate lined with paper towel.

» ½ cup (125 mL) all-purpose flour
» 1 Tbsp (15 mL) lemon zest (left to dry for 1 hour)
» 1 Tbsp (15 mL) ground cumin
» 1 tsp (5 mL) cayenne pepper
» 1 tsp (5 mL) paprika
» Eight 1 lb (500 g) perch fillets, skin on

TO SERVE

Place one-quarter of the bacon-thyme hash in the centre of each plate. Place two fillets of perch on top of each portion of hash. Top the fish with a heaping tablespoon (>15 mL) of the compote.

PAIRING SUGGESTION: A dry unoaked Chardonnay from the Niagara Peninsula (Ont). *Tom Firth:* Vineland Estates Elevation Chardonnay (Ont) or Pentâge Chardonnay Musque (Okanagan Valley, BC).

RESTAURANT
Boffins Club

TYPE
pickerel/walleye

CHEF
Rusty Penno

LOCATION
Saskatoon, sk

Pickerel with Pistachio Butter Sauce

Although there are many debates over the name of this fish—whether pickerel or walleye—it is the fish I caught with my grandpa while growing up. He called it pickerel and that's good enough for me. *Serves 4*

Mix the flour, salt, coriander, white pepper, and cardamom together in a large, shallow dish.

Heat half of the butter (¼ cup/60 mL) and all the canola oil in a large frying pan over medium heat. Once the butter has melted, dredge the fish fillets in the flour mixture and shake off any excess. Fry them, turning once, for about 5 minutes per side. Remove from the pan and keep warm, either on the back burner or in a preheated oven (250°F/120°C).

» ½ cup (125 mL) all-purpose flour
» ¼ tsp (1 mL) salt (approx)
» ¼ tsp (1 mL) ground coriander
» ¼ tsp (1 mL) ground white pepper
» Pinch ground green cardamom
» ½ cup (125 mL) cold butter
» ¼ cup (60 mL) canola oil
» Four 5 oz (150 g) skinless
   pickerel (walleye) fillets

PISTACHIO BUTTER SAUCE

Add the pistachios to the pan and sauté for 2 minutes, shaking the pan often. Deglaze the pan with the wine and stir it around with a wooden spoon to loosen all the bits on the bottom of the pan. Remove the pan from the heat, cut the remaining ¼ cup (60 mL) of butter into cubes and whisk them in, one or two cubes at a time, until all of it is incorporated. Season the sauce to taste with salt and pepper.

» ½ cup (125 mL) shelled pistachios,
   roughly chopped
» 1 cup (250 mL) Chardonnay
   or Pinot Gris
» Salt and pepper to taste

TO SERVE

Place the fillets on plates. Drizzle the sauce overtop, then sprinkle the pistachios and parsley over the fillets.

PAIRING SUGGESTION: The Chardonnay or Pinot Gris you are using to deglaze the pan will work just fine. *Tom Firth:* Burrowing Owl Pinot Gris or Road 13 Jackpot Chardonnay (both Okanagan Valley, bc).

» 2 Tbsp (30 mL) pistachios, toasted
» 1 Tbsp (15 mL) chopped parsley

RESTAURANT
Society Dining Lounge

TYPE
trout

CHEF
Brandon Thordarson

LOCATION
Vancouver, BC

Forno Baked Trout with Red Pepper–Basil Caponata and Grilled Eggplant Mascarpone

This rich, cheesy baked (*forno* is Italian for "oven") trout dish is ideal fare for a cool, damp afternoon. *Mangia bene! Serves 4*

NOTE: Leftovers of both the caponata and the eggplant mixture can be refrigerated for a few days—great on bruschetta, or use your imagination. If you cannot find mascarpone cheese, regular cream cheese will work.

RED PEPPER–BASIL CAPONATA

Heat ¼ cup (60 mL) of the olive oil in a medium frying pan over medium heat. Add the onions, fennel, and garlic and sauté them until they are tender, about 4 minutes. Add the red peppers and tomato paste and sauté the mixture for another 4 minutes. Once the fennel and peppers are tender, add the tomatoes. Lightly stir everything together for 20 seconds, and then remove the pan from the heat and let the caponata cool. Once it has cooled, add the fresh basil leaves and season the caponata to taste with salt and pepper.

» ¾ cup (185 mL) olive oil
» 2 large white onions, cut into ¼-inch (6 mm) dice
» 2 large fennel bulbs, cut into ¼-inch (6 mm) dice
» 4 cloves garlic, roughly chopped
» 2 large red peppers, cut into ¼-inch (6 mm) dice
» 2 Tbsp (30 mL) good-quality tomato paste
» 3 medium vine-ripened tomatoes, seeded and cut into ¼-inch (6 mm) dice
» 1 cup (250 mL) basil leaves (reserve a few leaves for garnish)
» Salt and freshly ground black pepper to taste

continued . . .

GRILLED EGGPLANT AND MASCARPONE CHEESE

Grill the whole eggplant on a barbecue at 400°F (200°C) or over the flame of a
gas burner, turning it periodically, until the skin is evenly charred. Set the eggplant aside until it is cool enough to handle, then peel away the charred skin.
Place the flesh of the eggplant in a food processor with ¼ cup (60 mL) of the
olive oil, the mascarpone cheese, lemon juice, shallot, and thyme. Blend them
together for 2 minutes, or until the mixture is smooth and well incorporated.
Season it to taste with salt and pepper.

» 1 medium round eggplant
» 1 cup (250 mL) mascarpone cheese
» Juice of 1 lemon
» 1 shallot, roughly chopped
» 1 Tbsp (15 mL) thyme leaves

TO STUFF, SEAR, AND BAKE THE TROUT

Preheat the oven to 375°F (190°C). Lay all four trout on the counter and open
the slits in the belly to expose the inside of the fish. Equally distribute all the
caponata stuffing between the four fish. Once all the fish are stuffed, season the
outside of them with a pinch of salt.

Heat a large frying pan over medium-high heat. Add the remaining ¼ cup
(60 mL) of olive oil and when the oil begins to smoke, gently lay the trout in
the pan. Sear the trout for 1 minute, flip them over, and place the pan in the
preheated oven. Bake the trout for 7 minutes, then remove them from the oven
and let them rest for 2 minutes before plating them.

» Four 10 to 12 oz (300 to 340 g)
whole trout, cleaned, deboned, but
with heads and tails still on

TO SERVE

Set out four plates. Smear one-quarter of the eggplant mascarpone cheese onto
each plate, lay a stuffed trout over it, and garnish the trout with the reserved
basil leaves.

PAIRING SUGGESTION: For an Italian grape variety I recommend a Pinot
Grigio, and there are excellent Pinots coming from the Interior of BC right
now. If you prefer red wine, a Pinot Noir would be equally good with this
dish. *Tom Firth:* Road 13 Jackpot Pinot Noir or Gray Monk Pinot Gris (both
Okanagan Valley, BC).

RESTAURANT
Jamie Kennedy Kitchens

TYPE
lake whitefish

CHEF
Jamie Kennedy

LOCATION
Toronto, ON

Hot Smoked Whitefish with Fennel and Onion Salad

I live in central Canada, nowhere near any oceans. For cooks living in locales similar to mine, it's important to look to the lakes for some or all of their supply of fish, wild or farmed—and lake whitefish is a great example. *Serves 6*

NOTE: If you do not have a smoker, I recommend using a charcoal barbecue with a cover to simulate a smoker.

TO SMOKE THE FISH

Season both fillets on the flesh side with salt and sugar. Salt the fish as you would if you were going to fry it in a pan, then add the same amount of sugar. Let the fillets absorb the salt and sugar for 4 hours in the refrigerator. Then heat the smoker to about 200°F (95°C). Place the fillets in the smoker. Place green apple wood chips in the smoker, and smoke the fish for about 45 minutes. Remove the fish from the smoker and refrigerate it for at least 2 hours before using. Meanwhile, prepare the salad.

» One 3 lb (1.5 kg) lake whitefish, filleted with skin left on, and cut in half
» Salt and sugar to taste
» Green (not dry) apple wood chips

FENNEL AND ONION SALAD

Mix all the sliced onions with the fennel in a bowl. Add the salt, black pepper, and vinegar.

» 1 medium red onion, finely sliced
» 1 medium Spanish onion, finely sliced
» 2 green onions, finely sliced on the bias
» 1 fennel bulb, finely sliced
» Salt and freshly ground black pepper
» ¼ cup (60 mL) white wine vinegar

TO SERVE

Place an equal amount of the salad on six room-temperature plates. Slice the fish into six fillets of equal size and place flesh side down on the salad on each plate. Peel back the skin on each of the fillets. Serve with buttered bread.

PAIRING SUGGESTION: *Tom Firth:* Quails' Gate Stewart Family Reserve Chardonnay or See Ya Later Ranch Riesling (both Okanagan Valley, BC).

RESTAURANT
*Trios Bistro, Toronto Marriot
Downtown Eaton Centre Hotel*

TYPE
walleye

CHEF
Morgan Wilson

LOCATION
Toronto, ON

Pan-Seared Walleye with Tomato, Lemon, and Olive

Walleye is a fish indigenous to the Great Lakes, and this dish is a great summer meal with super flavours. The dressing can be used for pretty much any other fish. *Serves 6*

NOTE: This dressing takes a bit of time but can be made well in advance and actually gets better after it has blended for a day or two. I like to make the oven-dried tomatoes in batches when the tomatoes are in season and at their sweetest. Once they are dried I cool them and store them in the refrigerator covered with olive oil, then take them out as I need them.

TO COOK THE LEMONS

Combine the sugar and water in a medium pot over medium-high heat. Bring the sugar water to a simmer and add the whole lemons. Simmer them for 15 minutes, or until they are somewhat soft, then drain off the water and let cool. Cut the lemons open, remove any seeds, and roughly dice them, rind and all. (Save any juices that come from the lemons for the dressing.)

» 1 cup (125 mL) sugar

» 4 cups (1 L) water

» 4 whole lemons, with a few slits cut through the skin

TO DRY THE TOMATOES

Preheat the oven to 175°F (79°C). Place the tomatoes, cut side up, on a baking sheet lined with parchment paper and sprinkle them with salt and pepper. Bake the tomatoes in the preheated oven, with the door slightly open, for 4 hours, or until they look about three-quarters of their original size. Remove them from the oven and let cool.

» 3 pints (6 cups/1.5 L) heirloom cherry tomatoes (various colours), halved

» Sea salt and freshly ground black pepper to taste

continued . . .

TO FINISH THE DRESSING

Combine the oven-dried tomatoes, diced lemons and their juices, olives, capers, anchovies, and shallot in a bowl with ½ cup (125 mL) of the extra virgin olive oil. Season the dressing to taste with sea salt and freshly ground black pepper. (Because the olives and capers are naturally salty, you may not need much salt.)

» ½ cup (125 mL) kalamata olives, pitted and roughly chopped
» ¼ cup (60 mL) capers
» 1 Tbsp (15 mL) minced anchovies
» 1 shallot, thinly sliced
» 1 cup (250 mL) extra virgin olive oil (approx)

TO BOIL THE POTATOES

In a large pot, cook the potatoes over medium heat until just tender, 10 to 12 minutes. Drain, return to the pot, and toss with the butter.

» 1 lb (500 g) new potatoes
» 1 Tbsp (15 mL) butter

TO SEAR THE FISH

Rub the walleye fillets generously with extra virgin olive oil and season them with salt and freshly ground pepper. Heat a large, heavy-bottomed frying pan to medium-high heat. Pour in 6 Tbsp (90 mL) of the extra virgin olive oil and heat it until it is smoking. Without crowding them, gently place the seasoned walleye fillets in the pan, skin side down. Sear them, turning once, until the flesh is firm and they are golden brown on both sides, 3 or 4 minutes per side. Remove the pan from the heat and pour half of the lemon juice over the fillets.

» 12 small walleye fillets, skin on
» Juice of 1 lemon

TO SERVE

Set out six plates. Toss the arugula and the remaining lemon juice and olive oil in a medium bowl. Heap the salad in the centre of each plate. Place a few of the potatoes around the plate or within the salad. Place two of the fillets on top of the salad and spoon some of the dressing over top. Garnish with parsley.

PAIRING SUGGESTION: *Tom Firth:* Villa Maria Private Bin Sauvignon Blanc (New Zealand) or Nk'Mip Cellars Riesling (Okanagan Valley, BC).

» 6 cups (1.5 L) baby arugula, stems picked off, washed, and dried
» ¼ cup (60 mL) roughly chopped Italian flat-leaf parsley

Harpoon-Caught Swordfish

Nicolas Budreski, Owner, Canesp Global Distributions, Halifax, NS

Many people don't want to know how fish gets from the ocean to their plates. But the effort fishers put into catching fish sustainably deserves acknowledgement and respect. Swordfish is a case in point.

My company, Canesp, provides high-end and fresh "niche" seafood to sushi restaurants and fine-dining establishments, including Ryan Duffy's, in downtown Halifax. Our clients are looking for the freshest possible products. Sustainable Ocean Wise fish fall into that category due to the method of and care taken in their harvesting.

Among our products is harpoon-caught swordfish, which we supply to gourmet grocery stores in eastern Canada and as far west as Winnipeg. East coast harpoon fishers travel into deep waters—there's a sweet spot called the "Hell Hole" where warm water streaming up from the Gulf of Mexico carries with it the bait fish, which are what the swordfish and other species feed on. They tend to pool in this hole and the fishers know this is a very prolific area. They usually find the mature swordfish sunning themselves at the surface of the water after a long night of dining on the little fish.

Unfortunately, the harpoon-caught swordfish season is very brief—typically two weeks in the summertime. If there were more demand for this product, the fishers would go back to the Hell Hole for more, but demand for this product seems to be in its infancy. However, there is enough supply. With the growing sustainability movement, this product is becoming more popular for two reasons: its freshness on delivery and the way it is caught.

The boats steam up right beside the swordfish and the fishers are able to catch the fish with relative ease. At the bow of the boat, the fishers hold a bronze harpoon tip at the end of a long pole, with a buoy line attached through the tip. They push the tip into the swordfish and take it out, leaving a buoy line deeply embedded within the fish. Once the swordfish has put up a fight against the buoys and been tired out, the fisher's work is done. Believe it or not, harpooning is one of the most efficient methods of catching fish.

When the swordfish arrives at the wharf, it goes to a sorting or distribution centre. From there, depending upon the size of fish the chef has ordered, it gets sorted and boxed. Chris Velden at Ryan Duffy's can get his fish within hours. Winnipeg chefs will get theirs shipped overnight—that's still very fresh.

The challenge, as for most sustainable fish products, is for the fishers to be properly compensated for the extra effort they take to fish in an ethical manner. In my opinion, we should pay more for swordfish. There's a positive ripple effect that starts at the consumer level: if we're willing to spend a few more bucks for an Ocean Wise entrée, that will eventually translate into more incentive for fishers to fish in a sustainable manner.

Champion Barbecue Tips

Rockin' Ronnie Shewchuk, bestselling cookbook author, Vancouver, BC

"I love using my grill in the summer, but how do I cook fish on it?" Competitive barbecue champion Rockin' Ronnie Shewchuk hears that question time and time again, and here's his short-form answer. Shewchuk's latest book, *Barbecue Secrets Deluxe!*, features in-depth techniques for grilling, planking, and smoking all kinds of foods, including fish.

GRILLING FISH

First get to know your grill—every grill has hot spots and cooler areas. Know where they are and use them to your advantage.

Start by preheating your gas or charcoal grill to medium. Then oil the cooking grate to minimize sticking. I often also drizzle a little oil on the fish itself. The best grilling fish are the firm-fleshed ones, like salmon, swordfish, and halibut. If you're going to grill delicate fish such as cod, it's better to butter or oil some foil and wrap the fish in the foil pack, so it steams rather than sticks.

When you're grilling fish, keep its skin on and cook it with the skin side down. If you cover the grill, you don't even need to turn the fish—it will grill and bake at the same time. When it's done, you can use a spatula to lift the fish right off its skin, which will stick to the grill. For a bonus snack, grill the skin for a few minutes, then pry it off with the spatula and sprinkle it with salt. It's crispy-chewy-good—the bacon of the sea.

If the fish is skinless, you do need to flip it, but don't turn it too early. On a hot cooking grate it will initially stick, then release. Turn your fish when it has actually popped off the grill (the fish will carbonize and shrink—wait at least a few minutes).

Barbecue most fish with the grill cover on. It cooks faster and gets more flavour by capturing more smoke and sizzle.

PLANKING FISH

Cooking fish on a cedar or hardwood plank is a great way to add flavour and create a gentle cooking environment. It's easy: just soak the plank for at least a couple of hours or preferably overnight in clean, fresh water. When you're ready to cook, preheat your covered grill on high.

When the grill is hot, put the plank on the cooking grate and close the cover. When you hear the plank starting to crackle and see wisps of blue smoke coming out of the grill, it's time to put your fish on the plank. As soon as you do this, close the cover and reduce the heat to medium. Your fish will cook perfectly and will take on the smoky flavour of the smouldering plank. Be sure to keep a spray bottle of water close to the grill in case the edges of your plank catch fire. It's easy to put the flame out by giving it a spritz!

SMOKING FISH

Most outdoor cooking these days happens on a covered gas or charcoal grill, but many backyard cooks are getting into smoking fish in the home version of a barbecue pit called a water smoker. The idea is to cook at a much lower temperature than grilling—somewhere around 200°F to 250°F (90°C to 120°C)—and for a longer period of time. This technique adds a lot of flavour and preserves the moisture in whatever you're cooking.

Even if you don't have a home smoker, you can still get a smoky flavour from your covered gas grill by filling an aluminum foil "cigar" with wood chips and placing it just beneath the cooking grate, so the chips will smoulder and inject flavour into your fish. Here are some suggested wood chip and other flavourings to use for smoking.

BEST MATERIALS FOR SMOKING FISH

» HICKORY WOOD. Sweet, strong. Some say it makes everything taste like ham. Good with salmon.

» ALDER WOOD. Classic way to smoke salmon. Fresh, pungent dry aroma and mild flavour. Good with salmon.

| Shellfish (oysters, scallops, or prawns) | 1 to 2 oz (30 to 60 g) per piece | ½ to 1 hour, as for fillets |

» BIRCH OR WILLOW. Sharply aromatic, pungent. Goes with any fish.

» APPLE, CHERRY, OR PEACH WOOD. Sweet, mild, fruity, very smooth. Great with almost anything.

» GRAPEVINE. Rich, fruity, aromatic. Goes with any fish.

» CEDAR. Distinctive sharp, astringent aroma. Excellent with fish. Requires planking technique.

» SEAWEED. Tangy, salty, smoky. Good with shellfish and all seafood. Wash and dry seaweed first.

» HERBS (BAY LEAVES, CINNAMON STICKS, WHOLE NUTMEG) AND HERB WOOD (BRANCHES OF ROSEMARY, SAGE, OR THYME). Whole other level of flavour. Goes with any fish.

Where can you find wood? Sometimes you can find it in someone's backyard, but most barbecue supply stores and general hardware or building supply outlets display bags of hardwood chunks and chips alongside grills and grilling utensils. If you want to source more obscure woods, call around to some high-end restaurants in your city; local chefs who use wood-fired ovens often know where to get the best cooking woods.

Don't oversmoke! The biggest mistake novice barbecuers make is to put too much hardwood on the coals. The end result is fish and seafood that tastes like smoke and not much more. Take it easy on the wood—barbecue is all about balance.

GUIDELINES FOR SMOKING TIMES

These guidelines are for smoking with alder, grapevine, hickory, and oak, the best flavours for smoking fish.

FISH	SIZE	COOKING TIME AND DONENESS TEST
Whole, small	1 lb (500 g)	¾ to 1½ hours, or until flesh is starting to firm up and almost flakes
Whole fillet, large	3 to 4 lb (1.5 to 1.8 kg)	2 to 3 hours, as above. If cooking salmon, use hickory or alder for best results.
Fillets or steaks	6 to 8 oz (175 to 250 g) per piece	½ to 1 hour, until just heated through and firm to the touch

PORTABLE BBQ: ON THE BEACH

I really love cooking fish on the beach. Smelling the ocean at the same time and hearing the surf crash makes the fish taste better. You can cook something as easy as fresh oysters or clams, still in their shells, simply tossed on top of an open fire. When they open, eat them as is—you don't even need utensils.

I like to bring a portable charcoal grill to the beach. I prefer hardwood charcoal but good old briquettes are fine. To add a little extra smoky flavour, I'll sprinkle a few hardwood chips on the coals just before I start grilling.

Nothing tastes better than fish you've caught yourself. One of my best memories is of catching rainbow trout on a fly rod, in one of Alberta's high mountain lakes. I just wrapped it in foil with a little butter, some onion, and a few slices of orange. Simple is best.

RESTAURANT
Darby's Pub

TYPE
catfish

CHEF
Alex Rotherham

LOCATION
Vancouver, BC

Pan-Fried Louisiana Catfish with Chips and Fresh Herb Mayonnaise

A variation on the classic fish and chips, Louisiana catfish has a rich, earthy flavour and light, flaky meat. It is a staple dish at Darby's Pub. *Serves 4*

NOTE: All the herbs and capers need to be minced very fine. You can do this in a food processor, but don't add mayonnaise to the food processor, as the high speed will cause it to separate. For the breading, it's important that all ingredients are a fine consistency in order to stick to the fish. Coating the fish with egg before breading it is an option, to make the breading stick more easily.

FRESH HERB MAYONNAISE

Mix the mayonnaise, basil, parsley, capers, and lemon juice together in a small bowl and refrigerate until ready to serve.

» ¾ cup (185 mL) mayonnaise
» ¼ cup (60 mL) finely chopped basil
» ¼ cup (60 mL) finely chopped parsley
» 2 tsp (10 mL) capers, drained and minced
» 1 Tbsp (15 mL) fresh lemon juice

BREADING FOR THE FISH

Mix the all-purpose flour, breadcrumbs, garlic powder, onion powder, black pepper, sea salt, and cayenne pepper together in a shallow dish.

» 1 cup (250 mL) all-purpose flour
» ½ cup (125 mL) fine dry breadcrumbs
» 1 Tbsp (15 mL) garlic powder
» 1 Tbsp (15 mL) onion powder
» ¼ tsp (1 mL) freshly ground black pepper
» ¼ tsp (1 mL) sea salt (approx)
» Pinch cayenne pepper

TO PREPARE THE POTATOES

Scrub the potatoes thoroughly. Cut them lengthwise into slices ¾ inch (2 cm) thick, then cut each slice lengthwise into sticks ¾ inch (2 cm) wide. Rinse the potatoes under cold running water until the water runs clear. Place the potatoes in a bowl, cover them with water, and let them soak for a few hours or overnight.

Reserve ¼ cup (60 mL) of canola oil for the fish. Heat the remaining oil in a deep fryer or a large pot with a basket to 325°F (160°C). Drain the potatoes and pat dry thoroughly with a kitchen or paper towel. Dip the frying basket in oil (this prevents the potatoes from sticking to it) and add a handful of potatoes to the basket. Lower into the hot oil and par-fry them until the potatoes are tender but not browned, 3 to 4 minutes. Lift the basket out of the oil to allow the potatoes to drain and then turn them onto paper towels. Repeat the procedure with the remaining potatoes. (At this stage the potatoes can be stored in the refrigerator for up to a day.)

To finish the fries, bring the same canola oil up to 375°F (190°C). Return the semi-cooked fries to the oil in batches until they are golden brown and crispy, 3 to 4 minutes. Drain again. Toss the fries in a mixing bowl with the rosemary, thyme, and a pinch of sea salt.

» 4 large russet potatoes
» 6 to 8 cups (1.5 to 2 L) canola oil
» ½ tsp (5 mL) chopped rosemary
» ½ tsp (5 mL) chopped thyme
» Pinch sea salt

TO FRY THE FISH

While the fries are cooking, heat the reserved ¼ cup (60 mL) of canola oil in two large frying pans (or one extra-large frying pan) over medium-high heat until it is almost smoking. Dredge the catfish in the flour mixture, pressing the breading firmly into the fish. Carefully place the fillets in the pans, making sure not to crowd them. Fry them, turning once, for 2 to 3 minutes per side. Remove the fillets from the oil and allow excess oil to drain on paper towels.

» Four 6 oz (175 g) skinless Louisiana catfish fillets, cut in half

TO SERVE

Distribute the fries among four plates. Place two pieces of catfish on top of each pile of fries. Garnish with a lemon wedge, and serve the fish and chips with the herb mayonnaise on the side.

PAIRING SUGGESTION: This dish will pair exceptionally well with a good Chardonnay or Pinot Blanc. *Tom Firth:* Perhaps a nice artisan or local beer, Poplar Grove Monster Pinot Gris (Okanagan Valley, BC), or Therapy Chardonnay (Okanagan Valley, BC).

» 1 lemon, cut into wedges, for garnish

SOURCE
Tapestry at The O'Keefe

TYPE
catfish

CHEF
Joseph Thomas

LOCATION
Vancouver, BC

Pan-Fried Catfish with Black Bean and Corn Salsa

This recipe comes from my love of both Spanish and Louisiana-style cooking. It is very simple to pull off, and the reward in flavour is awesome. It goes well with Spanish rice and a little drizzle of lemon juice. If possible, make the salsa a day ahead to maximize the flavour components. Here's to good eating. *Serves 4*

BLACK BEAN AND CORN SALSA

Make this ahead of time. Rinse and drain the corn and black beans in a colander. Transfer them to a small mixing bowl, add all the remaining ingredients, and mix well. Refrigerate for at least 1 hour.

» 1 cup (250 mL) corn kernels, canned or frozen
» ½ cup (125 mL) cooked black beans
» 1 small red onion, finely diced
» 1 medium red pepper, finely diced
» 3 cloves garlic, minced
» ½ bunch cilantro, roughly chopped
» 2 Tbsp (30 mL) olive oil
» 2 Tbsp (30 mL) fresh lemon juice

SPANISH RICE

Heat the oil in a large frying pan over medium heat. Add the onion, garlic, and pepper. Sauté for 2 minutes until softened. Add the rice and stir for about 5 minutes, or until the rice becomes a golden brown colour.

Slowly add the chicken stock and tomatoes and bring to a boil. Lower the heat, cover, and simmer for 20 to 25 minutes, stirring once or twice, until the rice is cooked. Fluff the rice with a fork. Gently fold in parsley and season to taste with salt and pepper.

» 2 Tbsp (30 mL) vegetable oil
» ¼ medium onion, finely chopped
» 3 cloves garlic, finely chopped
» 2 green peppers, seeded, ribs removed, and diced
» 1½ cups (375 mL) long grain rice
» 2 cups (500 mL) chicken stock (or vegetable stock)
» One 19 oz (540 mL) can crushed tomatoes
» ¼ cup (60 mL) finely chopped parsley
» Salt and pepper to taste

CATFISH

While the rice is cooking, mix the flour with the Cajun seasoning and half of both the salt and pepper. Lightly dust both sides of the catfish fillets with the flour mixture. Melt the butter in a large cast iron frying pan over medium heat. Season the catfish with a pinch of salt and pepper and place the fillets into the pan. Cook until they are golden brown on both sides, about 3 minutes per side.

» 1 cup (250 mL) all-purpose flour
» 1 tsp (5 mL) Cajun seasoning
» 1 tsp (5 mL) salt (approx)
» 1 tsp (5 mL) pepper (approx)
» Four 6 oz (175 g) catfish fillets
» ¼ cup (60 mL) butter
» 1 lemon, cut into wedges, for garnish

TO SERVE

Set out four plates. Place a mound of Spanish rice in the middle of each plate. Lay a catfish fillet over the rice. Spoon the black bean and corn salsa over the fish, and serve with lemon wedges.

PAIRING SUGGESTION: Black Hills Alibi (Okanagan Valley, BC), or Rodney Strong Chalk Hill Chardonnay (California).

SOURCE
Diversity Food Services Inc.
at the University of Winnipeg

TYPE
northern pike

CHEF
Ben Kramer

LOCATION
Winnipeg, MB

Hemp-Crusted Northern Pike with a Mixed Bean Cassoulet and Berry Compote

Northern pike is also known as jackfish. If you cannot get pike, substitute your favourite Ocean Wise white fish. *Serves 4*

NOTE: Hemp seed and oil are not marijuana! Marijuana and hemp both come from the same species of plant, *Cannabis sativa L.*, but from different varieties. Both the seed and oil have a nutty, earthy taste, almost like that of pine nuts, and are packed with omega-6 and omega-3 essential fatty acids.

MIXED BEAN CASSOULET

Simmer the adzuki beans and navy beans in the white wine in a medium saucepan until warm, 2 to 3 minutes. Stir in the butter, add all the rest of the beans and diced tomato, and simmer the cassoulet for 2 to 3 minutes. Season to taste with salt and pepper. Keep it warm until you are ready to serve.

» 2 cups (500 mL) cooked adzuki beans
» ½ cup (125 mL) cooked navy beans
» ½ cup (125 mL) dry white wine
» 1 Tbsp (15 mL) unsalted butter
» ¼ cup (60 mL) edamame beans, blanched until tender
» 10 green beans, blanched until tender, cut into 1-inch (2.5 cm) pieces
» 10 yellow beans, blanched until tender, cut into 1-inch (2.5 cm) pieces
» 2 Tbsp (30 mL) diced tomato
» Salt and pepper to taste

BERRY COMPOTE

Heat 1 Tbsp (15 mL) of the grapeseed oil in a heavy-bottomed saucepan over medium heat. Add the onion and sauté until soft, 3 to 4 minutes. Add the berries, cassis, bay leaf, and cinnamon stick, and reduce the mixture over medium heat until it has thickened to a jam-like consistency, 10 to 12 minutes. Remove the compote from the heat and stir in the thyme leaves.

» 2 Tbsp (30 mL) grapeseed oil
» 1 cup (250 mL) minced red onion
» 3 lb (1.5 kg) mixed fresh berries (use any of your favourite local fresh berries)
» 1 cup (250 mL) cassis
» 1 bay leaf
» One 3-inch (8 cm) cinnamon stick
» 1 Tbsp (15 mL) thyme leaves

BREADING FOR THE FISH

Melt the butter and combine it with the panko, hemp seeds, hemp oil, basil, chives, and parsley in a small bowl. Set aside until ready to use.

» ¼ cup (60 mL) unsalted butter
» ¼ cup (60 mL) panko (Japanese breadcrumbs)
» ¼ cup (60 mL) hemp seeds
» 1 Tbsp (15 mL) hemp oil
» 1 Tbsp (15 mL) finely chopped basil
» 1 Tbsp (15 mL) finely chopped chives
» 1 Tbsp (15 mL) finely chopped parsley

TO FRY THE FISH

Preheat the oven to 350°F (180°C). Season the fish with salt and pepper. Heat the remaining 1 Tbsp (15 mL) of grapeseed oil in a large frying pan over medium-high heat. Sear the fillets for 2 to 3 minutes per side. Distribute the herb crust onto the top of the fillets and press it into the fillets. Finish cooking the fish in the preheated oven for 5 to 6 minutes, or until it is cooked to your liking.

» Four 4 oz (115 g) northern pike fillets

TO SERVE

Spoon the bean cassoulet into the centre of four large bowls. Place a pike fillet on top of the cassoulet and garnish the dish with the berry compote.

PAIRING SUGGESTION: *Tom Firth:* Winery of Good Hope Chenin Blanc (South Africa) or Château des Charmes Riesling (Ont).

Pan-Roasted Northern Pike with Potato Pavé and Watercress Salad

You can cook the pavé a day ahead and warm it up before dinner. This dish is filling—if you plan to serve an appetizer beforehand or dessert afterward, you may want to keep them on the lighter side. *Serves 4*

POTATO PAVÉ

Preheat the oven to 350°F (180°C). Heat ¼ cup (60 mL) of the canola oil in a large frying pan over medium heat and sauté half the shallots until they are lightly cooked to golden brown, about 2 minutes. Add two-thirds of the thyme leaves and continue cooking the shallots for 30 seconds. Remove the pan from the heat and allow the mixture to cool at room temperature. Add the sliced potatoes to the pan, toss everything together, and season the mixture with kosher salt.

Line an 8-inch (20 cm) square ovenproof dish with parchment paper and grease it with a small amount of the canola oil. Evenly layer the potatoes in the pan. Place the dish in the oven and bake the potatoes for 45 minutes, or until a toothpick slides easily into the pavé. Remove the pavé from the oven, cover it with another piece of parchment paper, and let it rest on the counter with a heavy object—the size of the pan—resting on top of it. This will help set the pavé while it cools. When the pavé is done, it should have a golden brown colour on top and be soft throughout.

» ½ cup (125 mL) canola oil
» 2 large shallots, sliced into ⅛-inch (3 mm) rings
» 4 sprigs thyme, leaves picked off and roughly chopped
» 4 russet potatoes, peeled and cut lengthwise into ⅛-inch (3 mm) slices
» Kosher salt to taste

WATERCRESS SALAD

Heat 1 tsp (5 mL) of the remaining canola oil in a large frying pan over medium heat and sauté the bacon in it until the bacon fat turns translucent. Add the remaining shallots and cook the mixture until the bacon crisps and the shallots start to turn light brown, about 5 minutes. Remove the pan from the heat and add the watercress leaves, kosher salt, and fresh lemon juice to taste. Toss the salad until the watercress is slightly wilted.

» 2 oz (50 g) bacon, cut into ⅛-inch (3 mm) julienne
» 1½ cups (375 mL) watercress leaves
» Pinch kosher salt
» Juice of 1 lemon

NORTHERN PIKE

Preheat the oven to 500°F (260°C). Heat a pan large enough to fit all four fillets over medium-high heat. Place the pike, skin side up, on a tray and season it with the remaining thyme leaves, kosher salt, and freshly ground black pepper.

Pour the remaining canola oil into the preheated pan. Place each fillet, skin side down, in the pan and lightly press it so that the entire surface of the skin adheres to the pan. Season the flesh side with salt and pepper and cook the fish until the skin turns a light golden brown, 3 to 5 minutes.

Remove the pan from the stovetop, place it in the oven, and continue to cook the fish for 2 to 4 minutes, or until it is cooked through. Remove the fish from the pan and let it rest for 2 minutes before serving. The skin should be crispy and golden brown when done.

» Four 7 oz (200 g) northern pike fillets, skin on
» Kosher salt and freshly ground black pepper to taste

TO SERVE

Set out four plates. Divide the watercress salad among the plates. Put the pavé in the middle of the plates, and place the pike fillets atop the pavé.

PAIRING SUGGESTION: CedarCreek Pinot Gris (Okanagan Valley, BC). *Tom Firth:* Fielding Estate Pinot Gris (Ont).

RESTAURANT
C Restaurant

TYPE
*smoked
sturgeon*

CHEF
Quang Dang

LOCATION
Vancouver, BC

Smoked Sturgeon with Chive Crème Fraîche, Radish, and Wilted Cucumber

Land-based-aquaculture sturgeon is a great sustainable option; it has a rich, smoky flavour and buttery texture. Make the crème fraîche (see page 291) three days ahead of time. *Serves 4*

NOTE: Substitute smoked sablefish for the sturgeon.

TO PREPARE AND BAKE THE FISH

Preheat the oven to 350°F (180°C). Tear four 10- × 10- inch (25 × 25 cm) sheets of aluminum foil and lay them on the countertop. Divide the onion, garlic, bay leaf, thyme, parsley, and basil among the sheets of foil. Top them with a piece of fish. Rub each piece of fish with honey and season it with salt and pepper. Divide the white wine and 3 Tbsp (45 mL) of the butter equally among the packets. Wrap and seal the foil, place the packets on a baking sheet, and bake them in the preheated oven for about 20 minutes, or until the fish is opaque.

» 1 white onion, thinly sliced

» 4 cloves garlic, thinly sliced

» 1 bay leaf, broken into 4 equal pieces

» 4 sprigs thyme

» 4 sprigs parsley

» 4 sprigs basil

» Four 6 oz (175 g) smoked sturgeon fillets

» 1 Tbsp (15 mL) honey

» Salt and freshly ground black pepper to taste

» 3 Tbsp (45 mL) dry white wine

» 5 Tbsp (75 mL) butter

RADISHES AND CUCUMBER

While the fish is baking, bring the water and the remaining 2 Tbsp (30 mL) of butter to a boil in a large frying pan over medium heat. Add the radishes. Let them simmer until they are tender, about 8 minutes. As the radishes cook, the water will evaporate and the butter will become creamy. Once the butter is creamy, add the cucumber. Season the vegetables to taste with salt and pepper. Stir in the chopped parsley.

» ½ cup (125 mL) water
» 2 bunches radishes, tops removed, and sliced in ⅛-inch (3 mm) rounds
» 1 English cucumber, peeled, seeded, and cut into ½-inch (1 cm) wedges
» 3 Tbsp (45 mL) chopped parsley

TO SERVE

Open each packet of fish carefully (there will be a burst of hot steam and liquid) and slide its contents into four shallow soup bowls. Sprinkle the fish with the lemon juice and zest. Top each serving with the radish mixture, a dollop of crème fraîche, and some fresh chives.

PAIRING SUGGESTION: *Tom Firth:* Le Clos Jordanne Vineyard Chardonnay (Ont) or Sumac Ridge Pinnacle white (Okanagan Valley, BC).

» Zest and juice of 1 lemon
» 2 cups (500 mL) crème fraîche (see page 291)
» 1 cup (250 mL) chopped chives

RESTAURANT
Vij's

TYPE
tilapia

CHEFS
*Meeru Dhalwala
and Vikram Vij*

LOCATION
Vancouver, BC

Tilapia in Tomato, Onion, and Coconut Curry

We always have some version of this recipe on our menu at Vij's. The coconut masala is very versatile and accompanies many different types of seafood, including spot prawns and crab. In some versions of the curry we add more cumin and coconut milk, while at other times we add less coconut milk and more cilantro. *Serves 6*

NOTE: It's not exactly authentic, but you can mix this coconut masala with some linguini and spot prawns or Dungeness crabmeat—it's delicious. Since it already has oil in it, along with the coconut milk, you don't need to add any extra oil to the linguini if you mix it immediately after boiling.

TO PREPARE THE FISH

Rinse the tilapia fillets and set them aside in a colander to dry for a few minutes or pat dry with a kitchen towel. Cut the fillets into 12 pieces. In a large mixing bowl, gently toss the tilapia with 1 tsp (5 mL) each of salt and pepper. Set them aside in the refrigerator.

» 2½ lb (1.25 kg) tilapia fillets, trimmed with skin on
» 2 tsp (10 mL) salt
» 1 tsp (5 mL) pepper

TO MAKE THE CURRY

Heat the vegetable oil in a medium saucepan over medium-high heat for 1 minute. Add the cumin seeds and allow them to sizzle for 30 to 45 seconds, or until they turn a darker brown (but not black). Add the onions and sauté them for 5 to 8 minutes, or until they are dark brown but not burned. Stir in the tomatoes, coconut milk, remaining salt, and cayenne pepper. Simmer the mixture for 5 minutes. Add the vinegar and green onions, and stir well. (Don't add the water until you are ready to cook the tilapia.)

» ¼ cup (60 mL) vegetable oil
» 1 Tbsp (15 mL) cumin seeds
» 2 large onions, chopped
» 1½ cups (375 mL) tomatoes, chopped
» ⅓ cup (80 mL) coconut milk
» 1 tsp (5 mL) cayenne pepper
» 2 Tbsp (30 mL) red wine vinegar
» 3 bunches green onions, chopped
» 1½ cups (375 mL) water

Working in batches, place two pieces of tilapia in a large frying pan, skin side down, and add one-sixth of the tomato curry and the water. Cook the fish over medium-high heat until the curry boils, then reduce the heat to medium and cook each side of the fish for 1½ to 2 minutes, or until the flesh begins to flake.

Place two cooked fillets on each plate and spoon the curry over them. This dish is great with basmati rice on the side.

PAIRING SUGGESTION: Sancerre or Pouilly-Fumé. *Tom Firth:* Jolivet Pouilly-Fumé (France) or Santa Rita Reserva Sauvignon Blanc (Chile).

RESTAURANT
The Reef Caribbean Restaurant

TYPE
tilapia

CHEF
Kathleen Duncan

LOCATION
Vancouver, BC

Tilapia Rundown

This rich fish stew is traditionally from Jamaica and is found at many eateries in this tropical paradise. The name derives from the fish being cooked in a seasoned coconut milk until it just falls apart or literally "runs down." *Serves 6*

NOTE: If you like spicy food, you can substitute a habanero or Thai chili for the jalapeño. If you prefer milder food, use less jalapeño. Fully omitting the chili will alter the taste. Instead, choose one of the many mild chilies on the market, such as an ancho pepper.

Any kind of seafood will work with this dish. Think of it as a coconut milk–based stir-fry and have some fun with it. You can add a touch of honey or sugar if you like it sweet or a little chipotle pepper to give it a smoky finish. Lime leaves and ginger are also very flavourful additions.

Heat the vegetable oil in a large, deep frying pan (or a wok will do nicely) over medium heat for 30 seconds. Add the tomatoes, onions, garlic, jalapeño, thyme, and allspice, and sauté gently for 1 minute. Add the tilapia fillets and coconut milk. Simmer the fish over medium heat for 8 to 10 minutes, or until the fish is "run down," stirring gently 2 or 3 times. Try not to break up the fish too much. Season to taste with salt and pepper.

» 2 Tbsp (30 mL) vegetable oil
» 5 medium tomatoes, cut into wedges
» 2 medium yellow onions, sliced
» 5 cloves garlic, minced
» 1 jalapeño, finely chopped
» 2 sprigs thyme
» 1 tsp (5 mL) ground allspice
» 3 lb (1.5 kg) skinless tilapia fillets
» 4 cups (1 L) coconut milk
» 1 tsp (5 mL) salt
» 1 tsp (5 mL) black pepper

TO SERVE

Set out six plates. Serve the tilapia with white rice and grilled vegetables.

PAIRING SUGGESTION: Any unoaked Chardonnay would be ideal. A premier cru Chablis would also be complementary. *Tom Firth:* Mt. Boucherie Estate Collection Chardonnay (Okanagan Valley, BC) or William Fèvre Chablis (France).

› STRAIT OF GEORGIA EXHIBIT AT
  THE VANCOUVER AQUARIUM

RESTAURANT
The Fairmont Empress

TYPE
lobster

CHEF
Ken Nakano

LOCATION
Victoria, BC

Atlantic Lobster with Vanilla Butter Sauce

Atlantic lobster is another name for American or Maine lobster. The sweetness of lobster is really enhanced by fresh vanilla. Try this dish with saffron risotto (pictured) made with lobster stock, finished with a little bit of butter and fresh ginger instead of the usual Parmesan. *Serves 4*

NOTE: Spinach can also work in place of watercress here.

Add the juice of the lemon halves as well as the squeezed-out halves to a stockpot of salted water. Bring to a boil. Pierce each lobster between the eyes with a sharp knife. Hold the lobster belly side up and grasp the middle fanlike appendage at the end of the tail. Gently pull this out to remove the intestines. Remove the rubber bands from the claws and immerse the lobsters into the water. After 2 minutes, remove from the pot and leave until cool enough to handle.

Remove the heads and detach the claws. Remove the meat from the claws (save the heads to make lobster stock later on, if you like). With a pair of scissors, cut the underside of the shell on each tail in half lengthwise. Remove the meat and cut into ¼ inch (6 mm) thick medallions.

Melt 2 Tbsp (30 mL) of the butter in a small saucepan, and cook the shallots for a couple of minutes over low heat until translucent. Add the wine and vinegar, increase the heat to medium-high, and boil until the liquid is reduced to about 1 Tbsp (15 mL), about 5 minutes. Remove the pan from the heat and whisk in the remaining butter a few cubes at a time until it is uniformly incorporated. Scrape the seeds from the vanilla bean into the sauce, and stir to combine. Strain the sauce into a clean saucepan, and season with salt and pepper.

Heat a frying pan on medium heat, add 1 Tbsp (15 mL) of the olive oil, and gently heat the lobster medallions and claw meat for 2 to 3 minutes or until just opaque.

In a separate pan, sauté the watercress in the remaining 1 Tbsp (15 mL) of olive oil over high heat until wilted, 1 minute or so. Season lightly, remove from the pan, and gently squeeze the excess moisture onto kitchen towel.

Place a mound of watercress in the centre of each warmed plate and top with lobster tail medallions and claws. Pour 2 Tbsp (30 mL) of sauce over and around each plate.

PAIRING SUGGESTION: Nk'Mip Cellars Qwam Qwmt Chardonnay or Mission Hill Perpetua (both Okanagan Valley, BC). *Tom Firth:* Flat Rock Cellars The Rusty Shed Reserve Chardonnay (Ont).

» 1 lemon, halved
» Two 2 lb (1 kg) live Atlantic lobsters
» 2 Tbsp (30 mL) + ½ cup (125 mL) cold unsalted butter, cut into large dice
» 2 large shallots, finely chopped
» ½ cup (125 mL) dry Chardonnay
» 2 Tbsp (30 mL) white wine vinegar
» ½ vanilla bean split lengthwise
» ½ tsp (2 mL) sea salt
» Freshly ground white pepper to taste
» 2 Tbsp (30 mL) extra virgin olive oil, divided
» 1 lb (500 g) watercress leaves

SOURCE
Chef at Home (series on Food Network Canada)

TYPE
lobster

CHEF
Michael Smith

LOCATION
PEI

Mac and Cheese with Lobster

Few things are as good as a steaming bowl of homemade macaroni and cheese. I don't normally put lobster in mine—and this version is great without my favourite crustacean—but adding it is a delicious way to make the ordinary extraordinary. (You can ask your fishmonger to steam, shell, and even chop your lobster. If you want to do it yourself, see the previous recipe, Atlantic Lobster with Vanilla Butter Sauce, or the Butter-Poached Maine Lobster recipe on page 250.) *Serves 4 to 6*

NOTE: Because pasta absorbs moisture as it cooks, it's important to season the boiling water well. Combining the flour and butter into a roux first helps evenly distribute the flour throughout the sauce, preventing lumps. Aged cheddar cheese adds much more flavour than blander mild cheddar.

You may replace the lobster with a can or two of clams; if you use clams, replace some of the milk with their juice. Try replacing the cheddar with other semi-firm cheeses, like Swiss, Jack, or Emmenthal. Just about any minced fresh herb will add a wonderful aroma to the cheese sauce—I like thyme, tarragon, or dill.

TO COOK THE PASTA

Preheat the oven to 350°F (180°C). Meanwhile, cook the pasta in a large pot of boiling, salted water. Cook the pasta until it is al dente—tender, but still firm at the centre (it will finish cooking in the sauce). Drain it well but don't rinse it or you'll drain away the surface starch that the sauce likes to cling to.

» One 1 lb (500 g) package penne

TO MAKE THE SAUCE

Melt the butter in a saucepan over medium heat, add the garlic, and stir the mixture for several minutes as the garlic softens and flavours the butter. Add the flour and stir the mixture with a wooden spoon until a smooth paste forms (this is the roux). Continue cooking the roux for a few more minutes as it develops a bit of flavour. Slowly stir in the wine and continue mixing until the mixture is smooth again. Add both milks and switch to a whisk, mixing the sauce until it is smooth yet again. Continue whisking until the mixture is very thick, a few minutes longer. Stir in the cheese, mustard, paprika, cayenne, and salt.

» ½ cup (125 mL) butter
» 2 cloves garlic, chopped
» 2/3 cup (160 mL) all-purpose flour
» Big splash dry white wine
» One 12 oz (355 mL) can evaporated milk
» 4 cups (1 L) whole milk
» 1 lb (500 g) shredded aged cheddar
» 2 to 3 Tbsp (30 to 45 mL) Dijon mustard
» 1 Tbsp (15 mL) paprika
» Pinch cayenne pepper
» Salt to taste

TO ASSEMBLE AND BAKE THE MAC AND CHEESE

Stir the lobster meat into the cheese mixture along with the pasta. Pour everything into a 9- × 13-inch (23 × 33 cm) ovenproof casserole dish. Toss the bread with the olive oil, then sprinkle it evenly over the top. Bake the mac and cheese until the mixture is heated through and the pieces of bread are golden brown, about 30 minutes.

» Two or three 1 lb (500 g) lobsters, steamed, shelled, and chopped
» Half a loaf Italian bread, hand-torn into small pieces
» 1 to 2 Tbsp (15 to 30 mL) olive oil

TO SERVE

This dish goes well with garlic steamed broccoli, zucchini with tomatoes, or Caesar salad.

PAIRING SUGGESTION: *Tom Firth:* Noble Ridge Chardonnay (Okanagan Valley, BC) or Sokol Blosser Dundee Hills Pinot Noir (Oregon).

RESTAURANT
Jericho Tennis Club

TYPE
spot prawns

CHEFS
*David Beston
and Isaac Redfern*

LOCATION
Vancouver, BC

Spot Prawn Pad Thai

This dish was originally developed by our saucier, Isaac Redfern. He combined the classic Thai street food with sustainable West Coast seafood. *Serves 6*

TO COOK THE NOODLES

Boil 8 cups (2 L) of water. Place the rice noodles in a large bowl and pour the water over them, covering completely. Let the noodles soak until they are soft, about 15 minutes. Drain, rinse in cold water, and set aside.

» 1 lb (500 g) package wide rice noodles *(banh pho)*

TO MAKE THE PAD THAI SAUCE

Place the cilantro, ketchup, sambal oelek, ¼ cup (60 mL) of the peanuts, cooking wine, fish sauce, kecap manis, ginger, and garlic in a food processor or blender and combine thoroughly.

» 1 cup (250 mL) cilantro leaves, loosely packed
» 1 cup (250 mL) ketchup
» 5 Tbsp (75 mL) sambal oelek (Asian chili sauce)
» 1¼ cups (310 mL) peanuts, coarsely chopped
» ¼ cup (60 mL) Chinese cooking wine
» ¼ cup (60 mL) Vietnamese fish sauce
» 2 Tbsp (30 mL) kecap manis (Indonesian sweet soy sauce)
» 1 thumb-sized piece fresh ginger, peeled and minced
» 8 cloves garlic

continued . . .

TO COOK THE PAD THAI

Heat a large wok over medium heat. Add the vegetable oil until almost smoking and then add the prawns, tofu, and red pepper. Stir-fry until the prawns are translucent, a few minutes. Quickly add the beaten eggs and stir constantly as they scramble. Once the eggs are cooked, add the stock and 2 cups (500 mL) of the pad Thai sauce and bring to a boil.

Add the noodles and bean sprouts, and toss everything well. Cook the pad Thai until the excess liquid is absorbed, about 2 minutes. Remove the wok from the heat.

» ⅓ cup + 4 tsp (100 mL) vegetable oil
» 1 lb (500 g) shelled and deveined BC spot prawn tails
» 1 lb (500 g) fried tofu (or firm tofu), cut into 1-inch (2.5 cm) dice
» 2 large red peppers, julienned
» 6 large eggs, well beaten
» 1 cup (250 mL) chicken stock (or vegetable stock)
» 1 cup (250 mL) fresh mung bean sprouts (reserve some for garnish)

TO SERVE

Distribute the pad Thai onto six plates or into six large bowls. Garnish with the quartered limes, remaining chopped peanuts and fresh bean sprouts, and Thai basil leaves.

PAIRING SUGGESTION: La Frenz Alexandria (Okanagan Valley, BC). *Tom Firth*: Arrowleaf Snow Tropics Vidal (Okanagan Valley, BC).

» 2 limes, quartered
» ¼ cup (60 mL) Thai basil leaves, loosely packed

RESTAURANT
Cabana Bar and Grille

TYPE
crab

CHEF
Ned Bell

LOCATION
Kelowna, BC

Creamy Dungeness Crab Garganelli

This recipe keeps well for up to a week in the refrigerator; it can be reheated or baked (it also freezes nicely). At the Cabana we either serve it as an individual dish or on a larger family-style platter with caramelized red onions and roasted yellow peppers, and sprinkled with toasted fresh sourdough breadcrumbs. *Serves 4 to 6*

NOTE: Garganelli is a pasta that is diamond shaped, with grooves.

TO COOK THE PASTA

Make the pasta while the sauce is cooking. Bring a large pot of salted water to a boil over high heat. Cook the pasta in the boiling water until it is al dente, about 8 minutes. Drain the pasta.

» 1 lb (500 g) package garganelli (or your favourite type of pasta)

TO MAKE THE SAUCE

Heat the canola oil in a medium saucepan over medium heat. Add the onion and sauté it until it's tender, about 5 minutes. Add the cauliflower and sauté it with the onion until it's lightly caramelized. Add the garlic and chili flakes and sauté the mixture for a few more minutes. Add the milk and simmer the sauce over medium heat for 8 to 10 minutes, being careful not to let it boil. Add the cheeses and the mustard and stir the sauce until the cheeses melt. Remove it from the heat and purée the mixture in the pot with a hand blender until it's smooth.

» 2 Tbsp (30 mL) canola oil
» ½ white onion, diced
» 3 cups (750 mL) cauliflower, roughly chopped
» 2 to 3 cloves garlic, minced
» 1 tsp (5 mL) red chili pepper flakes
» 1 L (4 cups) whole milk
» 2 cups (500 mL) grated aged cheddar cheese
» 1 cup (250 mL) mascarpone cheese
» 1 small wheel Brie, cubed
» 2 Tbsp (30 mL) grainy Dijon mustard

TO SERVE

Toss the sauce with the cooked pasta, fresh crab, and chives.

PAIRING SUGGESTION: *Tom Firth:* Dry Creek Chenin Blanc (California) or any Louis Jadot Chablis (France).

» ½ lb (250 g) Dungeness crabmeat
» ½ cup (125 mL) finely chopped chives

RESTAURANT		TYPE
Araxi Restaurant		spot prawns, salmon
CHEF	LOCATION	
James Walt	Whistler, BC	

Spot Prawn Tortelloni with English Peas and Lemon-Thyme Sauce

Filled pastas like these tortelloni—which means "little twist" in Italian—are easy to make, especially with a little practice. In this dish, the subtle flavours of the prawns in the filling and the peas in the sauce go together well. Remember to taste some of the peas before you buy or pick them yourself to be sure they are perfect. *Serves 4 (about 24 tortelloni)*

NOTE: The "00" flour is a finely milled flour that's ideal for pasta and gnocchi and is available at most specialty grocery stores. If you cannot find it, use all-purpose flour.

SPECIAL EQUIPMENT: Pasta machine

PASTA DOUGH

Put the eggs, egg yolks, and olive oil in a large bowl and mix them together gently with a fork to break the yolks.

Place the flour and salt in a food processor and blend the mixture for 10 seconds to aerate it. With the machine running, slowly pour in the egg mixture and process the dough just until it is combined.

Turn the dough out onto a clean work surface. Bring it together with your hands and knead it for 5 to 7 minutes, or until it is smooth. Wrap the dough in plastic wrap and allow it to rest for 30 minutes before using it. Tightly wrapped in plastic wrap and refrigerated, it will keep for up to two days.

» 4 large eggs
» 5 large egg yolks
» 1 Tbsp (15 mL) olive oil
» 1 lb (500 g) Italian "00" flour
» 1 tsp (5 mL) salt

continued . . .

Chill the bowl of a food processor and a stainless steel bowl in the refrigerator for 30 minutes. Place the spot prawns and salmon in the food processor
bowl and pulse until the seafood is chopped and well combined. Add the salt,
nutmeg, lemon zest, and lemon juice, and pulse again to combine. Add the egg
and process the mixture at high speed until it is well mixed, about 2 minutes.
Transfer the mixture to the chilled stainless steel bowl and fold in the brandy,
followed by the cream and the dill. Refrigerate the prawn filling while you roll
out the pasta.

Lightly moisten a kitchen towel with cold water. Following the instructions on
your pasta machine, roll the dough into a sheet the thickness of a dime. Using a
3½- to 4-inch (9 to 10 cm) round cutter or a glass, cut the dough into 24 rounds.
Assemble the rounds in a stack and cover them with the damp cloth.

Lightly dust a baking sheet with flour and fill a small bowl with water. Fill
a large roasting pan with ice. Place the bowl of prawn filling on the ice while
you work with the dough.

Place one pasta round on a clean work surface. Spoon 2 tsp (10 mL) of the
filling onto the centre of the pasta, and then, with a pastry brush, lightly brush
the edges of the round with water. Fold the top half of the pasta over the bottom half to form a semicircle, being careful to completely enclose the filling.

To shape the tortelloni, lay one of the pasta semicircles across the middle
of your index finger with the flat edge toward you. There should be an even
amount of pasta on both sides of your finger. Dab a small amount of water on
one corner of the semicircle then fold the pasta around your finger, bringing
the two tips together. With the thumb and forefinger of your other hand, press
the tips together tightly to seal the tortelloni, then carefully slide it off your
finger. Place the tortelloni on the baking sheet, and continue filling and shaping the remaining tortelloni until you have used up all the pasta and the filling.
Reserve the pasta while you prepare the sauce. The tortelloni will keep in the
refrigerator, covered with plastic wrap, for one day.

» 1 lb (500 g) BC spot prawns, shelled
and well chilled (reserve the shells
for the sauce)
» 4 oz (120 g) skinless wild salmon
fillet, well chilled
» 1½ tsp (7 mL) kosher salt
» ¼ tsp (1 mL) freshly grated nutmeg
» Zest and juice of 1 lemon
» 1 large egg
» 1 Tbsp (15 mL) brandy
» ¾ cup + 3 Tbsp (230 mL)
whipping cream
» 1 tsp (5 mL) chopped dill
» 1 recipe fresh pasta dough
(recipe page 234)

ENGLISH PEAS AND LEMON-THYME SAUCE

Place the shallots and butter in a small saucepan over low heat and sauté them until they are softened but not coloured, about 5 minutes. Increase the heat to medium, add the vermouth, and reduce the sauce until almost all the liquid has evaporated, about 8 minutes. Add the prawn shells and cook them for 5 minutes, or until they turn red. Reduce the heat to medium-low, stir in the fish stock and one sprig of the lemon thyme, and simmer until the liquid is reduced by half, about 10 minutes. Pour in the cream, remove the saucepan from the heat and cover the pot with a lid or plastic wrap. Allow the sauce to infuse for 30 minutes.

Strain the sauce through a fine-mesh sieve into a clean saucepan and discard the solids. Bring the sauce to a simmer on medium heat and add the shucked peas. Cook the peas for 3 minutes, and then remove the pan from the heat.

» 2 shallots, minced
» 2 Tbsp (30 mL) unsalted butter
» 6 Tbsp (90 mL) dry vermouth
» Reserved prawn shells
» 1 cup (250 mL) fish stock
» 3 sprigs lemon thyme (or regular thyme)
» ½ cup (125 mL) table cream (18%)
» ¾ cup (185 mL) shucked fresh peas (reserve 4 whole pea pods for garnish)

TO COOK THE TORTELLONI

While the sauce is warming, bring a large pot of water to a boil over high heat. Add about 1 tsp (5 mL) of salt per 4 cups (1 L) of water. Add the tortelloni and cook it for 3 to 4 minutes. To check it for doneness, cut a tortelloni in half and look to see if the edges of the dough are cooked. Using a slotted spoon, transfer the cooked tortelloni to a medium bowl and toss them with the olive oil.

» 1 Tbsp (15 mL) olive oil

TO SERVE

Set out four pasta bowls. Place six tortelloni in each serving bowl and cover them with sauce. Split open the reserved whole pea pods to expose the peas and arrange a pod on each serving. Sprinkle each serving with pecorino Romano cheese and lemon thyme leaves. Serve the pasta immediately.

PAIRING SUGGESTION: There are lots of fun pairing possibilities with this dish, from Italian whites, like top-quality Soave or Falanghina, to Alsace or BC Riesling or Pinot Blanc. *Tom Firth:* Feudi di San Gregorio Falanghina (Italy) or CedarCreek Riesling (Okanagan Valley, BC).

» ¼ cup (60 mL) grated pecorino Romano cheese (Italian, from ewe's milk, strong-tasting, hard)

RESTAURANT
Bishop's

TYPE
scallops

CHEF
Andrea Carlson

LOCATION
Vancouver, BC

Qualicum Scallops with Lobster Mushroom, "La Ratte" Potatoes, and Ground Cherries

This dish is one of my current favourites from our seasonally evolving menus at Bishop's restaurant. Look for the vegetables at farmers' markets in the summertime. La Ratte potatoes are nutty fingerlings, but of course, other new potatoes will do. *Sunroot* is another name for sunchoke or Jerusalem artichoke; if you can't find it, try celery root or another root vegetable. New Zealand spinach has smaller, fuzzier leaves than regular spinach; baby spinach can replace it. Ground cherries, also known as husk tomatoes, are like cape gooseberries, covered in a papery husk, with a flavour profile that blends tomato and pineapple. Small cherry tomatoes, like Sun Golds, can fill in for them. *Serves 2*

TO MAKE THE SUNROOT PURÉE

Melt 2 Tbsp (30 mL) of the butter in a small saucepan over medium heat. Add two-thirds of the shallots and sweat them until they are translucent, about 5 minutes. Add the sunroots and sweat them for another 2 minutes. Add the cream and season the mixture to taste with salt. Cover the pot and simmer the sunroots over low heat until they are tender, about 8 minutes. Purée the mixture and pass it through a fine-mesh sieve. Put the purée back in the pot and keep it warm.

» 5 Tbsp (75 mL) unsalted butter
» 3 shallots, thinly sliced
» ¾ lb (185 mL) sunroots, scrubbed, peeled, and diced
» ¼ cup (60 mL) whipping cream
» Salt to taste

TO COOK THE POTATOES AND MUSHROOMS

Preheat the oven to 425°F (220°C). Heat 1 Tbsp (15 mL) of the olive oil in a large frying pan over medium-high heat. Sear the potato rounds, turning them once, until they are brown on both sides, about 8 minutes. Season the potatoes with salt and place them in the preheated oven to roast through, about 4 minutes.

Meanwhile, melt the remaining butter in a large frying pan over medium-high heat. Add the remaining shallots and sauté them until they are translucent, about 5 minutes. Add the lobster mushrooms and continue sautéing for a few minutes, until they are tender.

» 2 Tbsp (30 mL) olive oil
» ½ lb (250 g) fingerling potatoes, cooked in salted water, cooled, and sliced into 1-inch (2.5 cm) rounds
» ½ lb (250 g) lobster mushrooms, cleaned with a dry brush or cloth

continued . . .

TO SEAR THE SCALLOPS

While the mushrooms are sautéing, heat the remaining olive oil in a small frying pan over medium-high heat. Sear the scallops for about 2 minutes per side, turning them once.

» 6 large scallops

TO FINISH

While the scallops cook, add the roasted potatoes, spinach, ground cherries, and vegetable stock to the mushroom pan. Sauté the mixture over medium heat to wilt the spinach, about 2 more minutes.

» ½ cup (125 mL) spinach leaves (stems removed)
» 16 ground cherries, husks removed
» 2 Tbsp (30 mL) vegetable stock

TO SERVE

Create a "swoosh" of sunroot purée on each pre-warmed dinner plate. Place a mound of the sauté in the centre of each plate with three scallops around the edge of the mound. Top with salmon roe, if desired.

PAIRING SUGGESTION: *Tom Firth:* Mission Hill Five Vineyards Sauvignon Blanc (Okanagan Valley, BC) or Peter Lehmann Clancy's Semillon Sauvignon Blanc (Australia).

» Salmon roe, for garnish (optional)

Olive Oil–Poached Geoduck with Wild Mushroom Broth and Fresh Thyme

Geoduck (pronounced "GOO-ee-duk") is a species of very large saltwater clam, a marine bivalve mollusc in the family *Hiatellidae*. It has a very sweet flavour and light chewiness—and is a delicacy in many Asian cultures. *Serves 4*

NOTE: If you don't want to prepare the geoduck at home, geoduck siphon meat is available chilled or flash-frozen and then vacuum-packed.

TO CLEAN AND COOK THE GEODUCK

Bring a large pot of well-salted water to a boil. Remove it from the heat. Place the geoducks in the water. Let them sit for 5 minutes. To clean a geoduck, the shell should peel back off. If it does not, use a small paring knife to help. There is a skin wrapping the tube of the geoduck. Peel it back like a sock and the creamy-smooth flesh underneath will be exposed.

Place the olive oil in a large saucepan over medium heat. Add the lemon peel, half the garlic, and half the thyme. Bring to a simmer over medium high heat. Remove the pot from the heat. Place the cleaned geoduck tubes in the olive oil mixture. Let them sit for 30 minutes. The geoduck can be stored in the oil for up to one week. When ready to use the geoduck, slice it into thin rounds with a very sharp knife.

» 2 live geoduck (about 2.2 lb/1 kg each), shell attached
» 2 cups (500 mL) olive oil
» Zest of 1 lemon
» 4 cloves garlic, thinly sliced
» 4 sprigs thyme (more for garnish)

TO PREPARE THE MUSHROOM BROTH

Heat the vegetable oil in a large heavy-bottomed stockpot over medium heat. Add the onion, carrot, and remaining garlic. Sweat the vegetables until the onion is translucent, about 8 minutes. Add the mushrooms, the remaining thyme, and the bay leaf. Continue sweating the vegetables until the mushrooms become soft to the touch, about 5 minutes. Add the white wine and vermouth and continue cooking until the liquid has reduced by half, 5 to 8 minutes. Add the water and cracked peppercorns. Let simmer for 45 minutes to 1 hour. Strain through a fine-mesh sieve. Discard the vegetables and keep the broth for serving. Season to taste with salt.

» 2 Tbsp (30 mL) vegetable oil
» 1 white onion, thinly sliced
» 1 large carrot, thinly sliced
» 1 lb (500 g) wild or cultivated mushrooms, sliced
» 1 bay leaf
» ½ cup (125 mL) dry white wine
» ½ cup (125 mL) dry vermouth
» 10 cups (2.5 L) water
» 1 tsp (5 mL) black peppercorns, cracked
» Salt to taste

continued . . .

Set out four soup bowls. Divide the slices of geoduck between them. Top the geoduck with a sprinkle of the green onions and more freshly picked thyme leaves. Ladle the hot broth over the geoduck and serve.

PAIRING SUGGESTION: Poplar Grove Pinot Gris (Okanagan Valley, BC). *Tom Firth:* Desert Hills Gewürztraminer (Okanagan Valley, BC).

» 1 bunch green onions, thinly sliced
» Several sprigs thyme

ONE-POT
WONDERS

RESTAURANT
The Fish House in Stanley Park

TYPE
halibut

CHEF
Karen Barnaby

LOCATION
Vancouver, BC

White Halibut Chili

A fish chili may sound a little odd, but it's really tasty. If you want to make it in advance, add the halibut only when you reheat the chili. *Serves 6 to 8*

TO PREPARE THE BEANS

Place the beans in a large, heavy pot. Add enough cold water to cover the beans by at least 3 inches (8 cm), and soak them overnight. Drain the beans. Rinse them, and then return them to the pot. Cover them with water by 4 inches (10 cm) and bring them to a boil over high heat. Turn the heat down to low, reducing the boil to a simmer, and cook them for 45 minutes to 1 hour, or until the beans are almost tender. They should be firm when bitten. Drain the beans and set them aside.

» 1 lb (500 g) dried navy beans, rinsed and drained

In the same pot used to cook the beans, heat the oil over medium heat. Add the onion, garlic, jalapeño, cumin, and oregano, and sauté the mixture until the onion and the garlic are translucent, about 10 minutes. Add the beans and the chicken stock. Reduce the heat to low and simmer the beans for 1 to 1½ hours, or until they are tender, adding more stock or water if the mixture looks too dry. The texture should be that of beans in a beef chili. If the mixture has too much liquid and does not thicken, remove 1 cup (250 mL) of beans from the pot, mash them thoroughly, and return them to the pot.

Add the halibut and cook the chili over medium heat until the halibut can be flaked apart with a fork, about 10 minutes. When the fish is done, stir in the cheese until it melts. Season the chili to taste with salt and pepper.

» 2 Tbsp (30 mL) extra virgin olive oil
» 1 cup (250 mL) diced onion
» 4 cloves garlic, minced
» 1 medium jalapeño, minced
» 2 tsp (10 mL) cumin seeds
» 1½ tsp (7 mL) dried oregano
» 5 cups (1.25 L) chicken stock (approx)
» 1 lb (500 g) halibut (skinless, boneless), cut into bite-sized pieces
» 2 cups (500 mL) shredded aged cheddar
» Sea salt and freshly ground black pepper to taste

Sprinkle each serving with cilantro and serve it with the sour cream and salsa on the side.

PAIRING SUGGESTION: *Tom Firth:* Mission Hill Reserve Sauvignon Blanc (Okanagan Valley, BC) or Flat Rock Cellars Reserve Pinot Noir (Ont).

» 2 Tbsp (30 mL) coarsely chopped cilantro
» ½ cup (125 mL) sour cream
» 1 cup (250 mL) salsa

RESTAURANT
The Marina Restaurant

TYPE
mussels, smoked sablefish

CHEF
Matthew Rissling

LOCATION
Victoria, BC

Smoked Sablefish and Thyme Braised Salt Spring Island Mussels

This is an ideal dish on a cool day, but it's great any time of the year. Serve it with grilled baguette or crostini. A little more bread and a side salad make this a suitable main course for two. Sablefish adds the smokiness that many find appealing in bacon but is naturally much healthier to eat. *Serves 2 as a main course or 4 as an appetizer*

Wash the mussels well, taking care to remove their beards. Combine all the remaining ingredients—except the wine, salt, and pepper—in a food processor (or mix them by hand), and process the mixture until it is fairly smooth and all the ingredients are well incorporated. The mixture should not be completely puréed; it should have the consistency of chunky peanut butter. Place the butter mixture, wine, and mussels in a large frying pan or Dutch oven. Cover the pot and cook the mussels over medium-high heat until they open, about 7 minutes. Discard any mussels that are not open and season the broth to taste with salt and pepper.

» 2 lb (500 g) Salt Spring Island mussels (or any other plump, farmed variety)
» ⅓ lb (170 g) butter, salted or unsalted, room temperature
» ¼ lb (125 g) smoked sablefish (skinless, boneless)
» 2 cloves garlic, peeled
» 2 tsp (10 mL) honey
» 2 tsp (10 mL) fresh lemon juice
» 1 tsp (5 mL) chopped parsley
» 1 tsp (5 mL) chopped thyme
» 1 cup (250 mL) dry white wine
» Salt and pepper to taste

TO SERVE

For a hearty appetizer, divide the mussels and broth evenly into four large soup bowls, with grilled bread or crostini on top, and serve the dish at once.

PAIRING SUGGESTION: Mission Hill S.L.C. Sauvignon Blanc–Semillon (Okanagan Valley, BC). *Tom Firth:* Stag's Hollow Sauvignon Blanc–Semillon (Okanagan Valley, BC).

RESTAURANT
Shaughnessy Restaurant

CHEF
*David William
Grimshaw*

LOCATION
Vancouver, BC

TYPE
clams

Steamed Local Clams with VanDusen Herb and Chardonnay Beurre Blanc

Using fresh herbs is essential to the success of this recipe. We are particularly fortunate at Shaughnessy Restaurant to have a bounty of herbs just outside our windows in VanDusen Botanical Garden. This recipe can be served either as an appetizer or a main course and is best enjoyed with crusty bread to soak up the delicious broth. *Serves 2 as a main course or 4 as an appetizer*

NOTE: This recipe can be easily adapted to feature local mussels.

Sort through the clams and discard any that are not closed. Heat a deep-sided frying pan over high heat until it is very hot. Add the olive oil, shallots, and garlic. Stir the mixture constantly for 1 minute. Add the clams and wine, reduce the heat, cover, and simmer until the clams open, 5 to 8 minutes.

Remove the clams with a slotted spoon, transfer them to a bowl, and cover the bowl to keep them warm. With the pan over high heat, add the herbs and boil the broth until it has reduced by three-quarters. Lower the heat to medium so that the boiling reduces to a simmer and slowly add the butter cubes, one at a time, while constantly whisking the broth. Be careful not to allow the broth to boil; it should look creamy when all the butter has been incorporated. Add salt and ground pepper to taste.

» 2 lb (1 kg) local clams
» 2 Tbsp (30 mL) extra virgin olive oil
» 4 large shallots, minced
» 6 cloves garlic, minced
» 2 cups (500 mL) Chardonnay
» 1 Tbsp (15 mL) finely chopped thyme
» 1 Tbsp (15 mL) finely chopped chives
» 1 Tbsp (15 mL) finely chopped basil
» 1 Tbsp (15 mL) finely chopped dill
» ½ cup (125 mL) unsalted butter, chilled and cubed
» Salt and freshly ground black pepper to taste

TO SERVE

Return the clams to the broth, add the lemon juice, and bring to a simmer. Place the clams and broth in a big serving bowl or in individual bowls and serve with fresh crusty bread.

PAIRING SUGGESTION: Blasted Church Pinot Gris (Okanagan Valley, BC). *Tom Firth:* Sandhill Estate Vineyard Chardonnay (Okanagan Valley, BC).

» 2 Tbsp (30 mL) fresh lemon juice

RESTAURANT
Mosaic Restaurant,
Hyatt Regency Vancouver

TYPE
lobster, clams

CHEF
Daniel Chiang

LOCATION
Vancouver, BC

Butter-Poached Maine Lobster with Paella-Style Biodynamic Risotto

This dish has been on the Mosaic Restaurant menu with different seafood according to the season (Qualicum Bay scallops, sablefish, and wild salmon). *Serves 4*

NOTE: Biodynamic risotto rice is aged for between one and three years in chilled vats, during which time the proteins in the grains of rice mature, giving the rice its unique capacity to absorb more stock than regular risotto rice. The combination of organic farming and the aging of the rice grains gives it a more intense flavour than other risotto rice and enables it to retain a firm texture throughout the cooking process.

TO COOK THE LOBSTERS AND PREPARE THEIR MEAT

Place the lobsters in a tight-fitting heatproof container and cover them with cold water. Drain off the water, measure out 2 gallons (8 L), and pour it into a large stockpot. Place the pot over high heat, bring the water to a boil, and add the vinegar. Pour the boiling water over the lobsters and let them steep— 2 minutes for 1½ lb (750 g) lobsters and 3 minutes for 2 lb (1 kg) lobsters.

Remove the lobsters from the pot. One at a time, using a towel, grasp the tail and twist and pull to detach it. Twist and pull off the claws and return them to the hot water for 5 minutes. Reserve the bodies.

Hold each tail flat, twist the fan to one side, pull it off, and discard it. Use your fingers to gently push the meat through the tail end and pull the meat out through the large opening at the other end. Discard the shell. Lay the tail meat on its back and cut it lengthwise down the middle. Remove the vein running through the top of the meat. Lay the meat on a plate lined with paper towel, cover with plastic wrap, and refrigerate it until ready to poach.

After 5 minutes, remove the claws from the hot water. Twist off each knuckle to remove it. Hold the claw in your hand and pull down on the lower pincer to loosen it. Push it to either side to crack it and pull it straight off. Ideally, the cartilage from inside the claw should be attached to the pincer and the claw meat should remain intact. Still holding the claw, crack the top of the shell with the heel of the knife, about ¾ inch (2 cm) from the joint where the knuckle was attached. You want to go through the shell but not damage the meat. Wiggle

» Four 1½- to 2 lb (750 g to 1 kg) live lobsters
» ½ cup (125 mL) white wine vinegar
» 2 cups (500 mL) unsalted butter

your knife to loosen and crack the shell. If the shell does not pop off, it may be necessary to turn the claw over and repeat the procedure. Shake the claw to remove the meat.

Taking the reserved lobster bodies, pull back and discard the top shell of each lobster body, including the head and antennae, and discard it. You will be left with body and leg meat. Rinse this thoroughly under cold water and use it immediately.

Cut the butter into cubes. Bring the water to a boil in a medium saucepan. Reduce the heat to low and whisk in the butter a few cubes at a time so that it emulsifies. (This mixture is called a "beurre monté"—which should stay emulsified when heated.)

Bring the lobster meat to room temperature. Place it in one layer in a large saucepan and cover with the beurre monté. Place the pan over low heat and slowly poach the lobster in the butter for 5 to 6 minutes, or until it is just heated through.

TO COOK THE CLAMS

Soak the clams for 15 minutes in a brine solution of ⅓ cup (80 mL) salt to 1 gallon (4 L) cold water. Repeat with fresh brine for another 15 minutes. Bring 1 cup (250 mL) water to a boil in a large stockpot. Add the clams and cook them until they open, about 5 minutes. Remove the clams from the pot using a slotted spoon, discard any that did not open, and save the liquid for the risotto. Remove the clams from the shells and set them aside. Discard the shells.

» 1 lb (500 g) clams

continued . . .

TO MAKE THE RISOTTO

Add 1 Tbsp (15 mL) of the butter to a hot saucepan. Stir it until it melts, add the rice and bay leaf, and stir them over medium heat for 3 minutes. Add the onion to the mixture and cook until translucent. Add two ladles of the reserved clam liquid and stir the rice until the liquid has evaporated. Repeat this process until the rice is al dente. (Reserve ⅓ cup/80 mL + 4 tsp/20 mL of the clam liquid.) Set the risotto aside.

Sauté the sausage in a large saucepan over medium heat until it has browned, and then stir in the garlic, saffron, and risotto. Add the reserved clam liquid, tomatoes, peas, green onions, and clams, and stir the risotto until it becomes creamy. If it gets dry, add a little water. Finish the risotto by slowly stirring in the remaining 1 Tbsp (15 mL) of butter and the cheese and seasoning with salt and pepper to taste.

» 2 Tbsp (30 mL) butter
» 1 cup (250 mL) biodynamic or any other good-quality arborio rice
» 1 bay leaf
» 1 white onion, finely diced
» 3½ oz (100 g) Andouille sausage, finely diced
» 1 clove garlic, minced
» Pinch saffron
» 2 Roma tomatoes, chopped and seeded
» ⅓ cup (80 mL) fresh English peas (or frozen peas)
» 2 green onions, thinly sliced
» 5 Tbsp (75 mL) shaved Parmigiano Reggiano (Parmesan from Parma)
» Salt and white pepper to taste

TO SERVE

Set out four plates or bowls. Place a generous spoonful of the risotto in the centre of each, and top it with a lobster tail and two claws. Garnish with a sprinkle of saffron and parsley.

PAIRING SUGGESTION: *Tom Firth:* Sumac Ridge Black Sage Vineyard Chardonnay or Road 13 Viognier Roussanne Marsanne (both Okanagan Valley, BC).

» Saffron and chopped parsley, for garnish (optional)

Mussels Congolaise

A big bowl of these steaming mussels cooked with a tomato coconut cream, with a side of french fries—*moules frites*—is one of the most popular dishes at Chambar. If you can, get Salt Spring Island mussels; they are plump and juicy. *Serves 4*

NOTE: To make chipotle purée, blend canned chipotles in adobo until smooth. They are available at most grocery stores and Latin supermarkets.

Grind the cumin seeds, coriander, and fennel in a mortar and pestle or coffee grinder. Heat the olive oil in a heavy stockpot over medium heat and sauté the red onion until soft, about 2 minutes. Add the spices, including the black pepper, and stir to blend. Remove from the heat and allow the mixture to blend for a few hours.

Return the pot to medium heat. Add the garlic and cook for 2 minutes, until softened. Add the coconut milk and bring to a boil over high heat. Reduce the heat to medium, add the tomatoes, chipotles, and lemon juice and simmer until the sauce has thickened slightly. Bring it back to a boil and add the mussels. Cover and cook until the mussels have completely opened, about 5 minutes.

» 2 tsp (10 mL) cumin seeds
» 2 tsp (10 mL) coriander seeds
» ¾ tsp (4 mL) fennel seeds
» 1 Tbsp (15 mL) olive oil
» ¼ cup (60 mL) thinly sliced red onion
» 1 tsp (5 mL) freshly ground black pepper
» 1½ tsp (7 mL) minced garlic
» 2 cups (500 mL) coconut milk
» 1 cup (250 mL) chopped and seeded tomatoes
» 1 Tbsp (15 mL) chipotle purée (see note)
» ¼ cup (60 mL) fresh lemon juice
» 2 lb (1 kg) mussels, scrubbed and de-bearded

TO SERVE

Divide the mussels into four bowls, discarding any that are not fully open.

Season the sauce with salt, pepper, and sugar. Pour the broth over the mussels and sprinkle with cilantro just before serving.

PAIRING SUGGESTION: A Belgian wheat ale, such as Wittekerke. *Tom Firth:* Vineland Estates Elevation Chardonnay (Ont).

» Sea salt and freshly ground black pepper to taste
» Granulated sugar to taste
» ½ cup (125 mL) coarsely chopped cilantro, for garnish

RESTAURANT
Mangia E Bevi Ristorante

CHEF
Rob Parrott

TYPE
mussels, clams, spot prawns, sablefish (or halibut)

LOCATION
West Vancouver, BC

Cioppino

Cioppino is a fish stew thought to have originated in 1930s San Francisco from Italian immigrant fishermen. The day's catch turned into a communal stew, hence the many recipes for it, depending upon what is available, and where. *Serves 4*

In the oil, sauté the onion and fennel in a large frying pan over medium heat until they are soft and translucent, about 10 minutes. Add the garlic and cook the mixture for 1 minute, then add the Pernod and flambé it. The best way to flambé is to take the pot off the heat, light the Pernod-splashed mixture with a barbecue lighter, and return the pot to the heat when the flame burns out.

Add the crushed tomatoes and the fish stock and simmer the mixture for 10 minutes. Add the fresh herbs, salt, and chilies, then add the seafood and poach it for 5 minutes.

» ¼ cup (60 mL) olive oil
» 1 cup (250 mL) diced onion
» ½ cup (125 mL) diced fennel
» 1 Tbsp (15 mL) minced garlic
» 3 fl oz (90 mL) Pernod
» One 14 oz (398 mL) can crushed tomatoes
» 4 cups (1 L) fish stock (see page 289)
» ¼ cup (60 mL) chopped tarragon
» ¼ cup (60 mL) chopped basil
» ¼ cup (60 mL) chopped Italian flat-leaf parsley
» 2 tsp (10 mL) salt
» 1½ tsp (7 mL) crushed dried chilies
» 1 lb (500 g) mussels, scrubbed and de-bearded
» 1 lb (500 g) clams, scrubbed
» 1 lb (500 g) BC spot prawns, shell on
» 1 lb (500 g) sablefish or halibut pieces (skinless, boneless)

TO SERVE

Put a slice of garlic toast in each of four bowls and distribute the seafood and broth on top.

PAIRING SUGGESTION: Laughing Stock Blind Trust White (Okanagan Valley, BC). *Tom Firth:* JoieFarm A Noble Blend (Okanagan Valley, BC).

» 4 slices garlic toast

CANNED FISH and SEAFOOD

Let's face it, canned fish is a tough sell—a tuna sandwich or tinned sardines on toast are not perceived as thrill-a-minute fare. But with a little imagination, they can be. I grew up on tinned oily fish such as pilchards and mackerel mainly because they were economical and did not take any effort beyond opening the can and forking the contents over a piece of toast. My sisters and I certainly got our fair share of omega-3s, iron, vitamin B, and calcium—the latter from soft and edible fish bones.

Of course, we need to be aware that all canned products are not created equal. Most of the tuna on our grocery store shelves comes from Asia, where fish is typically canned well past its "best before" date. As well, mature fish can carry high levels of toxins, such as mercury. These fish are typically heavily disguised in oil or packed in tomato sauce. It's hard to read can labels to determine the source of the fish—it's usually in fine print—and you'll seldom find information on how it was caught.

Fortunately, Canadian products, such as those from BC's Raincoast Trading, are now appearing in our stores.

Raincoast is a member of Ocean Wise because it supports sustainable fishing practices and harvests only wild-caught tuna and salmon. Plus, its canned fish is single-cooked to preserve its natural oils, nutrition, and rich flavour, and Raincoast does not add water or oil to the fish during the canning process.

Next time you buy canned fish, look for wild salmon and pole- or troll-caught albacore tuna, both of which are harvested and canned on the West Coast. Most sardines and oysters are sourced and canned overseas, although some gourmet grocery stores carry local brands.

It's always good to have a few cans of fish in your cupboard, especially when you don't have the inclination or energy to cook from scratch. Most of the following recipes take only minutes to prepare and are sure to sell you on canned fish. Thanks to the students at the Pacific Institute of Culinary Arts and Barbara-jo McIntosh of the cookbook bookstore Barbara-Jo's Books to Cooks, also the author of *Tin Fish Gourmet* (Raincoast Books, 1998), who shared some of their favourite recipes.

CHEF
Barbara-jo McIntosh
Barbara-Jo's Books to Cooks

LOCATION
Vancouver, BC

TYPE
canned anchovies, tuna, sardines

Three-Tin Tapenade

Your can opener works overtime on this one! This flavour-ful Mediterranean appetizer is quick to prepare and has the added benefit of satisfying a small crowd. *Serves 6 to 8 as an appetizer*

Soak the anchovies in the milk for 10 to 15 minutes. Place all the ingredients in a food processor and blend them until they are coarsely combined, about 30 seconds.

» One 1¾ oz (50 g) can anchovies, drained
» ½ cup (125 mL) milk
» One 6 oz (170 g) can albacore tuna, drained
» One 3¾ oz (106 g) can sardines in water, drained
» 1 cup (250 mL) black olives, pitted and chopped
» ¼ cup (60 mL) coarsely chopped pimiento
» 5 Tbsp (75 mL) olive oil
» 2 Tbsp (30 mL) dry sherry
» 2 tsp (10 mL) chopped rosemary
» 1 tsp (5 mL) grainy Dijon mustard
» 1 clove garlic, coarsely chopped
» 1 small shallot, coarsely chopped

TO SERVE

Place the tapenade in a serving bowl with your favourite crackers nearby.

PAIRING SUGGESTION: Any robust red goes particularly well. *Tom Firth:* Black Hills Carmenere (Okanagan Valley, BC) or Fielding Estate Merlot (Ont).

SOURCE
Pacific Institute of Culinary Arts

TYPE
canned salmon

CHEF
Marlene J. Yong, Student

LOCATION
Vancouver, BC

911 Canned Salmon Party Platter

When it comes to food, I have often been caught "with my pants down." Yes, when I totally forgot the potluck gathering on my only day off . . . oops, no worry. Grill or toast some French baguette slices and jazz up some canned seafood for an elegant party platter in the shortest possible time.

Don't sweat over what you don't have in your pantry. No sea salt or kosher salt around? Use table salt or omit it totally. It's 911 . . . you are saving lives here—er, I mean saving a situation. By coming through with a tasty platter, you didn't douse the partying spirit. *Serves 8 as an appetizer*

Preheat the oven to broil with a rack in the upper-middle position. Cut the French loaves on the bias into slices 2 inches (5 cm) thick and brush both sides with the olive oil. Arrange them on a baking sheet and broil them for 2 to 4 minutes per side, until they are brown but still soft in the centre.

Drain the cans of salmon and, if you like, remove any skin and bones. Place the salmon in a medium bowl and flake it with a fork. Stir in all the remaining ingredients until they are well blended.

» 2 loaves French bread
» ¼ cup (60 mL) olive oil
» Two 5½ oz (156 g) cans wild salmon
» 1 cup (250 mL) plain yogurt
» ¼ cup (60 mL) finely chopped chives
» 1 Tbsp (15 mL) grainy mustard
» 1 tsp (5 mL) toasted fennel seeds (or caraway seeds)
» 1 tsp (5 mL) dried dill
» ½ tsp (2 mL) hot paprika
» Zest and juice of 1 lime
» Sea salt (or kosher salt) and coarsely ground black pepper to taste

TO SERVE

Spread the salmon mixture onto the grilled bread slices and sprinkle them with parsley.

PAIRING SUGGESTION: Champagne or sparkling white wine. *Tom Firth:* Summerhill Cipes Rosé N/V (Okanagan Valley, BC).

» ¼ cup (60 mL) chopped parsley, for garnish

CHEF
Jane Mundy

LOCATION
Vancouver, BC

TYPE
canned tuna

Spaghetti with Albacore Tuna

Try to buy good-quality sustainable albacore tuna from a brand such as Raincoast Trading—it really makes a difference. *Serves 4 as a main course*

Cook the spaghetti in a large saucepan until it is al dente and drain it, reserving ½ cup (125 mL) of the liquid.

Heat the oil in a large frying pan over medium heat. Add the garlic and shallots and cook, stirring the mixture, until the shallots are softened, about 2 minutes. Mix in the red pepper, parsley, lemon zest and juice, chili flakes, and capers. Add the tuna, gently flaking it with a fork. Add the pasta and toss it with the tuna mixture, adding enough pasta cooking liquid to moisten the pasta.

» 1 lb (500 g) package spaghetti
» 2 Tbsp (30 mL) olive oil
» 2 cloves garlic, minced
» 2 shallots, thinly sliced
» 1 large red pepper, roasted, peeled, and chopped
» ¼ cup (60 mL) chopped parsley
» Zest and juice of 1 lemon
» ½ tsp (2 mL) red chili pepper flakes
» 1 Tbsp (15 mL) capers, minced
» One 6 oz (170 g) can solid white albacore tuna, drained

TO SERVE

Set out four warmed plates. Place a tangle of tuna spaghetti on each plate, then top it with the toasted breadcrumbs and fresh herbs. Great with a green salad and fresh baguette.

PAIRING SUGGESTION: *Tom Firth:* Burrowing Owl Cabernet Franc or Van Westen Viognier (both Okanagan Valley, BC).

» ¼ cup (60 mL) fresh breadcrumbs, toasted
» Fresh herbs (basil, thyme, chervil)

CHEF
Jane Mundy

TYPE
canned tuna

LOCATION
Vancouver, BC

Tuna Fish Lagan

This recipe is a great Ocean Wise take on *lagan*—an Indian dish similar to a savoury cake. There are many versions of lagan, from sweet to savoury, like this one. *Serves 4 as an appetizer*

Preheat the oven to 350°F (180°C). Butter a deep 10-inch (25 cm) square baking pan with the 1 tsp (5 mL) of butter. Blend the ¼ cup (60 mL) of butter, pineapple juice, oil, eggs, parsley, green chili, garlic, red pepper flakes, and salt in a food processor—pulse the batter, do not purée it. Transfer it to a large bowl and add the onion, tuna, corn, and potatoes.

Fold in the flours, cornstarch, and baking powder. Mix in the pineapple chunks. The mixture should be the consistency of a cake batter. If it is not firm enough, add a little more all-purpose flour; if it is too stiff, add 2 Tbsp (30 mL) of milk.

Pour the batter into the buttered pan and bake for 25 minutes. Remove the pan from the oven and, with a spatula, cover the top of the lagan with the whisked egg white and sprinkle with hemp seeds. Bake for another 10 minutes, or until golden brown.

TO SERVE

Remove the lagan from the oven and let it rest a few minutes before removing it from the pan. Cut it into thick slices and serve with green chutney, basmati rice, and, if you have time to prepare them, curried vegetables.

PAIRING SUGGESTION: *Tom Firth:* Tree Brewing Hophead India Pale Ale or Alvear's Amontillado.

» ¼ cup (60 mL) + 1 tsp (5 mL) butter, room temperature
» ½ cup (125 mL) pineapple juice (canned is okay)
» ¼ cup (60 mL) vegetable oil
» 2 eggs, lightly beaten
» ¼ cup (60 mL) finely chopped parsley
» 2 tsp (10 mL) finely chopped fresh green chili (or curry paste, page 292)
» 2 cloves garlic, finely chopped
» 1 tsp (5 mL) red chili pepper flakes
» ¼ tsp (1 mL) salt
» 1 medium onion, grated
» One 5½ oz (156 mL) can solid white albacore tuna, drained and flaked
» ½ cup (125 mL) fresh or frozen corn kernels
» ½ cup (125 mL) cooked cubed potatoes
» ⅓ cup (80 mL) chickpea flour
» ⅓ cup (80 mL) all-purpose flour (approx)
» ⅓ cup (80 mL) cornstarch
» 1 tsp (5 mL) baking powder
» ½ cup (125 mL) pineapple chunks (canned is okay)
» 2 Tbsp (30 mL) milk (optional)
» 1 egg white, whisked
» 1 Tbsp (15 mL) hemp seeds
» Green chutney to taste

CHEF
Jane Mundy

LOCATION
Vancouver, BC

TYPE
canned tuna

tuna

Mexican Tuna Tacos

Again, make sure you purchase good-quality Ocean Wise tuna. Raincoast Trading's albacore tuna is hook-and-line caught in the Pacific Northwest and is available at most high-end grocery stores. Serve these tacos cold—ceviche style—or hot. *Serves 6 as an appetizer*

Place the fish in a medium glass dish or bowl and sprinkle it with the taco seasoning, salt, and pepper. Mix in the corn, tomatoes, red onion, cilantro, 2 Tbsp (30 mL) of the salsa, pickled jalapeños, lime juice, and jalapeño juice. Cover the mixture and chill it for 1 to 2 hours to blend the flavours.

If you like ceviche-style tacos, just heat the corn tortillas. Lightly sprinkle each one with water (if desired), wrap them in waxed paper, and microwave them on high power for 30 seconds.

Alternatively, pour about 1 inch (2.5 cm) of water into a medium saucepan and place a vegetable steamer on top. Cover the pot and bring the water to a boil over medium-high heat. Wrap the tortillas in a heavy kitchen towel. Place them over the boiling water in the steamer, cover, and steam them for 2 minutes. Turn the heat off and let the tortillas stand, covered, for 15 minutes.

If you want crispy taco shells, place hard taco shells on a baking sheet and bake them in a preheated oven at 300°F (150°C) for 6 to 8 minutes.

» Two 5⅓ oz (150 g) cans solid white albacore tuna, drained
» 1 Tbsp (15 mL) taco seasoning mix (or ancho chili powder)
» Fine sea salt and freshly ground black pepper to taste
» One 14 oz (398 mL) can sweet corn kernels, drained
» 1 cup (250 mL) chopped seeded tomatoes
» ¾ cup (185 mL) chopped red onion
» ½ cup (125 mL) chopped cilantro
» ½ cup (125 mL) + 2 Tbsp (30 mL) salsa
» 2 Tbsp (30 mL) sliced pickled jalapeños (from a jar)
» 2 Tbsp (30 mL) fresh lime juice
» 1 Tbsp (15 mL) pickled jalapeño juice (from a jar)
» 12 soft corn tortillas (or hard taco shells)

TO SERVE

Arrange the shredded lettuce, diced avocado, and sour cream on a large platter. Fill the warm tortillas or taco shells with the tuna mixture and shredded cheese, and top with a dollop of salsa. If you prefer hot tacos, preheat the oven to 350°F (180°C). Place the tuna mixture on 12 corn tortillas and top them with cheese and salsa. Roll up the tortillas and wrap aluminum foil around each one. Bake them in the oven until the cheese melts, about 8 minutes.

Your guests can help themselves to the toppings.

PAIRING SUGGESTION: *Tom Firth:* Lagunitas Pale Ale, Big Rock Warthog Cream Ale, or Hester Creek Semillon Chardonnay (Okanagan Valley, BC).

» ½ large head of romaine lettuce, very thinly sliced crosswise
» 1 large avocado, peeled, pitted, and diced
» 1 cup (250 mL) sour cream
» 1 cup (250 mL) shredded cheddar

CHEF
Barbara-jo McIntosh
Barbara-Jo's Books to Cooks

TYPE
canned
salmon

LOCATION
Vancouver, BC

Curried Salmon Loaf

I grew up with a basic salmon loaf that my granny called her own. She was an English cook and it was a staple of her recipe files. Salmon loaf continues to remind me of her and I love the memory, but I had to create my own version to satisfy my spice-loving palate. *Serves 2 as a main course*

Preheat the oven to 350°F (180°C). Place the rack in the middle of the oven. Grease an 8- × 4-inch (1.5 L) loaf pan with 1 tsp (5 mL) of the butter.

Put the salmon in a medium bowl and set it aside. Melt the remaining butter in a small saucepan over medium heat. Add the curry powder and cook it for 30 seconds, being careful not to let the mixture burn. Stir in the green onion, tomato, carrot, and parsnip. Turn the heat down to medium low and cover the saucepan. Cook the mixture for 2 minutes, being careful not to let it brown.

Remove the pan from the heat and add the mixture to the salmon. Add the egg and Parmesan cheese. Mix well but gently, being careful not to turn the mixture into mush. Place the mixture in the loaf pan and cook it in the pre-heated oven, covered with aluminum foil, for 35 minutes. Uncover and cook the loaf for 2 more minutes.

» 1 Tbsp (15 mL) butter
» One 7½ oz (213 g) can wild salmon, drained
» 1½ tsp (7 mL) curry powder
» 1 large green onion, finely sliced
» 1 medium tomato, finely chopped
» 1 small carrot, grated
» 1 small parsnip, peeled and grated
» 1 large egg, lightly beaten
» ¼ cup (60 mL) grated Parmesan cheese

TO SERVE

Slice the loaf and fan a few pieces on each plate. Serve with a green salad and garnish with lemon wedges.

PAIRING SUGGESTION: *Tom Firth:* Church & State Hollenbach Family Vineyard Pinot Noir or Red Rooster Gewürztraminer (both Okanagan Valley, BC).

» 2 lemon wedges, for garnish

SOURCE
Pacific Institute of Culinary Arts

CHEF
*Erin Kelly,
Administrator*

TYPE
*canned
anchovies*

LOCATION
Vancouver, BC

Puttanesca Sauce for Pasta

This is a super-fast sauce that makes a great weekday meal, using canned anchovy fillets and a couple of fresh ingredients. *Serves 4 as a main course*

Cook the pasta in a large saucepan until it is al dente, and drain it, reserving 2 Tbsp (30 mL) of the water.

Heat the oil in a large saucepan over medium heat and sauté the garlic for 1 minute, being careful not to burn it. Add all the remaining ingredients and simmer them over medium heat for 10 minutes, or until the water from the tomatoes evaporates a bit. Add the reserved pasta cooking liquid and simmer the sauce over low heat for another 5 minutes.

» One 1 lb (500 g) package pasta, any kind
» 2 Tbsp (30 mL) olive oil
» 2 to 3 cloves garlic, minced
» 4 large tomatoes, chopped (or 30 cherry tomatoes, halved)
» 12 large green olives, pitted and sliced (with pimiento or without)
» One 1¾ oz (50 g) can anchovies, drained and chopped
» ½ cup (125 mL) chopped Italian flat-leaf parsley
» 2 Tbsp (30 mL) basil chiffonade (finely sliced)
» ½ tsp (2 mL) red chili pepper flakes

TO SERVE

Toss the pasta with the sauce and serve right away, with a generous sprinkling of fresh herbs and a crusty bread.

PAIRING SUGGESTION: *Tom Firth:* Feudi di San Gregorio Greco di Tufo (Italy) or JoieFarm Muscat (Okanagan Valley, BC).

» Finely chopped fresh herbs (basil, parsley, chervil), for garnish

CHEF
Barbara-jo McIntosh
Barbara-Jo's Books to Cooks

TYPE
canned
sardines

LOCATION
Vancouver, BC

Sardine and Potato Pancakes with Lemon and Chive Mayonnaise

You may not think of the humble sardine as glamorous, but this recipe will change your way of thinking. *Makes 18 small pancakes*

LEMON AND CHIVE MAYONNAISE

Mix the mayonnaise, lemon juice, chives, and pepper together in a small bowl and refrigerate until you are ready to serve the pancakes.

» ½ cup (125 mL) mayonnaise
» 1 Tbsp (15 mL) fresh lemon juice
» 1 Tbsp (15 mL) chopped chives
» Freshly ground black pepper to taste

SARDINE AND POTATO PANCAKES

Chop the sardines into small pieces and place them in a medium mixing bowl. Cook the potato in a small pot of boiling water for 5 minutes. Remove it from the water, let it dry for 5 to 10 minutes, and then grate it. Add the warm potato and the onion to the sardines.

In another bowl, mix together the flour and baking powder. Whisk in the buttermilk, egg, and vegetable oil. Combine the two mixtures and season with the rosemary and more pepper.

Melt the butter and olive oil together in a large frying pan over medium heat. When the butter is bubbly, use a soup spoon (one spoonful per pancake) to drop the potato mixture into the pan, a few spoonfuls at a time. When small bubbles form on the top of the pancakes, flip them over and cook them until they are golden brown, about 2 minutes per side.

» One 3¾ oz (106 g) can sardines in water, drained
» 1 large russet potato, peeled and cut in half
» 1 small yellow onion, diced
» ½ cup (125 mL) all-purpose flour
» 1 tsp (5 mL) baking powder
» ¾ cup (185 mL) buttermilk
» 1 large egg
» 2 Tbsp (30 mL) vegetable oil
» 2 Tbsp (30 mL) chopped rosemary
» 1 tsp (5 mL) butter
» 1 tsp (5 mL) olive oil

TO SERVE

Dollop the mayonnaise over the cakes—that's it!

PAIRING SUGGESTION: *Tom Firth:* Masi Soave (Italy) or Sandhill Gamay Noir (Okanagan Valley, BC).

CHEF
Jane Mundy

LOCATION
Vancouver, BC

TYPE
canned clams

clams

Clam Fritters

This is a classic recipe for clam fritters. Try to buy good-quality canned clams; they are really flavourful and, of course, convenient. *Serves 4 as an appetizer*

SWEET AND SOUR SAUCE

Mix the brown sugar and cornstarch in a small saucepan. Stir in the rest of the ingredients. Heat and stir the sauce over medium-high heat until it boils and thickens. Set it aside.

» 1½ cups (375 mL) brown sugar
» 4 tsp (20 mL) cornstarch
» ½ cup (125 mL) water
» ½ cup (125 mL) white wine vinegar
» 2 Tbsp (30 mL) soy sauce
» 1 Tbsp (15 mL) ketchup

CLAM FRITTERS

Mix all the ingredients, except the egg whites and vegetable oil, in a medium bowl or food processor. It should be a bit lumpy. In a separate bowl, beat the egg whites until they form soft peaks. Fold them into the batter. Heat the oil to 350°F (180°C) in a large, deep saucepan. Using a tablespoon or small scoop, drop portions of the batter, a few at a time, into the pot. Fry them until they are golden brown, then remove them with a slotted spoon. Place them on a kitchen or paper towel.

» 1¼ cups (310 mL) all-purpose flour
» ½ tsp (2 mL) baking powder
» ½ tsp (2 mL) lemon pepper
» ¼ medium onion, diced
» 1 celery stalk, diced
» Half a 10 oz (284 mL) can baby clams with nectar
» 2 large egg whites
» 2 cups (500 mL) vegetable oil (or enough to make pot 2 inches/ 5 cm full)

TO SERVE

Serve the fritters with the sweet-and-sour sauce for dipping.

PAIRING SUGGESTION: *Tom Firth:* Granville Island English Bay Pale Ale, Leacock Rainwater Madeira (Portugal) (for the bold), or McAuslan St. Ambroise Griffon Rousse.

CHEF
Jane Mundy

LOCATION
Vancouver, BC

TYPE
canned oysters

oysters

Asian Smoked Oysters

These fried oysters are almost as addictive as chocolate!
Serves 4 as an appetizer

SAUCE

Mix all the sauce ingredients thoroughly and set aside.

» 2 Tbsp (30 mL) honey
» 1 Tbsp (15 mL) soy sauce
» 1 Tbsp (15 mL) mirin (sweet rice wine)
» 1 Tbsp (15 mL) grated fresh ginger (peeled)
» 1 Tbsp (15 mL) toasted sesame seeds
» 1 Tbsp (15 mL) chopped chives
» 1 green onion, finely chopped
» 1½ tsp (7 mL) sesame oil
» 2 tsp (10 mL) red chili pepper flakes

TO COOK THE OYSTERS

Drain the oysters in a mesh sieve.

Heat the oil to 350°F (180°C) in a deep pan. Dust the oysters with flour. Dip the oysters in the egg, then double-dip in panko. Fry the oysters until golden.

» One 3 oz (85 g) can sustainable smoked oysters
» ½ cup (125 mL) vegetable oil
» 2 Tbsp (30 mL) all-purpose flour
» 1 egg, lightly beaten
» ¼ cup (60 mL) panko (Japanese breadcrumbs)

TO SERVE

Sprinkle with salt and serve immediately as an appetizer with dipping sauce on the side, or plate with basmati rice and bok choy and drizzle the sauce over the oysters.

PAIRING SUGGESTION: *Tom Firth:* Sparkling wine such as Seaview Brut (Australia) or See Ya Later Ranch Non Vintage SYL Brut Sparkling Wine (Okanagan Valley, BC).

» Salt to finish

SOURCE
Pacific Institute of Culinary Arts

CHEF
*Marlene J. Yong,
Student*

LOCATION
Vancouver, BC

TYPE
*canned smoked
oysters*

Smoked Oyster Omelette

This is one of my favourite all-day dishes. It's great for breakfast served with plain rice congee, for lunch with rice pilaf, or just on its own as a snack. *Serves 2 as a main course*

POTATO BATTER

Blend the sweet potato flour with the chicken stock in a small bowl to form a batter. Mix in the white wine, sesame oil, fish sauce, and ginger powder and a pinch of salt. Set the seasoned potato batter aside.

Whisk the eggs, black pepper, and cayenne pepper and a pinch of salt together in a second bowl and set aside.

Heat 1 Tbsp (15 mL) of the vegetable oil in a medium saucepan over medium-high heat. Pour the potato batter into the pan and spread it out evenly. Cook it until the bottom starts to crisp, about 3 minutes, then push it over to one side of the pan. Add the remaining 1 Tbsp (15 mL) of oil to the empty side of the pan and sauté the garlic and julienned green onion until they are soft. Add the pepper and carrot and sauté them for another minute, and then add the egg mixture and oysters. Gently combine all the components in the pan and cook until set. Do not overcook.

» 2 Tbsp (30 mL) sweet potato flour
» ½ cup (125 mL) chicken stock (or water)
» 1 Tbsp (15 mL) dry white wine
» 1 tsp (5 mL) sesame oil
» ¼ tsp (1 mL) fish sauce
» Pinch ground ginger
» Salt
» 2 large eggs
» Pinch freshly ground black pepper
» Pinch cayenne pepper
» 2 Tbsp (30 mL) vegetable oil
» 1 clove garlic, minced
» 1 Tbsp (15 mL) julienned green onion (white part only; green part for garnish)
» ½ cup (125 mL) julienned green, red, or yellow pepper
» ¼ cup (60 mL) julienned carrot
» One 3 oz (85 g) can sustainable smoked oysters

TO SERVE

Turn the omelette over onto a plate, season it to taste with more salt and freshly ground pepper, and then garnish it with the iceberg lettuce, cilantro, and chopped green onion.

PAIRING SUGGESTION: Heineken Pilsner Beer or Côtes de Provence Rosé (France).

» ½ cup (125 mL) iceberg lettuce, shredded
» 1 Tbsp (15 mL) chopped cilantro
» 1 Tbsp (15 mL) chopped green onion (green part only)

MAKEOVERS

think of "makeovers" as comfort food, reminiscent of my childhood, when my British granny made delicious haddock cakes, a creamy fish pie with mashed potatoes, or steaming rustic soups from the remainder of a lovely piece of fish we'd eaten the night before. To be honest, I liked the second day's meal better.

Probably because I grew up in a large family and because I used to cook for hundreds of people daily when I was a film caterer, I still tend to cook too much for one meal. And, like most people, I don't have the luxury of grocery shopping daily, so I also tend to buy too much. As my mother said, "Your eyes are bigger than your belly." Like Granny, however, I never throw food away, especially when it comes to fish and seafood.

Given a little creativity, along with a well-stocked pantry, my bits and pieces of fish and seafood don't have to wind up in little baggies, tossed into my freezer only to be turfed out later.

Last night's fish fillet resurfaces the next day as a wondrous curry—maybe I'll add a handful of mussels or squid to gussy it up. If the fridge is looking a little bare, I'll think back to my granny's meals and, with a few simple ingredients, assemble salmon cakes in no time. I hope the following chart will encourage you to think of leftovers as makeovers—delicious, easy, time-saving, and economical.

Note: For optimum food safety, the rule of thumb is to refrigerate fish and seafood within 2 hours of cooking and to use it within 3 or 4 days. And don't microwave remakes—the texture will be leathery.

HOW TO USE LEFTOVERS

IF YOU HAVE LEFTOVER	ADD (5 INGREDIENTS OR LESS)	TO MAKE
any cooked fish	mashed potatoes, parsley sauce (up a notch: add grated cheese)	fish pie or fish cakes
any cooked fish	egg, mayonnaise, panko or dry breadcrumbs, hemp seed or flaxseed	fish sticks
any seafood	avocado, Clamato juice, cucumber, cilantro	gazpacho (cold soup)
any seafood or fish	coconut milk, onion, garlic, curry powder, cilantro	seafood curry
any firm fish cut into cubes	zucchini, red pepper, firm fruit such as pineapple, lemon or lime juice (and skewers)	seafood kabobs
any seafood, any smoked fish	eggs, onion, butter, sour cream	seafood or smoked fish omelette
smoked fish	rice, egg, butter, cayenne pepper	kedgeree
white fish	canned tomatoes, onion, garlic, hot pepper flakes (up a notch: add a spoonful of pesto at the last minute)	rustic fish soup
albacore or canned tuna	spaghetti, garlic, parsley, lemon, red pepper flakes	spaghetti with tuna
albacore or canned tuna	mayonnaise, celery, lemon juice, Dijon mustard, sourdough bread (up a notch: top with Parmesan)	tuna melt
pollock	mayonnaise, clam nectar, egg, breadcrumbs, dill	faux crab cakes
sablefish	potato, milk, butter, parsley	brandade (recipe facing page)
salmon	breadcrumbs, egg, onion	salmon cakes
smoked salmon	pasta, peas, cream, herbs	salmon alfredo
smoked salmon	cream cheese, cream, dill	smoked salmon mousse
shrimp	ramen noodles, Chinese vegetables	Chinese hot pot
clams	egg, flour, milk, onion	clam fritters
squid, shrimp, or oysters	flour, egg, garlic, green onions, soy sauce	Asian seafood pancakes

RESTAURANT
River Café

TYPE
sablefish

CHEF
Scott Pohorelic

LOCATION
Calgary, AB

Sablefish Brandade

When sizing and cutting sablefish at the restaurant for our main course, we always end up with a few extra pieces that are not large enough for a portion. We salt these pieces to preserve them and use them later to make brandade. Traditionally brandade is made with salt cod, but this is our Ocean Wise–friendly version. Note that it takes one month to cure the fish. *Serves 6 to 8 as an appetizer*

TO CURE THE FISH

Place the fish in a glass or plastic container. Cover it with the coarse salt and bay leaves. Seal the container and refrigerate to cure for one month. Drain the excess liquid every few days.

» 1 lb (500 g) sablefish (skinless, boneless), cut into ½-inch (1 cm) slices
» ½ cup (125 mL) coarse salt
» 2 bay leaves

TO MAKE THE BRANDADE

The day before you plan to make the brandade, rinse the cured fish with cold water to remove all the salt and discard the bay leaves. Place it in a clean container, cover it with cold water, and let it soak in the refrigerator overnight. In the morning, rinse the fish again and soak it in fresh water for 1 hour.

Rinse the fish again and place it in a large saucepan. Cover the fish with 8 cups (2 L) of cold water. Simmer the fish over medium heat for 20 minutes, or until it is tender. Remove the fish from the water with a slotted spoon and reserve it for later. Also reserve the hot water.

Place the potatoes in the same hot water used to cook the fish. Simmer them over medium heat until they are tender enough to mash, about 15 minutes. Strain the potatoes and discard the liquid.

Place the olive oil, canola oil, and garlic in the same pot and place it back over medium heat. Let the garlic cook for about 3 minutes, or until it is soft and translucent. Add the milk and butter. When the milk is hot and the butter has melted, add the cooked fish and potatoes. Mash them with a potato masher, leaving a few chunks. Stir in the parsley and season to taste with salt and pepper.

» 1 lb (500 g) yellow potatoes (such as Yukon Gold), cut into 1⅛-inch (3 cm) rounds
» ¼ cup (60 mL) extra virgin olive oil
» ¼ cup (60 mL) canola oil
» 1 Tbsp (15 mL) minced garlic
» ½ cup (125 mL) whole milk
» 3 Tbsp (45 mL) butter
» 2 Tbsp (30 mL) chopped parsley
» Salt and pepper to taste

TO SERVE

Serve the warm brandade in a bowl as a spread for toasted baguette slices.

SOURCE
Pacific Institute of Culinary Arts

TYPE
any fish

CHEF
Marlene J. Yong,
Student

LOCATION
Vancouver, BC

Fish Soup with Chinese Preserved Eggs and Spinach

This light soup dish came to mind when I was one of several culinary students from the PICA who volunteered to plate canapés at a posh shopping mall for 1,500 people under the direction of chef Robert Clark. We used sablefish, which is delicate yet versatile, but any leftover seafood will work. What could be more delicate than a traditional all-season century-egg and spinach soup? *Serves 2 as a main course or 4 as an appetizer*

NOTE: Century eggs, a preserved delicacy, can be bought from Asian markets or supermarkets. Instead of regular spinach, use Chinese spinach (yin choy) or baby spinach leaves.

Slice the fish into strips 1 inch (2.5 cm) thick. Wash the spinach and cilantro under cold running water and discard all older leaves.

Place the fish stock, ginger, whole sprigs of cilantro, and century eggs in a medium saucepan and simmer them over medium-high heat for 5 minutes. Add the wine, salt, and pepper. Add the spinach and cook it for 1 minute. Add the fish and cook it until it is heated through, about 2 more minutes.

» One 7 oz (200 g) cooked fish fillet (approx)
» 4 cups (1 L) packed spinach leaves
» 4 sprigs cilantro
» 4 cups (1 L) fish stock (see page 289)
» One 1-inch (2.5 cm) piece fresh ginger, peeled and julienned
» 2 century eggs
» ½ cup (125 mL) dry white wine
» Salt and pepper to taste

TO SERVE

Sprinkle with cilantro and serve immediately with steaming hot jasmine tea.

» Finely chopped cilantro, for garnish

CHEF
Jane Mundy

TYPE
any white fish

LOCATION
Vancouver, BC

Puff Pastry Fish Pie

Ready-made puff pastry turns everyday fish pie into an elegant main course, and no one would guess it drapes leftover seafood. To take this recipe up another notch, add a handful of shrimp. *Serves 4*

Melt the butter in a large frying pan over low heat, add the onion, and cook until golden, about 20 minutes. Flake the fish and add it to the onion. Season with the herbs, salt, and pepper, and stir in the crème fraîche. Allow the mixture to cook for a few minutes, until it has a creamy consistency.

Preheat the oven to 400°F (200°C). On a lightly floured board, roll the pastry into two rectangles about 8 × 14 inches (20 × 35 cm). Spread the fish mixture along the centre of one rectangle, leaving about 2 inches (5 cm) bare around the edge of the pastry. Brush a little beaten egg around the edge, then lay the second rectangle of pastry over the top. Seal the edges together by pinching them all along with your thumb and forefinger—it is important that the two pieces be sealed tightly. Brush the top of the pastry with more beaten egg, and cut a few slits in the top to allow the steam to escape.

Transfer the pie to a large baking sheet and bake it for about 20 minutes, or until it has puffed up and is a golden colour. Take it out of the oven and check that the pastry is cooked underneath. If not, give it another 5 minutes.

» 2 Tbsp (30 mL) butter (or vegetable oil)
» 1 medium onion, chopped
» 1 lb (500 g) cooked white fish (any type) and/or smoked fish, such as albacore tuna or haddock
» ½ cup (125 mL) chopped fresh herbs (thyme, parsley, chervil, dill)
» Salt and pepper to taste
» 1 cup (250 mL) crème fraîche (see page 291)
» 1 lb (500 g) puff pastry
» 1 medium egg, lightly beaten

TO SERVE

Cut into hearty wedges, add a dollop of peas or green beans on the side, and sprinkle with parsley.

» Parsley for garnish

CHEF
Jane Mundy

TYPE
pollock

LOCATION
Vancouver, BC

Faux Crab Cakes (Pollock)

Even among seafood lovers, pollock is not a popular fish, but it deserves more credit. When poached in clam nectar, it is very similar to crabmeat and very inexpensive. This recipe makes eight to twelve small cakes or four burger-sized patties—slide them into soft buns with lettuce. *Serves 4 as a main course or 8 as an appetizer*

Season the fish with salt and pepper. Pour the clam nectar into a large frying pan over medium-high heat. Add the pollock and simmer it until it flakes with a fork, about 8 minutes. Remove the pan from the heat and drain the fish. Set it aside to cool.

Mix the egg, lemon juice, and mayonnaise in a large bowl. Gently fold in the cooled pollock, panko, green onion, parsley, dill, and Old Bay Spice. If the mixture does not look firm enough, add more panko. Shape into cakes, cover, and refrigerate for 30 minutes or overnight.

Spread out the flour on a large plate. Dredge both sides of the cakes with flour. Heat the grapeseed oil in a large pan over medium-high heat. Working in batches and being careful not to overcrowd the pan, cook the cakes until the outsides are golden brown, about 4 minutes per side. Drain on a kitchen towel or paper towels.

» 1 lb (500 g) pollock
» Salt and pepper to taste
» One 14 oz (398 mL) can clam nectar
» 1 large egg, lightly beaten
» Juice of 1 lemon
» ¼ cup (60 mL) mayonnaise
» ½ cup (125 mL) panko (Japanese breadcrumbs)
» ½ cup (125 mL) finely chopped green onion
» 1 Tbsp (15 mL) chopped parsley
» 1 Tbsp (15 mL) chopped dill
» ½ tsp (2 mL) Old Bay Spice (see page 294)
» ¼ cup (60 mL) all-purpose flour
» 3 Tbsp (45 mL) grapeseed oil

TO SERVE

Serve with the tartar sauce as an appetizer or "burger-style" for a main course.

» Tartar Sauce (see page 294)

CHEF
Jane Mundy

LOCATION
Vancouver, BC

TYPE
*pollock, any
white fish*

Fish Stix

Some kids don't much care for fish, but these fish stix are in a different category, especially when served with a side of fries. Hemp seed and ground flaxseed make them healthy. And adults love them too. *Makes 8 fish stix*

Combine the mashed potato, pollock, white fish, salt and pepper, green onion, and flaxseed in a food processor and pulse until they are combined. Transfer the mixture to a medium bowl. Beat the eggs in another medium bowl. Combine the breadcrumbs and hemp seeds on a large plate.

Shape the seafood mixture into "stix," about 4 × 1½ inches (10 × 4 cm). Coat each stick with the beaten egg and then gently roll it in the breadcrumb-hemp seed mix. Heat the oil in a large frying pan over medium heat. Fry the fish stix until they are golden brown all over, 2 to 3 minutes per side.

» 1 lb (500 g) russet potatoes, peeled, cooked, and mashed
» ½ lb (250 g) cooked pollock
» ½ lb (250 g) leftover white fish
» Salt and pepper to taste
» ¼ cup (60 mL) finely chopped green onion
» 1 Tbsp (15 mL) ground flaxseed
» 2 eggs
» ½ cup (125 mL) dry breadcrumbs
» 2 Tbsp (30 mL) hemp seeds
» 2 Tbsp (30 mL) canola oil

TO SERVE

Accompany with french fries, mayo, ketchup (upon request!), and raw veggie sticks.

CHEF
Jane Mundy

TYPE
any white fish

LOCATION
Vancouver, BC

Fish Cakes with Horseradish Mayonnaise

When I was growing up, it seemed as if my mother made fish cakes several times a week, so they didn't get me too excited. But she probably didn't have the ingredients to give her recipe zing. This one gets its heat from the spicy mayonnaise and is enhanced by fresh herbs. A green salad would complement this dish. I recall that at home we had butter lettuce with Crosse & Blackwell salad cream. (Not too exciting.) *Serves 4 as a main course or 8 as an appetizer*

FISH CAKES

Cook the potatoes in a large saucepan of boiling, salted water for 15 to 20 minutes, or until they are tender. Drain the potatoes well, mash them, and set them aside, covered.

Pick through the fish for any skin and bones and flake it into chunks. Gently fold the fish, parsley, dill, capers, lemon zest, and egg yolks into the mashed potatoes. Season with salt and pepper. Shape the mixture into eight fish cakes (about the size of a golf ball about 1 inch / 2.5 cm thick). Cover and refrigerate for 20 minutes or overnight.

» 1 lb (500 g) russet potatoes, peeled and roughly chopped
» ¾ lb (375 g) cooked white fish, and/or any smoked fillet
» ¼ cup (60 mL) chopped parsley
» 1 Tbsp (15 mL) chopped dill
» 1 Tbsp (15 mL) capers, drained and chopped
» Zest of 1 lemon
» 2 medium egg yolks
» Salt and pepper to taste

HORSERADISH MAYONNAISE

Place the mayonnaise in a small bowl. Mix in the horseradish, lemon juice, and salt and pepper to taste. Cover the horseradish mayonnaise and refrigerate it until you are ready to serve it.

» 1 cup (250 mL) good-quality mayonnaise (or make you own—see page 292)
» 2 Tbsp (30 mL) prepared hot horseradish
» Juice of 1 lemon

TO FRY THE FISH CAKES

Heat the olive oil in a large frying pan over medium heat. Dust the fish cakes with a little flour and, working in batches, fry them for 3 to 4 minutes per side, or until they are golden.

» 2 Tbsp (30 mL) olive oil
» All-purpose flour, for dusting the cakes

TO SERVE

Serve the fish cakes with the horseradish mayonnaise and lemon wedges.

» 1 lemon, cut into wedges, for garnish

SOURCE
Diversity Food Services Inc.
at the University of Winnipeg

TYPE
northern pike

CHEF
Ben Kramer

LOCATION
Winnipeg, MB

Fish Cakes with Wasabi Pea Purée and Wilted Pea Shoot Salad

This recipe is a great way to use up leftover cooked pike or any white fish. The sauce and accompanying salad capture the taste of fresh peas—a sure sign of summer in Manitoba. *Serves 4 as a main course or 8 as an appetizer*

FISH CAKES

Combine the pike meat and 1 cup (250 mL) of the panko in a medium bowl. Add the onion, celery, pepper, mayonnaise, 1 Tbsp (15 mL) of the lemon juice, parsley, hot sauce, and egg. Do not overmix. Season to taste with salt and pepper and form the mixture into the desired number of cakes (bigger for a main course).

Place the remaining 1 cup (250 mL) of panko on a small plate. One at a time, gently press both sides of each fish cake into the breadcrumbs. Cover the cakes and refrigerate until you are ready to cook them.

» 1½ lb (750 g) skinless, boneless northern pike (or any Ocean Wise white fish)
» 2 cups (500 mL) panko (Japanese breadcrumbs)
» ⅓ cup (80 mL) finely minced white onion
» ⅓ cup (80 mL) finely minced celery stalks
» ⅓ cup (80 mL) finely minced red, green, or yellow pepper
» ¼ cup (60 mL) mayonnaise
» 2 Tbsp (30 mL) fresh lemon juice
» 1 Tbsp (15 mL) finely chopped parsley
» ½ tsp (2 mL) hot pepper sauce
» 1 large egg, lightly beaten
» Salt and pepper

WASABI PEA PURÉE

Combine the peas, orange juice, olive oil, wasabi powder, and basil leaves in a blender and purée until smooth. Season the purée to taste with salt and pepper. Pour it into a small saucepan and warm over low heat. Do not let it boil.

» 1 cup (250 mL) shelled fresh peas, blanched
» ¼ cup (60 mL) freshly squeezed orange juice
» 1 tsp (5 mL) olive oil
» 1 tsp (5 mL) wasabi powder
» 6 basil leaves

TO FRY THE FISH CAKES

Preheat the oven to 350°F (180°C) if making larger cakes. Heat the vegetable oil in a non-stick frying pan over medium heat. Working in batches, gently place the fish cakes in the pan and sear them, turning once, until they are golden brown on both sides, 1 to 3 minutes per side. (If the cakes are large, finish them in the preheated oven for 5 to 8 minutes, or until warmed through.)

» 2 Tbsp (30 mL) vegetable oil

WILTED PEA SHOOT SALAD

Heat the olive oil in a small frying pan over medium heat. Add the pea shoots and toss them quickly until they are just barely wilted. Add the remaining 1 Tbsp (15 mL) of the lemon juice and the chopped tomato and orange, heat through, and season the salad to taste with salt and pepper.

» 2 tsp (10 mL) olive oil
» 4 cups (1 L) pea shoots
» 1 large tomato, finely chopped
» ¼ orange, peeled, segmented, and chopped

TO SERVE

Set out the desired number of plates. Pool the wasabi pea purée on each plate, and place the salad and fish cake(s) side by side.

CHEF
Jane Mundy

LOCATION
Vancouver, BC

TYPE
any fish, scallops, and shrimp, crab or lobster

Seafood and Fish Sausages

You can use any leftover fish and seafood to make these sausages, with the exception of oysters. The sausages can be served as a main course or thinly sliced as an hors d'oeuvre. *Makes 8 sausages*

NOTE: Make sure all your cooking equipment—even the food processor—is cold. Instead of using plastic wrap, you could stuff the sausage mixture into casings with a pastry bag.

TO MAKE THE STUFFING

Heat the butter in a medium frying pan over medium heat and add the onion. Cook until soft, then add the grated carrot and cook the mixture for another minute. Remove the pan from the heat.

Flake the fish with a fork and grind it in a food processor until it is smooth. Add the egg whites and continue processing until the two are blended. With the processor running, slowly add the cream, cooked onion and carrot, and seasonings, until everything is well mixed. Transfer the ground fish mixture to a chilled medium bowl and stir in the scallops, shellfish, parsley, and mushrooms. Add the rest of the fresh herbs and minced green onion. Refrigerate the mixture for 10 minutes.

If you want to do a "test run," bring some water to a simmer in a small saucepan. Poach a spoonful of the stuffing in the water, then season the seafood mixture with salt and pepper to taste. You may want to add a dash of Pernod, white wine, or Worcestershire sauce.

» 1 Tbsp (15 mL) butter (or olive oil)
» 1 medium onion, minced
» 1 medium carrot, grated
» 1½ lb (750 g) cooked fish (skinless, boneless)
» 2 egg whites, chilled
» 1½ cups (375 mL) whipping cream, chilled
» 2 tsp (10 mL) salt
» ½ tsp (2 mL) ground white (or green) pepper
» ¼ tsp (1 mL) ground nutmeg
» 1 cup (250 mL) diced cooked scallops
» 1 cup (250 mL) cooked shrimp, crab, or lobster meat, cut into ¼-inch (6 mm) pieces
» ½ cup (125 mL) chopped parsley
» ¼ cup (60 mL) chopped mushrooms
» 2 Tbsp (30 mL) fresh herbs (tarragon, chervil, lemongrass, or thyme)
» 1 Tbsp (15 mL) minced green onion
» Salt and pepper to taste
» Dash Pernod, white wine, or Worcestershire sauce (optional)

TO MAKE THE SAUSAGES

Spread a large sheet of plastic wrap on the counter. Place one-eighth of the seafood mixture in the centre of the wrap, shaping it into a log, about 5 inches (12 cm) long and 1½ inches (4 cm) wide. Wrap it tightly, twist each end, and secure the ends with an elastic band or kitchen string. Repeat with the remaining seafood and refrigerate the sausages until they are firm, about 2 hours.

TO BOIL THE SAUSAGES

Bring a large stockpot of water to a boil over high heat. Add the plastic-wrapped sausages and simmer them for 15 minutes, turning them halfway through the cooking time. Remove the sausages from the water and drain them in a colander. Remove the plastic wrap and cut into slices.

TO SERVE

Serve with lemon aioli (see page 292) or tartar sauce (see page 294).

SOURCE
Pacific Institute of Culinary Arts

CHEF
*Marlene J. Yong,
Student*

TYPE
*shrimp (or pollock
or tuna)*

LOCATION
Vancouver, BC

Seafood Pizza

This colourful pizza is bound to cheer anyone up. I consider it my ultimate comfort food. You can create your own topping with whatever ingredients you have left over; I like the combination of fish and pineapple. *Makes two 12-inch (30 cm) pizzas*

NOTE: If you're in a hurry, purchase two pre-made pizza bases.

PIZZA DOUGH

Combine the flour and olive oil in a large mixing bowl. You may knead the dough by hand or use a stand mixer with a dough hook on the slowest speed. Mix the water, yeast, and sugar in a small bowl and let the mixture stand for 10 minutes.

Combine the yeast mixture with the flour mixture. Continue to knead or beat the dough on slow speed until it becomes soft and pliable. Flour a large board, cut the dough in half, and roll each piece out until it will fit into a 12-inch (30 cm) pizza pan. Fit the dough into the pans and let it relax for about 15 minutes.

» 1 lb (500 g) bread flour, preferably organic
» ¾ cup (185 mL) olive oil
» 1¼ cups (310 mL) lukewarm water
» 1 package active dry yeast (about 2½ tsp/12 mL)
» 1 tsp (5 mL) sugar

› AT STEVESTON, BC

Preheat the oven to 400°F (200°C). Check all the seafood for bones and season with salt and pepper if necessary. Layer the pizza toppings onto the dough, starting with the tomato sauce, then adding the seafood, and ending with the cheeses.

Bake the pizzas until the cheese has melted and the crust is golden brown, about 20 minutes.

» 1½ cups (375 mL) leftover cooked shrimp or pollock, or canned albacore tuna
» Salt and pepper to taste
» One 7½ oz (213 mL) can tomato sauce or homemade tomato sauce
» 3 Roma tomatoes, sliced
» ½ cup (125 mL) sliced white onion
» 3 red, green, and yellow peppers, seeded and sliced (three different colours)
» One 7½ oz (213 g) can sliced pineapple
» ½ cup (125 mL) grated Swiss cheese
» ½ cup (125 mL) grated aged cheddar
» ½ cup (125 mL) grated mozzarella

Fish Stock

Jane Mundy

Fish stock keeps for four to five days in the refrigerator and about three months in the freezer. You can also freeze it in ice cube trays for smaller portions when needed. *Makes 5 cups (1.25 L)*

» 2 lb (1 kg) heads and bones of any white fish
» 10 cups (2.5 L) cold water
» ½ cup (125 mL) dry white wine
» 2 carrots, chopped
» 2 celery stalks, chopped
» 1 large onion, chopped
» 1 shallot, chopped
» 2 cloves garlic
» 6 sprigs parsley
» 1 sprig thyme
» 1 bay leaf
» 6 whole black peppercorns
» 1 Tbsp (15 mL) sea salt

Soak the fish head and bones in a large bowl of cold water for a few hours to remove any traces of blood. Drain them and place them in a large stockpot with the water. Bring the water to a boil and add all the other ingredients. Simmer over low heat for about 2 hours. Drain the stock and filter it through cheesecloth or a fine-mesh sieve.

Dashi

Frank Pabst, Blue Water Café and Raw Bar,
Vancouver, BC

Dashi is a basic Japanese stock made with kelp (kombu seaweed) and flakes from dried and smoked bonito (tuna) fish. You can find these ingredients at Asian supermarkets. *Makes 8 cups (2 L)*

» 1 piece dried kombu seaweed, about 12 inches (30 cm) long
» 8 cups (2 L) water
» 2 cups (500 mL) bonito flakes

Wipe the kombu gently with a moistened towel to remove any loose impurities. Combine the kombu and water in a medium saucepan, and bring the water to a simmer over medium-high heat. When the kombu rises to the surface, remove it from the pot with tongs or a slotted spoon. Turn off the heat, add the bonito flakes, and allow them to infuse for 30 seconds. Use a slotted spoon to skim any impurities off the surface.

Fill a large bowl with ice. Strain the broth immediately through a fine-mesh sieve into a medium bowl. Discard the solids. Set the bowl of dashi over the large bowl of ice and let it cool to room temperature. Refrigerate the dashi in an airtight container for up to one week.

Prawn Bisque Sauce

Don Letendre, Elixir Bistro,
Opus Hotel, Vancouver, BC

Makes 3 cups (750 mL)

» 1 Tbsp (15 mL) olive oil
» 10 prawn heads and shells
» 1 Tbsp (15 mL) Pernod (or cognac)
» 4 cups (1 L) fish stock (recipe above)
» 2 medium onions, peeled and chopped
» 2 medium carrots, chopped
» 2 celery stalks, chopped
» 3 cloves garlic, peeled
» 1 Tbsp (15 mL) tomato paste
» 4 sprigs tarragon
» 1 bay leaf
» 1 whole star anise
» 2 cups (500 mL) whipping cream
» Lemon juice to taste
» Salt to taste

Heat the olive oil in a large frying pan over medium-high heat. Add the prawn heads and shells and cook them until they are bright pink and the shells are crispy, about 2 minutes. Deglaze the pan with the Pernod and reduce the liquid to about 2 Tbsp (30 mL). Put the mixture in a medium stockpot with enough of the fish stock just to cover it.

Sauté the onions, carrots, celery, and garlic in a medium saucepan for 8 to 10 minutes, or until the onions are caramelized. Add the tomato paste, tarragon, bay leaf, and star anise. Simmer the mixture over medium heat, being careful not to boil it. Periodically skim off any foam or scum from the surface of the stock. After 2 hours add the cream and simmer the bisque for another 15 minutes. Strain it through a fine-mesh sieve and discard the solids. Pour the bisque into a blender and blend it until it is smooth. Add lemon juice and salt to taste.

Rich Shellfish Stock and Bisque

Jane Mundy

Makes 4 cups (1 L) stock or bisque starter

SHELLFISH STOCK

» 2 Tbsp (30 mL) olive oil
» 2 to 3 lb (1 to 1.5 kg) seafood shells (lobster, prawn, or shrimp)
» 3 cloves garlic, cut in half
» 3 celery stalks, roughly chopped
» 1 tomato, roughly chopped
» 1 large onion, roughly chopped
» 1 large fennel bulb, roughly chopped
» 1 carrot, roughly chopped
» ½ cup (125 mL) field mushrooms, roughly chopped
» ½ cup (125 mL) brandy
» ½ cup (125 mL) dry sherry
» 1 tsp (5 mL) whole black peppercorns
» 6 cups (1.5 L) fish stock (see previous page)
» 1 tsp (5 mL) salt
» 3 sprigs thyme
» 2 bay leaves
» 1 tsp (5 mL) fennel seeds

BISQUE

» ¼ cup (60 mL) tomato paste
» ½ cup (125 mL) whipping cream
» 1½ Tbsp (22.5 mL) cornstarch

» 2 Tbsp (30 mL) water
» 1 lb (500 g) cooked seafood (lobster, prawns, or scallops)

SHELLFISH STOCK

Heat the olive oil in a large stockpot over medium-high heat and sauté the seafood shells, stirring them occasionally, for about 8 minutes. Add the garlic, vegetables, brandy, sherry, and peppercorns and simmer the mixture, stirring, for about 5 minutes. Add the fish stock, salt, thyme, bay leaves, and fennel seeds and simmer, uncovered, for about 1 hour, skimming the surface when necessary.

Pour the mixture through a fine-mesh sieve into a large bowl, pressing it to get every drop. Discard the solids. At this point you can refrigerate the stock in an airtight container or freeze it.

BISQUE STARTER

Pour the stock into a large saucepan. Whisk in the tomato paste and simmer until the stock is reduced to about 3 cups (750 mL), about 10 minutes. Add the cream and simmer another 5 minutes. Mix the cornstarch and water in a small bowl, and then whisk them into the stock, stirring constantly for 2 minutes.

Add the cooked seafood, and simmer the bisque until it is heated through, about 1 minute.

Clarified Butter

Jane Mundy

Clarified butter has had the milk solids and water removed. It is called for in recipes that require a higher smoke point, so you can cook with butter without browning and burning. *About 1¼ cups (310 mL) of butter will produce 1 cup (250 mL) of clarified butter*

To clarify butter, melt the butter slowly in a heavy pot. Let it sit for a bit to separate. Skim off the foam that rises to the top, and gently pour the butter off the milk solids, which will have settled to the bottom. Pour into a glass jar with a tight-fitting lid and refrigerate.

Crème Fraîche

Jane Mundy

Crème fraîche, a soured cream, is a staple in French cooking. It has a slightly sour, nutty taste and velvety texture. *Makes about 2 cups (500 mL)*

» 2 cups (500 mL) whipping cream
» ¼ cup (60 mL) buttermilk

In a small saucepan, heat the cream until it is just warm to the touch (about 100°F/40°C). Remove from the heat and stir in the buttermilk, and then transfer the mixture to a large Mason jar. Put cheesecloth over the top and secure it with an elastic band. Let the jar sit in a warm place in the kitchen for two days. Once you see the crème fraîche thicken, refrigerate for one day.

You can whip the crème fraîche to make it even thicker. If you like, add 1 Tbsp (15 mL) each of lemon zest and chives.

Hollandaise Sauce

Jane Mundy

This sauce is best served immediately, but you can also keep it warm for a few hours in a Thermos or covered over a pan of warm water. *Makes 1 cup (250 mL)*

» 2 Tbsp (30 mL) water
» 2 egg yolks
» 1 cup (250 mL) clarified butter, warmed (recipe on facing page)
» Juice of ½ lemon
» ½ tsp (2 mL) cayenne pepper
» ¾ tsp (4 mL) salt

Put the water and egg yolks into a metal or glass bowl over a pot of simmering water. Make sure the base of the bowl does not touch the water. Whisk until light and creamy.

Remove the bowl from the water and gradually whisk in the clarified butter until thick. Next, whisk in the lemon juice, cayenne pepper, and salt.

Beurre Blanc

Jane Mundy

Literally translated, beurre blanc means "white butter," a rich butter sauce that is the base for a number of sauces. *Makes 1½ cups (375 mL)*

» ½ cup (125 mL) minced shallots
» ½ cup (125 mL) dry white wine
» 2 Tbsp (30 mL) white wine vinegar
» ⅓ cup (80 mL) fish stock (see page 289)
» 3 Tbsp (45 mL) whipping cream
» ¾ cup (185 mL) unsalted butter, cubed
» Salt and white pepper to taste

Put the shallots, wine, and vinegar into a small saucepan over medium-high heat and simmer until nearly all the liquid is evaporated, leaving about 2 Tbsp (30 mL). Add the fish stock and cream and simmer until reduced a bit more.

Lower the heat and gradually whisk in the butter, one cube at a time. Season to taste with salt and pepper.

Tapenade

Don Letendre, Elixir Bistro, Opus Hotel, Vancouver, BC

Makes ¾ cup (185 mL)

» ½ cup (125 mL) black olives, pitted (not canned)
» 1 large shallot, chopped
» 2 cloves garlic
» 1 Tbsp (15 mL) caperberries, rinsed
» 3 canned white anchovy fillets
» 2 Tbsp (30 mL) balsamic vinegar
» 1 Tbsp (15 mL) fresh lemon juice
» ¼ cup (60 mL) olive oil
» Salt and pepper to taste

Place the olives, shallot, garlic, caperberries, anchovies, balsamic vinegar, and lemon juice in a food processor and pulse into a paste. Continue pulsing the paste while adding the olive oil in a steady stream. Season the tapenade to taste with salt and pepper.

Curry Paste

Jane Mundy

Red or green curry paste is readily available at most supermarkets, but it can easily be made from scratch. *Makes ⅔ cup (160 mL)*

» 12 cloves garlic, chopped
» 10 fresh green or red chilies, chopped
» 3 stalks lemongrass, minced
» 2 Tbsp (30 mL) minced fresh ginger (peeled)
» 2 Tbsp (30 mL) finely chopped cilantro
» 2 Tbsp (30 mL) peanut oil
» 1 Tbsp (15 mL) ground coriander
» 2 tsp (10 mL) cumin seeds
» 1 tsp (5 mL) cayenne pepper
» 1 tsp (5 mL) salt
» 1 tsp (5 mL) anchovy paste
» Zest of 1 lime

Pulse all the ingredients in a food processor, using a spatula to push the ingredients down the sides of the bowl, until a smooth paste forms. Refrigerate in an airtight container for up to one month.

Anchovy Butter

Barbara-jo McIntosh, Barbara-Jo's Books to Cooks,
Vancouver, BC

A great thing to have in the freezer is a prepared butter that will accent numerous dishes. This butter is wonderful tossed on pasta or served with a strong-flavoured fish like salmon or albacore tuna. Anchovy paste spread on bread and butter at teatime was a favourite in Victorian England. *Makes 1 lb (500 g)*

» 1 lb (500 g) butter, room temperature
» One 1¾ oz (50 g) can anchovy fillets
» ½ cup (125 mL) chopped Italian flat-leaf parsley
» ½ cup (125 mL) diced pimiento
» 2 shallots, finely chopped

Pulse all the ingredients in a food processor, using a spatula to push them down, until they are uniformly distributed throughout the butter.

Lay 16 inches (40 cm) of waxed paper lengthwise on a clean work surface. Place all the anchovy butter one-third of the way up the wax paper. Fold the end nearest you up and over the butter and roll it to form a uniform 2-inch (5 cm) cylinder. Tightly wrap the ends. Wrap the waxed paper roll with plastic wrap and store it in the freezer.

When required, simply cut ⅓ inch (8 mm) of the roll per serving.

Mayonnaise

Jane Mundy

This recipe will keep in the refrigerator for up to one week. You can either whisk it by hand or use a food processor. *Makes 1¼ cups (310 mL)*

» 1 large egg
» 1 large egg yolk
» 2 tsp (10 mL) white wine vinegar (or lemon juice, to make lemon mayonnaise)
» ½ tsp (2 mL) salt
» 1¼ cups (310 mL) sunflower oil (or olive oil)

Have all the ingredients at room temperature. Place the egg, egg yolk, vinegar, and salt into a large metal bowl or food processor. Slowly add the oil in a steady stream, while whisking constantly, until the mixture is emulsified.

At this point, you can whisk in fresh herbs and lemon zest, mustard, or Pernod and chopped fennel. Experiment!

Aioli

Jane Mundy

Aioli is a staple condiment, the Mediterranean's answer to mayonnaise. It can be used as a dip, or to dollop on

soup—it's very versatile. Aioli is typically served at room temperature. Leftover sauce should be refrigerated and served within a week. *Makes ¾ cup (185 mL)*

» 4 cloves garlic, minced
» ½ tsp (2 mL) salt
» 1 large egg yolk
» 3 tsp (45 mL) fresh lemon juice
» ¾ cup (185 mL) extra virgin olive oil

Sprinkle the minced garlic with the salt and pound it in a mortar and pestle or grind in a coffee grinder. Transfer it to a medium bowl and add the egg yolk and lemon juice. Beat the mixture together with a hand-held electric mixer. Slowly add the olive oil in a steady stream to make a thick mixture, almost like mayonnaise.

Tartar Sauce

Jane Mundy

Needs no introduction! *Makes about ¾ cup (185 mL)*

» ½ cup (125 mL) mayonnaise (see page 292)
» 1 Tbsp (15 mL) chopped chives
» 1 Tbsp (15 mL) chopped parsley
» 1 tsp (5 mL) minced green olives
» 1 tsp (5 mL) minced sweet gherkins
» 1 tsp (5 mL) minced capers

Mix all the ingredients together. Instead of homemade, you could use a good-quality store-bought mayonnaise.

Salsa Verde

Jane Mundy

This recipe adds zest to just about any grilled fish. *Makes 1½ cups (375 mL)*

» ½ cup (125 mL) each baby spinach and arugula leaves
» 1 bunch Italian flat-leaf parsley
» 6 anchovy fillets (from a can)

» 2 cloves garlic, minced
» 2 Tbsp (30 mL) capers, drained
» 1 Tbsp (15 mL) mint leaves
» 1 Tbsp (15 mL) Dijon mustard
» Juice of 1 lemon
» 1 cup (250 mL) sunflower oil (or olive oil)

Blanch the spinach and arugula leaves in boiling water for 1 minute. Drain them and cool them under cold running water. Squeeze them dry. Put all the ingredients except the oil in a blender or food processor and blend them until they are smooth. Slowly add the olive oil in a steady stream until the mixture looks like a thin mayonnaise.

Old Bay Spice

Jane Mundy

Old Bay Spice, a chef's choice spice combo, originated in the 1940s in Maryland's Chesapeake Bay area. *Makes about ¼ cup (60 mL)*

» 1 Tbsp (15 mL) bay leaves
» 2½ tsp (12 mL) celery seeds
» 1½ tsp (7 mL) mustard seeds
» ¼ tsp (1 mL) cardamom seeds
» 1 tsp (5 mL) paprika
» 1 tsp (5 mL) ground black pepper
» ½ tsp (2 mL) ground white pepper
» ½ tsp (2 mL) ground nutmeg
» ½ tsp (2 mL) ground cloves
» ½ tsp (2 mL) ground ginger
» ¼ tsp (1 mL) ground allspice
» ¼ tsp (1 mL) red pepper flakes

Grind the bay leaves, celery seeds, mustard seeds, and cardamom seeds in a mortar and pestle (or a coffee grinder). Add the remaining ingredients and mix well. Transfer the mixture to an airtight container and store it in a cool cupboard for up to several weeks.

Shichimi Togarashi

Jane Mundy

This is the basic recipe for togarashi, also known as Japanese seven-spice. If you can't find sansho or lemon pepper, use black peppercorns. *Makes ¼ cup (60 mL)*

NOTE: Sansho, also called Szechuan pepper, can be found at Chinese or other Asian grocery stores.

» 1 Tbsp (15 mL) sansho powder (or lemon pepper)
» 1 Tbsp (15 mL) ground chili pepper
» 1 Tbsp (15 mL) poppy seeds
» 2 tsp (10 mL) black or golden sesame seeds
» 1 Tbsp (15 mL) dried tangerine (or orange) peel
» 2 tsp (10 mL) dried garlic flakes
» 1 tsp (5 mL) nori flakes (or dry and crumble a nori sheet)

Grind the sansho powder, chili powder, poppy seeds, and sesame seeds in a mortar and pestle (or a coffee grinder). Stir in the tangerine peel, garlic, and nori. Transfer the mixture to an airtight container. Refrigerated, it will keep for one month.

Spice Bundle

Jane Mundy

These spices re-create the taste of New Orleans and are a typical addition to the traditional shrimp boil in late summer. You can buy commercial brands, but it's more rewarding to make your own. *Makes ⅓ cup (80 mL)*

» 3 Tbsp (45 mL) coriander seeds
» 1 Tbsp (15 mL) crumbled bay leaves
» 1 Tbsp (15 mL) mustard seeds
» 1 Tbsp (15 mL) dill seeds
» 8 whole allspice berries
» 4 to 6 small dried hot chilies

Place a 12-inch (30 cm) square piece of cheesecloth onto a clean work surface. Spoon the spices into the centre and crush the seeds using a rolling pin to release the aromas. Gather the edges of the cloth together and tie them with kitchen string. Store in a tightly closed container in a cool, dry, dark place; shelf life is about six months.

best
FLAVOURS *and*
SEASONINGS

You can't go wrong combining ingredients such as lemon juice, salt and pepper, butter, shallots, *fines herbes* (i.e., chervil, chives, parsley, and tarragon), and a splash of white wine with just about any seafood. Many fish recipes call for fennel, garlic, and ginger. And some fish are like a blank slate—they work well with any flavour. Fortunately we are blessed with many options in Canada, and if you can step outside the cooking comfort zone, there are many different herbs and spices, veggies, and other foods that marry beautifully with seafood, some of them unexpected.

Texture is equally important to flavour when it comes to balancing a dish. Something crunchy like hemp seed, for instance, works well with silky sablefish, and it adds immensely to the dish's "wow" factor.

After perusing and testing the recipes submitted for this book by innovative and knowledgeable chefs, I put together the following list that matches specific fish and seafood with their most compatible ingredients. Of course, this is a matter of personal taste, and you will inevitably come up with your own favourite flavour pairings.

FRUITS AND VEGETABLES	
apple	herring, mackerel, trout
apricots	shrimp and prawns
artichoke	halibut, lobster
arugula	catfish, pickerel, shrimp and prawns, walleye
Asian pear	arctic char
asparagus	crab, halibut, sablefish
avocado	albacore tuna, catfish, crab, lobster, mahi mahi, scallops
beets	albacore tuna, mackerel, mahi mahi, sablefish, salmon, sardines
beets, pickled	herring

FRUITS AND VEGETABLES (CONT'D)	
blueberries	salmon
Brussels sprouts	barramundi
butternut squash	arctic char, scallops
cabbage, Savoy	mahi mahi, Pacific cod, scallops
cantaloupe	scallops
cauliflower	mahi mahi
celeriac (celery root)	albacore tuna, Pacific cod
celery	clams
coconut	mahi mahi, sablefish
corn	crab, lobster, scallops, shrimp and prawns
cranberries	crab
cucumber	albacore tuna, mackerel, salmon, sturgeon
eggplant	albacore tuna
eggplant, smoked	mackerel, swordfish, trout
endive	trout
escarole	octopus
figs, green	squid
grapefruit	crab, halibut, sardines
ground cherries	scallops
Jerusalem artichoke (or sunroot or sunchoke)	scallops
leek	clams, halibut, oysters
lemon, preserved	anchovies, sardines

mango	mahi mahi, scallops, trout (green mango)
melon (any kind)	mahi mahi, shrimp and prawns
mushrooms	Pacific cod, sablefish, scallops
onion, red	herring
orange	arctic char, barramundi, crayfish, lobster, mahi mahi (blood oranges), octopus, salmon, sardines, striped bass, swordfish
papaya or passion fruit	squid
peas	lobster (snap peas), spot prawns, shrimp, swordfish
pineapple	salmon
plums	squid
radicchio	albacore tuna, octopus
radishes	anchovies, trout
shallots	halibut, mackerel, mussels, oysters
sorrel	arctic char, crayfish
spinach	scallops
squash	clams, pollock
sweet potato	barramundi
tomatillos	mahi mahi, swordfish
tomatoes	lingcod, pickerel and yellow perch (green tomatoes)
watercress	Atlantic croaker, mahi mahi, northern pike, sablefish, sardines, sea urchin, trout

HERBS AND SPICES

basil	arctic char, clams, halibut, lingcod, lobster, mussels, Pacific cod, salmon, scallops, shrimp and prawns, squid, striped bass, trout
bay leaf	mussels, Pacific cod
Cajun spice	pickerel
cayenne pepper	scallops
chervil	salmon, scallops

chilies, cracked	anchovies
chili peppers	albacore tuna, shrimp and prawns, squid (red chilies)
chipotle peppers	mussels, octopus, sablefish, trout
chives	albacore tuna, crab, scallops
cilantro	albacore tuna, arctic char, crab, mahi mahi, salmon, scallops, squid, swordfish
curry (leaves, powder, or paste)	catfish, herring, mussels, oysters, squid, trout
dill	salmon, trout
fennel seeds	sardines, sturgeon
ginger	catfish, oysters, scallops, striped bass, sea urchin
jalapeños	octopus
juniper berry	salmon
lemongrass	crab, lobster, mahi mahi, shrimp and prawns
lime leaves	Atlantic croaker
masala	shrimp and prawns
mint	mackerel, mahi mahi, octopus, Pacific cod, scallops, shrimp and prawns, sturgeon
nutmeg	shrimp and prawns
paprika, smoked	squid
parsley	anchovies
peppercorns, green	albacore tuna
rosemary	halibut
saffron	crayfish, lobster, mussels, oysters, shrimp and prawns, Pacific cod, yellow perch
sage	trout
shiso (Japanese basil)	shrimp and prawns
tarragon	crayfish, lobster, trout

HERBS AND SPICES (CONT'D)	
Thai basil	Atlantic croaker, scallops, tilapia
thyme	albacore tuna, clams, crayfish, halibut, mussels, oysters, Pacific cod, northern pike, sardines, striped bass
vanilla	lobster

NUTS AND SEEDS	
almonds	anchovies, barramundi, mackerel, striped bass, trout
cashews	barramundi
hazelnuts	barramundi, mackerel
hemp seed	northern pike, sablefish
pine nuts	halibut, mackerel, sablefish, swordfish, trout
pistachios	arctic char, pickerel, walleye

BEANS AND LENTILS	
black beans	catfish, sablefish, shrimp and prawns
du Puy lentils	arctic char, Pacific cod, salmon
edamame (green soybeans)	scallops
fava beans	albacore tuna, salmon
garbanzo beans (or chickpeas)	albacore tuna, octopus
white navy beans	anchovies, clams, halibut, northern pike, sardines, squid

OTHER INGREDIENTS	
bacon	albacore tuna, arctic char, catfish, clams, mackerel, mussels, northern pike, scallops, sturgeon, trout
balsamic vinegar	trout
black bean sauce	crab

OTHER INGREDIENTS (CONT'D)	
brown butter	sablefish, swordfish, trout
buttermilk	pollock
capers	anchovies, mackerel, sablefish, sardines, any oily and deep-flavoured fish
chorizo sausage	clams, mussels, octopus, shrimp and prawns
coconut milk	albacore tuna, mussels, oysters, scallops, squid, tilapia
cornmeal	pickerel, trout
currants	swordfish
feta cheese	mahi mahi
harissa (hot red pepper paste)	mussels
honey	salmon, sturgeon
horseradish	lake whitefish, oysters, salmon
maple syrup	Pacific cod, salmon
maple-soy glaze	mackerel
miso	Pacific cod, sablefish, salmon
mozzarella	lingcod
olives	arctic char (kalamata), catfish (green olives), mackerel, Pacific cod, sablefish (black olives), swordfish
pistou (basil sauce)	shrimp and prawns
ponzu (Japanese citrus-based sauce)	oysters
prosciutto	sablefish
raisins, yellow	sardines
rouille	lake whitefish
smoked ham hock	clams
sour cream	northern pike
soy sauce	salmon, swordfish

OTHER INGREDIENTS (CONT'D)	
sun-dried tomatoes	sardines
tamarind	lobster, sablefish, squid
truffles	shrimp and prawns
wasabi	albacore tuna, Pacific cod, salmon
yogurt	sturgeon

ALCOHOL	
brandy	any seafood
champagne	oysters
muscadet	oysters
Pernod	mussels
sake	octopus
sherry	shrimp and prawns
vodka	shrimp and prawns
white wine	any fish or seafood

FISH	FRUITS AND VEGETABLES	HERBS AND SPICES	NUTS AND SEEDS	BEANS AND LENTILS	OTHER INGREDIENTS (INCLUDING ALCOHOL)
albacore tuna	avocado beets celeriac cucumber eggplant radicchio	chili peppers chives cilantro green peppercorns thyme		fava beans garbanzo beans	bacon coconut milk wasabi
anchovies	preserved lemon radishes	cracked chilies parsley	almonds	white navy beans	capers
arctic char	Asian pear butternut squash orange sorrel	basil cilantro	pistachios	du Puy lentils	bacon kalamata olives
Atlantic croaker	watercress	lime leaves Thai basil			
barramundi	Brussels sprouts orange sweet potato		almonds cashews hazelnuts		
catfish	arugula avocado	curry (leaves, powder, or paste) ginger		black beans	bacon green olives
clams	celery leek squash	basil thyme		white navy beans	bacon chorizo sausage smoked ham hock
cod, Pacific	celeriac mushrooms Savoy cabbage	basil bay leaf mint saffron thyme		du Puy lentils	maple syrup miso olives wasabi
crab, Dungeness and stone	asparagus avocado corn cranberries grapefruit	chives cilantro lemongrass			black bean sauce
crayfish	orange sorrel	saffron tarragon thyme			
haddock. *See* cod, Pacific					

FISH	FRUITS AND VEGETABLES	HERBS AND SPICES	NUTS AND SEEDS	BEANS AND LENTILS	OTHER INGREDIENTS (INCLUDING ALCOHOL)
halibut, Pacific	artichoke asparagus grapefruit leek shallots	basil rosemary thyme	pine nuts	white navy beans	
herring	apple pickled beets red onion	curry (leaves, powder, or paste)			
lingcod	tomatoes	basil			mozzarella
lobster	artichoke avocado corn orange snap peas	basil lemongrass saffron tarragon vanilla			tamarind
mackerel, king and Spanish	apple beets cucumber shallots smoked eggplant	mint	almonds hazelnuts pine nuts		bacon capers maple-soy glaze olives
mahi mahi	avocado beets blood oranges cauliflower coconut mango melon (any kind) Savoy cabbage tomatillos watercress	cilantro lemongrass mint			feta cheese
mussels	shallots	basil bay leaf chipotle peppers curry (leaves, powder, or paste) saffron thyme			bacon chorizo sausage coconut milk harissa (hot red pepper paste) Pernod
octopus	escarole orange radicchio	chipotle peppers jalapeños mint		garbanzo beans	chorizo sausage sake

FISH	FRUITS AND VEGETABLES	HERBS AND SPICES	NUTS AND SEEDS	BEANS AND LENTILS	OTHER INGREDIENTS (INCLUDING ALCOHOL)
oysters	leek shallots	curry (leaves, powder, or paste) ginger saffron thyme			champagne coconut milk horseradish muscadet ponzu (Japanese citrus-based sauce)
pickerel	arugula green tomatoes	Cajun spice	pistachios		cornmeal
pike, northern	watercress	thyme	hemp seed	white navy beans	bacon sour cream
pollock	squash				buttermilk
prawns. *See* shrimp and prawns					
sablefish	asparagus beets coconut mushrooms watercress	chipotle peppers	hemp seed pine nuts	black beans	black olives brown butter capers miso prosciutto tamarind
salmon	beets blueberries cucumber orange pineapple	basil chervil cilantro dill juniper berry		du Puy lentils fava beans	honey horseradish maple syrup miso soy sauce wasabi
sardines	beets grapefruit orange preserved lemon watercress	fennel seeds thyme		white navy beans	capers sun-dried tomatoes yellow raisins
scallops (bay, sea, Pacific, or diver)	avocado butternut squash cantaloupe corn ground cherries Jerusalem artichoke mango mushrooms Savoy cabbage spinach	basil cayenne pepper chervil chives cilantro ginger mint Thai basil		edamame (green soybeans)	bacon coconut milk

FISH	FRUITS AND VEGETABLES	HERBS AND SPICES	NUTS AND SEEDS	BEANS AND LENTILS	OTHER INGREDIENTS (INCLUDING ALCOHOL)
shrimp and prawns	apricots arugula corn melon peas	basil chili peppers lemongrass masala mint nutmeg saffron shiso (Japanese basil)		black beans	chorizo sausage pistou (basil sauce) sherry truffles vodka
squid (calamari)	green figs papaya passion fruit plums	basil cilantro curry (leaves, powder, or paste) red chilies smoked paprika		white navy beans	coconut milk tamarind
striped bass	orange	basil ginger thyme	almonds		
sturgeon	cucumber	fennel seeds mint			bacon honey yogurt
swordfish	orange peas smoked eggplant tomatillos	cilantro	pine nuts		brown butter currants olives soy sauce
tilapia		Thai basil			coconut milk
trout	apple endive green mango radishes smoked eggplant watercress	basil chipotle peppers curry (leaves, powder, or paste) dill sage tarragon	almonds pine nuts		bacon balsamic vinegar brown butter cornmeal
urchin, sea	watercress	ginger			
walleye	arugula		pistachios		
whitefish, lake					horseradish rouille
yellow perch	green tomatoes	saffron			

ABOUT THE CONTRIBUTORS

ERIC AKIS (VICTORIA) is a food writer and chef and makes numerous food-related appearances on radio and television and at culinary events. Prior to becoming a journalist, Eric trained as a professional chef and pastry chef, and worked for 15 years in a variety of operations, from fine hotels to restaurants to catering operations.

TED ANDERSON (REFUEL, VANCOUVER) has cooked at restaurants in Australia and Japan and travelled the world, but his culinary career was launched at home in Vancouver. "At Refuel we pursue the best-tasting product available, as this is the only way to ensure the quality the guests deserve." Ted's high standards and cooking ability helped Refuel (formerly called Fuel) snag 2007's Best New Restaurant nod from *Vancouver* magazine.

KAREN BARNABY (THE FISH HOUSE IN STANLEY PARK, VANCOUVER) is an award-winning executive chef, cookbook author, *Vancouver Sun* food columnist, and cooking teacher. Karen also manages to squeeze in some volunteer time for a number of worthwhile causes. Her philosophy is keep it simple, keep it tasty, and keep thinking outside the box.

ROBERT BELCHAM (REFUEL RESTAURANT AND CAMPAGNOLO RESTAURANT, VANCOUVER), chef and proprietor of Refuel, was named 2009 Chef of the Year by *Vancouver* magazine. He is committed to local and sustainable foods and believes that "the best-tasting ingredients come from our own backyard. Mother Nature has given us this bounty and we must remember to protect what she has given us for the generations of chefs and diners to come."

NED BELL (CABANA BAR AND GRILLE, KELOWNA, BC) has always had a passion for cooking. Ned began his career in Vancouver under the tutelage of Le Crocodile's Michel Jacob, then served as sous-chef at Rob Feenie's Lumière. He became a regular on Food Network Canada's *Cook Like A Chef* and has been voted one of *Western Living*'s Top 40 Foodies (Under Forty).

DAVID BESTON (JERICHO TENNIS CLUB, VANCOUVER) started cooking at the age of 14 and has never looked back. His life journey has been about turning local bounty into a meaningful culinary craft. Today, David's philosophy of embracing and protecting nature's bounty is reflected in the on-site herb and vegetable gardens at Jericho and through side projects such as the Chefs to the Field culinary competition that raises funds for agriculture in BC's Fraser Valley.

JULIAN BOND (PACIFIC INSTITUTE OF CULINARY ARTS (PICA), VANCOUVER) landed in BC in 1995 after graduating from culinary college in the UK and honing his skills there. He soon became a founding member of the Green Table Network, an organization that aims to make food service sustainable. Now executive chef and program director at PICA (the first culinary school in Canada to partner with Ocean Wise), Julian combines his energy, talents, and passion for teaching to promote kitchen sustainability among the next generation of chefs.

WALTER BONN (BARLEY STATION BREW PUB, SALMON ARM, BC) has been in the industry for a good 30 years and prefers to do things from scratch—such as filleting fish.

ALLAN BOSOMWORTH AND KARL GREGG (2 CHEFS AND A TABLE, VANCOUVER) combine talents to create inventive menus built around the seasonal foods available to them. Whether they're serving up hearty lunches to locals or creating custom menus for the catering business they run out of their 27-seat bistro, they showcase their passion in everything they do.

NICHOLAS BUDRESKI (OWNER, CANESP, HALIFAX) is the owner of a boutique seafood distribution company. When he is not trying to develop new local sustainable fare, Nick is a part-time professor of international trade and a full-time father of three. He can also be seen huffing and puffing on the soccer pitch, desperately trying to put the ball in the back of the net.

ANDREA CARLSON (BISHOP'S, VANCOUVER) honed her culinary skills under Rob Clark at C Restaurant, first as a pastry chef and later as sous-chef. Next up, the Sooke Harbour House on Vancouver Island. Andrea returned to Vancouver as chef de cuisine at Raincity Grill, where she created the city's first "100-Mile Menu." In 2007, she jumped at the chance to become executive chef at Bishop's, where she brings her next-generation sensibilities to the "locavore" movement started by Mr. Bishop more than 20 years ago.

PAUL CECCONI (LOCAL LOUNGE & GRILLE, SUMMERLAND, BC) became interested in food at 13. He honed his skills and developed his style by working at a variety of establishments, ranging from a bakery to various fine-dining restaurants around Vancouver. After a number of years at Four Seasons hotels in Vancouver and Australia, Paul moved to Summerland. He believes "the closer to home the better."

ANDY CHAN (UBC FOOD SERVICES, VANCOUVER) has won two gold medals and one silver medal in culinary competitions for Canadian and North American college and university associations. When away from work, Andy can often be found at one of his neighbourhood farmers' markets, getting inspiration from their abundant selection. His kitchen philosophy is simple: cook with love, and love your food.

MARY-ANNE CHARLES (FRESH OFF THE BOAT OCEAN FOODS, WHITE ROCK, BC) strives to offer the freshest seafood available at Fresh Off The Boat, a family-run business that started by delivering fresh seafood to the doors of homes, restaurants, and catering companies around BC's Lower Mainland. The company grew through word of mouth and now sells its catch at Surrey farmers' markets.

DANIEL CHIANG (MOSAIC RESTAURANT, HYATT REGENCY VANCOUVER) began his culinary training in his dad's butcher shop at age 16. He went on to graduate from VCC's culinary arts program and Dubrulle Culinary Institute. During his tenure at the Hyatt Regency, Daniel worked with two-Michelin-star chef Ron Siegel at Masa's in San Francisco, where he learned to use fresh and simple ingredients.

JONATHAN CHOVANCEK (CULINARY CAPERS CATERING, VANCOUVER) worked in award-winning restaurants, such as the Sooke Harbour House on Vancouver Island. In 2006 he earned rave reviews from international patrons at the Olympic Winter Games in Torino, Italy, where he spearheaded the Culinary Capers kitchen at British Columbia–Canada Place. As exclusive caterer for the British Columbia–Canada Pavilion in Beijing, China, Jonathan once again oversaw Culinary Capers' cuisine during the 2008 Olympic Summer Games.

ROBERT CLARK (C RESTAURANT, VANCOUVER) believes that "as chefs, our job is not only about serving great-tasting food, but encouraging our staff and guests to learn how to get sustainably produced food to the table." Robert was honoured at the 2006 Monterey Bay Aquarium's Cooking for Solutions as the year's Canadian seafood ambassador and recognized for his outstanding dedication to working with sustainably harvested seafood. He continually promotes BC as a burgeoning seafood and agri-food producing region, and participates in exchange programs where he promotes local products and shares his philosophies.

DAMIAN CONNOLLY (INDISHPENSABLE, VANCOUVER) hails from Ireland, where he began working in kitchens at 15. He was fortunate to learn from some of Ireland's best chefs and later in Greece and aboard the QE2. Damian joined Indish in 2007. He was drawn to the concept of taking the restaurant to the customer and the challenge of making every customer a chef in their home.

FRÉDÉRIC COUTON (THE CANNERY SEAFOOD RESTAURANT, VANCOUVER (NOW DEFUNCT)) trained at Michelin-starred restaurants in France, honing his culinary skills in the kitchens of the Paris and Geneva Hiltons, and then pursued his career in Montreal, Bangkok, and Vancouver. Frédéric joined The Cannery in 1996 and found it the perfect setting for his passion for seafood. In 2004 he wrote *The Cannery Seafood House Cookbook*.

DAVID CYMET (PACIFIC INSTITUTE OF CULINARY ARTS (PICA), VANCOUVER) is a newcomer to the industry. He is driven by a passion for cooking and by the energy found in the kitchen. A recent graduate of PICA, David has launched his career in the kitchen of a Vancouver-area hotel.

QUANG DANG (DIVA AT THE MET, VANCOUVER) exemplifies the new breed of chef making the Pacific Northwest's food scene avant-garde and ultra-modern. His is a blend of styles, mixing magic with kitchen improvisation in take-no-prisoners fashion. Quang was previously chef de cuisine at C Restaurant—Robert Clark, executive chef at C, says: "He has studied the food chain. He knows where food is coming from, where it was harvested, who fished it, and how it was handled. He is an ardent advocate of sustainability and respects every element and aspect needed to retain and maintain it."

PETER DEBRUYN (STRATHCONA HOTEL, VICTORIA) completed a Bachelor of Commerce in Entrepreneurial Management at Royal Roads University. Peter has worked in restaurants in BC and Alberta, including Milestones, Ric's Grill, and the Six Mile Public House. As executive chef, Peter's philosophy is to serve quality food made from scratch while using as many local ingredients as possible.

MEERU DHALWALA (VIJ'S, VANCOUVER) earned a degree in developmental studies and worked with various human rights and international development organizations before marrying Vikram Vij and joining Vij's in 1994. Meeru is committed to community involvement and devoted to regional ingredients on and off the job, especially those grown and gathered sustainably.

TRISH DIXON (BREAKERS FRESH FOOD CAFÉ, TOFINO, BC) has owned and operated Breakers for over 12 years. Trish worked and lived in Vancouver for about six years until her love of the ocean brought her to Tofino, where she spent the next five years training under one of the town's most accomplished chefs. She jumped at the chance to develop her own restaurant, and has launched a Breakers Fresh Food Café franchise concept.

KATHLEEN DUNCAN (THE REEF CARIBBEAN RESTAURANT, VANCOUVER) is a Red Seal chef with over 20 years' experience in the hotel and restaurant industries. She has travelled the globe and has a vast repertoire of cooking experience that ranges from working in high-end European hotels to helming the kitchens of small family-run restaurants.

ROB ERICKSON (WILD RICE, VANCOUVER) launched his career south of the border in Seattle and returned to BC where he worked at Vancouver's Bin 942, then went on to Langara Fishing Lodge. In the lodge's off-season, he taught Western-style cooking to Chinese students in Taiwan. In turn, under the tutelage of China's many culinary masters, he learned to cook the country's abundant regional cuisines.

ROB FEENIE (CACTUS CLUB CAFE, VANCOUVER). From France to North America, Rob Feenie is revered for his mastery of French cuisine. Under Rob's guidance, his former restaurant Lumière received the Relais Gourmand designation, and was awarded the Traditions et Qualité designation and an AAA Five Diamond rating. In addition to publishing three cookbooks and starring in *New Classics with Chef Rob Feenie* on Food Network Canada for five seasons, he is most noted for claiming the lucrative Iron Chef title. Feenie's dishes are clean and simple in construction, allowing premium ingredients to take the lead role. Only the best-quality ingredients, sourced from nearby purveyors of meat, seafood, produce, and baked goods, are used in each "Rob Feenie Signature" dish at the Cactus Club.

MANUEL FERREIRA (LE GAVROCHE, VANCOUVER) grew up and developed a love of food and wine in Portugal and France. In 1994, Manuel became sole owner of "Le Gav." Ferreira is a member of the American Wine Society, and November 2003 marked his induction into the exclusive Commanderies de Bordeaux.

BRIAN FODOR (THE LOBBY, PINNACLE HOTEL AT THE PIER, NORTH VANCOUVER) served a tour of duty as an officer in the Canadian navy while dreaming about becoming a cook and working in the restaurant industry. Travels to Italy and France, in particular, motivated him to get into the kitchen. He realized that food could mean more than mac and cheese and hot dogs. Brian has been the executive chef in many busy restaurants in locales such as Whistler, Toronto, and the Okanagan.

CHRISTIAN GAUDREAULT (TOMATO FRESH FOOD CAFÉ, VANCOUVER) says that fresh food and family have always played a major role in his life, from his childhood in Quebec where he worked in his family's restaurant to his adult life, when he began exploring the hospitality field in Europe, Asia, India, and Australia. Christian spent several years developing his skills under Umberto Menghi, opened a pastry shop, and was sales and marketing director for Yves Veggie Cuisine and general manager of the café at two Capers organic food stores before opening Tomato.

PATRICK GAYLER (AURA RESTAURANT, INN AT LAUREL POINT, VICTORIA) has always loved cooking. He started competing at 15, which led to his joining Culinary Team Canada to compete at the World Cup in Luxembourg in 2010 and then at the IKA/World Culinary Olympics in Erfurt in 2012. Competitions help him to perfect aspects of his cooking, from organizing to presenting finished plates. He has also had the privilege of cooking for Queen Elizabeth II and for many celebrities.

DINO L. GAZZOLA (THE OBSERVATORY/GROUSE MOUNTAIN VISITOR FOOD SERVICES, NORTH VANCOUVER) was inspired by his grandmother. "As a child, my grandmother or some other family member always seemed to be cooking; it was common to have 30 people at the table on special occasions." Everything was made from scratch, the vegetables more often than not came from his grandfather's garden, and everyone participated in the preparation. This is the model Dino follows in his Grouse Mountain kitchens today.

WARREN GERAGHTY (WEST RESTAURANT, VANCOUVER) has a distinguished résumé that features stints in various three-Michelin-star establishments, including a position as executive chef at Marco Pierre White's L'Escargot restaurant in Soho, London. Having been drawn to Vancouver by its rising status on the world's culinary stage, Warren is energized by the region's unparalleled diversity. "It is entirely about using the ingredient at its natural peak, thoughtful preparation, and working with trusted purveyors."

KUNAL GHOSE (RED FISH BLUE FISH, VICTORIA) dreamed of a restaurant concept that wouldn't take a toll on the planet. Victoria's 100 percent Ocean Wise Red Fish Blue Fish changed that dream into reality in 2007. Kunal's love of the bounty of BC waters and the desire to keep it that way moulded his creative inspiration. "Adhering to Ocean Wise guidelines is a joy, not a challenge."

DAVID WILLIAM GRIMSHAW (SHAUGHNESSY RESTAURANT, VANCOUVER), a winner of the Escoffier Society Award, joined the Shaughnessy Restaurant in 1999 after stints at various fine dining establishments in Ontario and the eastern United States. He is committed to sourcing fresh ingredients from trusted suppliers in his area, and draws on international tastes and techniques to fashion unique dishes.

RYAN GUSTAFSON (EPIC RESTAURANT, FAIRMONT ROYAL YORK, TORONTO) is at the forefront of the sustainable food movement. He is committed to safeguarding traditional quality foods and is dedicated to sourcing local products. He is an enthusiastic supporter of the hotel's rooftop herbs, beehives, and grapevines.

ERIK HECK (GLOWBAL GRILL STEAKS & SATAY, VANCOUVER) was inspired by his father's culinary prowess and took great joy in helping put the family's daily meals on the table. Erik applied his gastronomic zeal to cooking positions in Vancouver restaurants Earls and Joe Fortes, before joining Glowbal Grill in 2006 as sous-chef. Erik is thrilled to put his own philosophies to work in the kitchen of Glowbal.

LUC JEAN (VELVET GLOVE, FAIRMONT WINNIPEG) recently returned home to Winnipeg from a world tour of culinary experiences. Stints in England, Sweden, and France paved the way for Luc's tenure at Charters Towers, at Jupiters Hotel & Casino on the Gold Coast of Australia. Under Luc's direction this Australian hot spot was voted best restaurant in Queensland for 2008.

ERIN KELLY (PACIFIC INSTITUTE OF CULINARY ARTS (PICA), VANCOUVER) says some of her earliest memories involve beachside bonfires and eating fresh clams that her dad would bring home while living on the East Coast. Happy to relocate to Vancouver after years in Toronto, she now enjoys the (sustainable) gifts the west coast waters have to offer and often champions the Ocean Wise cause at her workplace, the Granville Island–based Pacific Institute of Culinary Arts.

JAMIE KENNEDY (JAMIE KENNEDY KITCHENS, TORONTO) has respect for the products he buys and sells, and the world we live in. With a string of successful ventures that spans almost 30 years, Jamie is recognized as a pioneer of Canadian cuisine. In 2000, Jamie was honoured with the Gold Award as Chef of the Year by the Ontario Hostelry Institute, and published the cookbook *Jamie Kennedy's Seasons*. Jamie has spoken for causes including the Endangered Fish Alliance, World Wildlife Foundation, Living Ocean Society, and Seafood Watch.

ALBERT KIRBY, EVA MARIA JOE, AND KEN WRIGHT (CAFÉ, SQUAMISH LIL'WAT CULTURAL CENTRE, WHISTLER, BC). As the leading culinary ambassadors for the Squamish Lil'wat Cultural Centre, Eva Maria Joe (Lil'wat Nation) and Ken Wright (Squamish Nation) bring their traditions and culture together to create a unique culinary experience. Eva's deep roots in the Lil'wat culture enable her to infuse the menu with her nation's traditions and flavours. Her passion for her history speaks through the food she creates. Ken Wright's Squamish background in meat and fish preparation adds an element that most people outside the nations have never experienced. His experience as a hunter and provider in the community helps keep the original aspects of our cured products true to form. With the aid of Café manager Albert Kirby, Eva and Ken unite the traditional flavours and preparations of each nation in a contemporary setting, with recipes made nearly as they were many years ago using the simplest ingredients.

BEN KRAMER (DIVERSITY FOOD SERVICES INC. AT THE UNIVERSITY OF WINNIPEG) says, "These days, people want to know where their food comes from. They want to know that the choices they make are not having a negative impact on the world." In 2009, Ben made *Western Living* magazine's prestigious Top 40 Foodies (Under Forty) listing. Ben now oversees three on-campus restaurants and a demanding catering schedule.

DON LETENDRE (ELIXIR BISTRO, OPUS HOTEL, VANCOUVER) is a founding member of the Green Table Network, an organization dedicated to making food service sustainable. Don's contemporary and innovative cooking style blends diverse experience gained in Asia, at Tokyo's famed Domani Cucina restaurant and the Soba Ni Umazake Yoshimura, in Europe, at the Michelin-starred Le Manoir aux Quat'Saisons and L'Odéon, and at home, in some of Vancouver's top dining rooms. Don sits on the board of directors for the Chefs' Table Society of BC.

JEFF MASSEY (RESTAURANT 62, ABBOTSFORD, BC) has always enjoyed working with food and wine, putting an emphasis on quality ingredients. While working in some of Vancouver's top kitchens, Jeff became especially fond of cooking fresh seafood. "My philosophy has always been to create and maintain a menu that is simple and clean."

MIKE MCDERMID (VANCOUVER AQUARIUM AND OCEAN WISE, VANCOUVER) became fascinated with sea creatures at an early age, and continues to be amazed "that the most fantastical creature a child's imagination can dream up probably already exists in some form in the ocean." It's not surprising that he studied marine biology at university and chose to dedicate his career to sharing his passion for the ocean and its creatures—and, ultimately, to conserving them. In the course of his career, Mike has conducted research at the University of British Columbia and the Department of Fisheries and Oceans; he has been an educator at the Vancouver Aquarium, and has worked as a diver in a commercial fishery on the coast of BC. Now, as Ocean Wise Program Manager at the aquarium, he has the fortune to combine two great passions: his love for the oceans and his love of food.

BARBARA-JO MCINTOSH (BARBARA-JO'S BOOKS TO COOKS, VANCOUVER) is an award-winning food professional with over 25 years' experience in the food and hospitality industry. She opened Barbara-Jo's Elegant Home Cooking restaurant in 1990 and in 1997, she opened Barbara-Jo's Books to Cooks. Author of the bestselling *Tin Fish Gourmet*, Barbara-jo served on the James Beard Foundation Awards cookbook selection committee for six years. In 2003, *Vancouver* magazine honoured her with a lifetime achievement award for her many contributions to the local culinary scene.

DAVID MCRAE (PACIFIC URCHIN HARVESTERS ASSOCIATION) is a member of the board of directors of the Pacific Urchin Harvesters Association. David and his vessel the *Kuroshio* were featured on the Food Network in an episode of *Glutton for Punishment*, where David trained the host of the show, Bob Blumer, in the fine art of sea urchin diving.

COLIN METCALFE (CATCH RESTAURANT, CALGARY) graduated from the SAIT School of Hospitality and Tourism in 2005 and started working at Catch shortly thereafter. In 2009 he helped Catch win the Gold Medal Plates culinary competition in Calgary. Colin implemented the Ocean Wise program at Catch in 2007. He loves the challenge that cold prairie winters pose in making seasonal choices and he is proud to be a part of keeping the slow food movement going strong in southern Alberta.

MICHAEL MINSHULL (THE MARK AND THE PACIFIC RESTAURANTS, HOTEL GRAND PACIFIC, VICTORIA) grew up with the ocean, hailing from Sointula, a small fishing village on BC's west coast. He has worked at the Chateau Whistler and the Delta Whistler, the Fairmont Empress in Victoria, the Aerie Resort and Spa in Victoria (where he began to form closer bonds with local producers and learn the value of their products), and Dock 503 in Sidney, BC.

PAUL MON-KAU (THE DISTRICT SOCIAL HOUSE, NORTH VANCOUVER) was born in the Netherlands and grew up with a mix of European and North American cultures that now accents the unique vibe of his restaurants. He worked as a bartender, server, cook, bouncer, general manager, owner—and everything else in between. Eventually Paul realized that he had accomplished all he could working for others so, at the age of 31, he opened The District.

GEOFFREY MORDEN (FAIRMONT CHÂTEAU LAURIER, OTTAWA) travelled the world while growing up. After completing his culinary education in 1993, he began working at the Château Laurier, and passion and perseverance helped him climb the culinary ladder within the Fairmont hotel chain. He was executive sous-chef at the Château Laurier and the Fairmont Chateau Lake Louise, and executive chef at the Fairmont Winnipeg and the Fairmont Chateau Lake Louise. In 2008, Geoffrey returned to the Fairmont Château Laurier as executive chef.

KEN NAKANO (FAIRMONT EMPRESS, VICTORIA) was raised on traditional Japanese cuisine and developed an appreciation for homegrown seasonal ingredients from his parents, who also taught him the art of foraging wild foods such as clams, fiddleheads, and mushrooms. Ken has been executive sous-chef at The Fairmont Empress since 2006 and is a member of the Canadian Culinary Federation as well as of the Island Chefs' Collaborative.

DANIEL NOTKIN (RESTAURANT L'ORIGNAL, MONTREAL) is a self-proclaimed oysterologist. When not researching the most interesting advances in his avocation and the best seafood available, he can be found shucking oysters, cracking lobster, and waxing philosophical about seafood at L'Orignal, the small raw bar he runs in Montreal's Old Port.

FRANK PABST (BLUE WATER CAFÉ AND RAW BAR, VANCOUVER) is recognized for his creative flair, deft technique, and dedication to responsible seafood practices (as exemplified by his acclaimed "Unsung Heroes" menu). Thanks to his tenures in Michelin-starred restaurants throughout Germany and France, Frank's skills were honed in the classical discipline that shapes his cooking style today. Frank was named the 2008 Vancouver Culinary Champion in the Gold Medal Plates culinary competition and Silver Medalist at the Canadian Culinary Championships in 2009.

CHRISTABEL PADMORE AND PATRICK SIMPSON (LITTLE PIGGY CATERING, VICTORIA) have been cooking together for nearly six years. After several years as partner-owners of The Little Piggy, a bakery-café and event catering company, the two were married in Christabel's family home in France. At The Little Piggy they express their culinary values while working to increase their community's access to tasty and honest food.

ROB PARROTT (MANGIA E BEVI RISTORANTE, WEST VANCOUVER) has owned and cooked in Mangia E Bevi since April 2007. Prior to opening his own restaurant, he was chef at various Quattro group venues—some of Vancouver's top Italian restaurants—from 1993 until 2007.

ERIC PATEMAN (EDIBLE BRITISH COLUMBIA, VANCOUVER) created the culinary tourism company Edible BC in 2005. Eric has worked in the hospitality industry for over 15 years, both as a chef and as a hotel consultant. He is a past director of the BC Culinary Tourism Society and is a current member of the Chefs' Table Society.

RUSTY PENNO (BOFFINS CLUB, SASKATOON) has been in the food service industry for over 18 years, working in almost all facets of it. He finds his calling rewarding despite its many challenges. Rusty is proud to be from Saskatchewan and works hard to get the word out that it has much to offer in the way of agriculture, meats, and, of course, beautiful freshwater fish.

WILLIE PETZ (HOODOOS AT SUN RIVERS, KAMLOOPS, BC) has a passion for food, wine, and golf. He is a classically French-trained, award-winning chef who has been in the industry for over 35 years. Willie has also offered his time and expertise to two culinary apprenticeship boards, including that of Thompson Rivers University.

SCOTT POHORELIC (RIVER CAFÉ, CALGARY) began working in the industry at 16 and took over his first kitchen at 19. Scott completed the highly regarded culinary program at SAIT in Calgary and found his way to River Café, where he became chef. Scott's food philosophy stems from spending summers on his grandparents' farm where he experienced the taste of homegrown vegetables. Scott believes that "there is a direct correlation between a person's passion and the quality of the work they do. This is just as true for farmers as it is for cooks. It is the link that binds us."

PINO POSTERARO (CIOPPINO'S MEDITERRANEAN GRILL & ENOTECA, VANCOUVER) came to Canada from Italy at 12 and soon found himself working in his brother's restaurant. Pino returned to Europe, cooked in several well-known restaurants there, and then helmed the Ristorante Bologna in the Marina Mandarin Hotel in Singapore. In 1999, Pino opened the award-winning Cioppino's. In 2008, he was named Chef of the Year by *Vancouver* magazine, and in 2009, Cioppino's was named Restaurant of the Year.

ALESSANDRA AND JEAN-FRANCIS QUAGLIA (PROVENCE RESTAURANTS, VANCOUVER) met while rubbing shoulders in the kitchens of the south of France. They married in 1992 and moved from Jean-Francis' hometown of Marseilles to Vancouver, where they realized their dream of opening their own restaurant. In 1997, they opened Provence Mediterranean Grill in Point Grey, followed by Provence Marinaside in Yaletown in 2002.

ISAAC REDFERN (JERICHO TENNIS CLUB, VANCOUVER) became interested in cooking when his father, who had friends in the restaurant industry, took him to a "posh Italian restaurant before dinner service had started, and I tasted grilled octopus and crispy calamari (in the kitchen) for the first time. I can still taste and smell them 30 years later."

MATTHEW RISSLING (THE MARINA RESTAURANT, VICTORIA) grew up watching cooking shows on TV, tuning in to see stars like Julia Child, Graham Kerr, Jacques Pépin, Jeff Smith, and Vancouver's James Barber. Also, the unfussy cooking styles of his mom and aunts proved to be lasting influences. Matthew earned his Red Seal in 2004 and became executive chef at The Marina Restaurant in 2009.

ALEX ROTHERHAM (DARBY'S PUB, VANCOUVER) is a true local chef, having spent 90 percent of his culinary career in Vancouver. His training is in classic French cuisine, although he spent 10 years specializing in Italian cuisine. Alex now enjoys putting his personal stamp on classic pub fare at Darby's. His interpretation of fish and chips illustrates his unique culinary direction.

ANDRÉ ROY (L'AQUARIUM DU QUÉBEC, QUEBEC) has worked in a variety of hotels and restaurants throughout Quebec and Ontario, and became director of l'Aquarium du Québec in 2006. André's mission no longer involves preparing fish dishes in a restaurant kitchen; rather, he and his team work relentlessly to preserve precious species and their environment with Quebec's Menu Bleu Marin, in collaboration with Ocean Wise and the Vancouver Aquarium.

MARCO SANTOS (L'ORIGNAL, MONTREAL) is self-taught, which allowed him to develop his own style. "Cooking for me is a state of mind. Although my deepest passion and inspiration come from my Portuguese background, I love to support and nurture as much local produce as I can possibly find."

NICO SCHUERMANS (CHAMBAR RESTAURANT, VANCOUVER) was schooled at the prestigious CREPAC School of Culinary Arts in Belgium. He worked as chef de partie for Comme Chez Soi, a three-Michelin-star establishment that is often considered Belgium's finest restaurant, where he cooked for a number of celebrities including Mick Jagger, Prince, and Bill Clinton.

MYKE SHAW (VANCOUVER AQUARIUM CATERING AND EVENTS, VANCOUVER) has been part of the catering team at the Vancouver Aquarium since 2004 and is proud to be the first caterer to become partners with Ocean Wise.

ROCKIN' RONNIE SHEWCHUK (AUTHOR OF BARBECUE SECRETS DELUXE!, NORTH VANCOUVER). The self-proclaimed "barbecue evangelist" is never far from a grill or a smoker, whether he's teaching cooking classes, appearing as a guest chef on TV, hosting one of the Internet's most popular barbecue podcasts, blogging about grilling and barbecue, writing articles for food publications, or cooking up a storm on the competitive circuit. "For me, barbecue is not just a pastime, it's a lifestyle," says Ron, who was named by Food & Wine magazine as one of America's greatest grillers.

MICHAEL SMITH (FORTUNE BAY, PEI) is an award-winning chef, television personality, cookbook author, newspaper columnist, roving Canadian cuisine ambassador, and home cook. Since his television debut on the Life Network in 1998, Michael has been featured in a number of shows that have aired on a variety of networks and in more than 40 countries around the world.

DAVID SPEIGHT (ARAMARK AT ROGERS ARENA (FORMERLY GM PLACE), VANCOUVER) served as chef at two Vancouver restaurants after receiving his Red Seal and before joining ARAMARK as executive chef in 2008. Soon after, David earned his Pro-Chef Level II certification at the Culinary Institute of America.

STAR SPILOS (TOMATO FRESH FOOD CAFÉ, VANCOUVER) says her lifelong interest in food and in baking began by watching her mother create desserts. Star received a Les Dames d'Escoffier scholarship to the Culinary Institute of America in Napa Valley. Star and her husband, Tomato co-owner Christian, are the authors of the award-winning bestseller As Fresh as It Gets: Everyday Recipes from the Tomato Fresh Food Café.

WAYNE SYCH (THE CANNERY SEAFOOD RESTAURANT, VANCOUVER (NOW DEFUNCT)) offered a tempting variety of regional and imported seafood at the Cannery, blending his vibrant west coast style with the freshest local and Pacific Rim ingredients. Wayne now spends several evenings a month teaching cooking classes throughout Vancouver and the Lower Mainland.

JOSEPH THOMAS (TAPESTRY AT THE O'KEEFE, VANCOUVER) started his culinary career as a dishwasher at age 15. He was called up to the line to help out on a busy night and "the rest is history." He has worked with top chefs across Canada, and apprenticed as both cook and baker with some of the finest chefs in Ontario.

BRANDON THORDARSON (SOCIETY DINING LOUNGE, VANCOUVER) says that "coming from a very large family, food has always been the main attraction at all [our] gatherings since I was a child." Brandon travelled across Canada, working his way through some of the best private golf and country clubs, and worked behind the stoves throughout hotels and restaurants in Australia and Europe. He brings a worldly view to the Society team.

DAVID TOMBS (MANTLES RESTAURANT & LOUNGE, DELTA SUN PEAKS RESORT, SUN PEAKS, BC) trained at the Dubrulle culinary school in Vancouver and later moved to the famed Sooke Harbour House where he developed a profound respect and admiration for local cuisine. David has worked to establish Delta Sun Peaks Resort as a culinary destination for those interested in experiencing regional cuisine.

MICHAEL TRAQUAIR (BANQUET & CATERING SERVICES, RAMADA PLAZA AND CONFERENCE CENTRE, ABBOTSFORD, BC) moved to the Fraser Valley with his family as a pioneer of sorts, to raise the bar in awareness and appreciation of fine culinary fare at the Ramada Plaza and Conference Centre. Michael's professional relationships with many farmers in the area guarantee him the freshest ingredients for his creations.

WILLIAM TSE (GOLDFISH PACIFIC KITCHEN, VANCOUVER) leapt over the pond from England at the age of seven and quickly developed a passion for food. He found inspiration in Toronto's international cultures and global flavours, combined with his upbringing in the Tse family restaurant. While working alongside his father, William learned the fundamentals of Asian cuisine. In 2008 and 2010 William had the pleasure of hosting the Chefs for Life event.

CHINDI VARADARAJULU (CHUTNEY VILLA, VANCOUVER). Born in Singapore, Chindi moved to Canada in 1996 and worked at several restaurant chains until she opened Chutney Villa in 2003. Chindi uses age-old recipes passed down to her by her grandmother and mother. She is passionate about her food and culture, leading culinary tours to South India and bringing back new recipes and ideas.

CHRIS VELDEN (RYAN DUFFY'S, HALIFAX) is a European-trained chef with over 25 years' experience working in Europe, Canada, and the US. Before coming to Halifax and transforming Ryan Duffy's into a modern-day steak house, Chris spent several years in Vancouver as executive chef and program director for the Pacific Institute of Culinary Arts, one of Canada's top culinary schools. He is now the Ocean Wise Atlantic Canada representative. However, if you ask him to describe himself, you get a simpler synopsis: "I am a cook who loves to teach."

VIKRAM VIJ (VIJ'S, VANCOUVER) opened the first incarnation of Vij's in 1994. Now the lineups at his renowned Indian restaurant are legendary. He is passionate about the health of our oceans and is a member of the Canadian Chefs' Congress and the Chefs' Table Society of BC. Vikram works closely with a number of Lower Mainland farmers, fishers, and winemakers, in keeping with his philosophy of using authentically Indian spices and cooking techniques while drawing on Canadian products.

MICHAEL VILORIA (MANHATTAN RESTAURANT, DELTA VANCOUVER SUITES HOTEL, VANCOUVER) developed his culinary career at several hotels in Metro Vancouver. His career highlight prior to Delta Vancouver Suites was joining the Pacific Palisades as executive chef at its new concept restaurant, Zin. It was one of the first restaurants to provide a new culinary experience by focusing on using local ingredients and global cuisine to reflect Vancouver's multicultural population.

JAMES WALT (ARAXI RESTAURANT, WHISTLER, BC) has had a stellar culinary career, including a post as executive chef to the Canadian Embassy in Rome. Now living in the heart of Pemberton, a BC farming community near Whistler, James makes regular visits to nearby farms where he personally selects the freshest ingredients for Araxi. James is Whistler's only chef to have cooked at the celebrated James Beard House in New York City, where he has performed three times.

CHRIS WHITTAKER (O'DOUL'S RESTAURANT & BAR, LISTEL HOTEL, VANCOUVER) has been an integral player in some of Vancouver's most interesting kitchens. Chris has garnered praise for his eclectic cooking style and his passion for local products and ethically sound ingredients. Since his arrival at O'Doul's, Chris has been the driving force behind its Ocean Wise program. He is also involved with the Green Table Network.

MORGAN WILSON (TRIOS BISTRO, TORONTO MARRIOT DOWNTOWN EATON CENTRE HOTEL) gained expertise while competing in culinary competitions. In 2005, Morgan represented Canada in the Bocuse d'Or culinary competition in Lyon, and placed eighth among non-European chefs. Morgan believes that "great cuisine combines two basic components: top-quality products and flawless technique."

JOSH WOLFE (COAST RESTAURANT, VANCOUVER) learned the speed and precision necessary to cater fine dining to upward of 300 guests at Centro Grill & Wine Bar in Toronto. Josh refined his cooking and honed his management skills at The Fifth, which was voted top restaurant by *Toronto Life* magazine. While Josh's training is classical, his inspiration is contemporary and his style is fuelled by both products and seasons.

MARLENE J. YONG (PACIFIC INSTITUTE OF CULINARY ARTS (PICA), VANCOUVER) attended PICA in 2009, but her stint in school was not the beginning of a career, but the next stage in a journey to a new career. Marlene was trained as a nutritionist and naturopath and gained experience operating her own catering business before attending PICA to hone her skills. Marlene is well known for cooking with a smile.

JEFFERY YOUNG (AUBERGINE GRILLE, WESTIN RESORT & SPA, WHISTLER, BC) thrives under pressure, both as executive chef and in competition. Jeffery has won a total of 20 gold, silver, and bronze culinary awards during his 19-year culinary career, including top chef in BC at the 10th annual BC Chefs' Association competition in 2009, and he was a member of Team British Columbia, which brought home the gold at the XXVIII Culinary Olympics in Germany.

ACKNOWLEDGEMENTS

This book wouldn't exist without the collaboration of Mike McDermid and the team at Vancouver Aquarium's Ocean Wise program, who provided me with chef contacts, photographs, and lots of information about sustainability. To the chefs who contributed to the book from across Canada, thanks for your terrific recipes and wine suggestions.

Speaking of wine, a profound thanks to Tom Firth at *Wine Access* for his insightful wine and beer pairings; to my dear friend Kate Zimmerman for her support, witticisms, recipe testing, and editing; and to Amber Shute, who kindly also helped edit the recipes. I couldn't have done it without them.

A big thanks to Vancouver chefs Robert Clark, Quang Dang, Frank Pabst, Karen Barnaby, and Josh Wolfe, who gave up their time to help create the Ocean Wise videos. And to "barbecue evangelist" Rockin' Ronnie Shewchuk, Barbara-jo McIntosh (owner of Barbara-Jo's Books to Cooks), and the folks at the Pacific Institute of Culinary Arts all of whom went above and beyond the call of duty.

I am also indebted to Carol Jensson, who helped with food styling, and to the many photographers whose pictures bring these great recipes to life.

Many thanks, too, to Bob Fraumeni of Finest at Sea, Steve Johansen of Organic Ocean, and the folks at Raincoast Trading for providing me with fish and seafood. Without their support my recipe testing budget would have gone overboard.

I also appreciate the generosity of Nicolas Budreski, David McRae, and Daniel Notkin, who all shared their knowledge with me.

My mum, Pamela Sangster, deserves some credit for nurturing my love of seafood—even though she also fed me cod liver oil. Mum, all is forgiven.

Last, but most importantly, I'd like to thank Robert McCullough and Taryn Boyd of Whitecap Books for giving me the green light; without them, this book would never have reached solid land. And to all the fishes—may they forever run.

INDEX

JANE MUNDY is a freelance writer and editor. Her articles have appeared in a number of newspapers and magazines including the *Globe & Mail*, the *National Post*, the *Vancouver Sun*, and *More* (www.more.ca). She studied marine biology at the University of Victoria, but her passion for food and writing led her down a different path. As owner of Reel Appetites—which catered to the film industry in BC—she gained 20 years of experience as a professional cook. She lives in Vancouver with Lizzie, her border collie.

TRACEY KUSIEWICZ is a commercially trained freelance photographer specializing in food and beverages and everything epicurean. She creates "tasty images" for cookbooks, magazines, and advertisements in the culinary and hospitality industries of BC. Recent accolades include an award in 2010 for her creative photography in *Applied Arts* magazine. Visit her website at www.foodiephotography.com.

TOM FIRTH, whose wine suggestions are featured throughout *The Ocean Wise Cookbook*, got his start in wine back in 1996, working for one of Canada's largest private wine retailers. He joined *Wine Access* magazine in 2006 as events and promotions manager, and manages the magazine's Canadian Wine Awards and International Value Wine Awards. Lacking talent in the kitchen, he is more than happy to bring the wine when invited out for dinner.

Credits

Photography by Tracey Kusiewicz, except as follows:

pages iv, 13, and 243 (top)
    by FAS Seafood Producers Ltd.
pages v, 139 (top), 197, and 235
    by John Sherlock
pages 2, 23, and 211 by Jane Mundy
pages 10, 21 (right), 24, 76, 148, 181,
    and 242 by Mike McDermid
pages 11, 69 (top), 85 (bottom),
    and 286 by Margaret Butschler
pages 21 (left), 50, and 225 (top)
    by Neil Fisher
page 22 by Riccardo Cellere
page 31 © 2010 Bruce Law Photography
page 44 by Geoffrey Morden
page 51 by Ron Sangha
pages 52, 92, 99, 113, 145, 155, 161, 180,
    195, 232, 243 (bottom), 251, and 295
    by Mauve Pagé
pages 67 and 69 (bottom)
    by Voth Photography
page 79 by Heather Goldsworthy
page 85 (top) by Jackie Connelly
    Photography
pages 90, 91, and 114 (bottom)
    by David McRae
pages 100 and 104 by Patrick Gayler
pages 114 (top, both photos) and 115
    courtesy of Quang Dang
page 133 (top) by KmarkyW/stock.xchng
    (www.sxc.hu)
pages 133 (bottom) and 192 (top)
    by Wendy McElmon/
    www.wendymcelmon.com
page 139 (bottom) by Duncan Holmes
page 192 (bottom) by andrewatla/stock
    .xchng (www.sxc.hu)
page 225 (bottom) by John Healey
pages 244 and 254 (top and bottom left)
    by Kelly Johnson